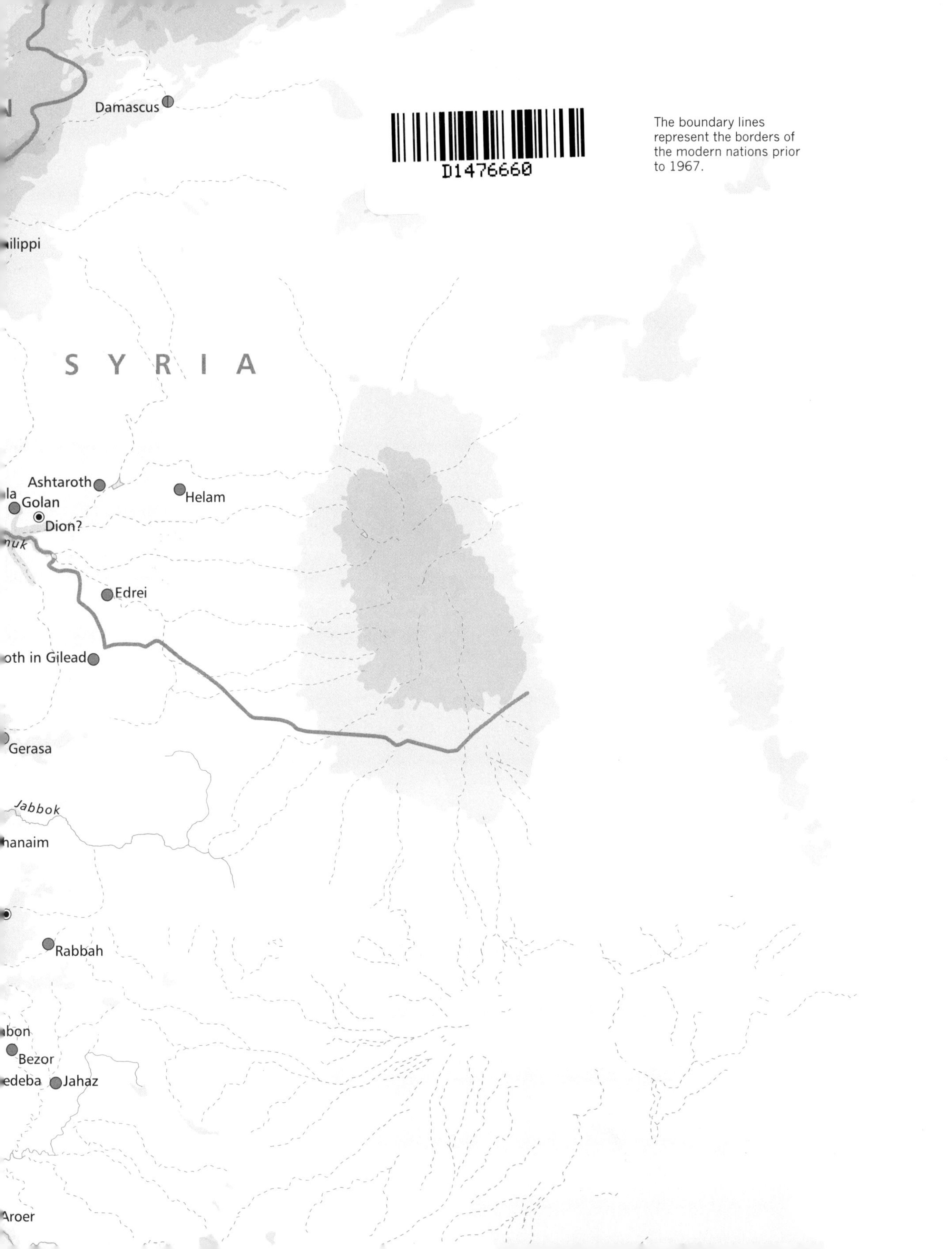
Damascus
The boundary lines represent the borders of the modern nations prior to 1967.
ilippi
S Y R I A
Ashtaroth
la
Golan
Helam
Dion?
nuk
Edrei
oth in Gilead
Gerasa
Jabbok
hanaim
Rabbah
bon
Bezor
edeba
Jahaz
Aroer

The Lion Guide to the Bible

Happy Birthday Pat.

Wishing you hours of
enjoyment as I have
Love & Blessings
Karen
Aug /24.

For my many friends at Wycliffe
(staff and students, past and present),
with thanks for all we have learned together
of Christ and his Word.

Peter Walker

The Lion
Guide to
the
Bible

Copyright © 2010 Peter Walker
This edition copyright © 2010 Lion Hudson

The author asserts the moral right
to be identified as the author of this work

A Lion Book
an imprint of
Lion Hudson plc
Wilkinson House, Jordan Hill Road,
Oxford OX2 8DR, England
www.lionhudson.com

ISBN 978 0 7459 5292 5

Distributed by:
UK: Marston Book Services, PO Box 269, Abingdon, Oxon, OX14 4YN
USA: Trafalgar Square Publishing, 814 N. Franklin Street, Chicago, IL 60610
USA Christian Market: Kregel Publications, PO Box 2607, Grand Rapids, MI, 49501

First edition 2010

10 9 8 7 6 5 4 3 2 1 0
All rights reserved

Acknowledgments
p. 79: Scripture quotation taken from the *Holy Bible, New International Version*,
copyright © 1973, 1978, 1984 International Bible Society. Used by permission of
Zondervan and Hodder & Stoughton Limited. All rights reserved. The 'NIV' and 'New
International Version' trademarks are registered in the United States Patent and
Trademark Office by International Bible Society. Use of either trademark requires the
permission of International Bible Society. UK trademark number 1448790.
All other scripture quotations taken from the *Holy Bible, Today's New International
Version*. Copyright © 2004 by International Bible Society. Used by permission of Hodder
& Stoughton Publishers. A member of the Hachette Livre UK Group. All rights reserved.
'TNIV' is a registered trademark of International Bible Society.

A catalogue record for this book is available
from the British Library

Typeset in 10/12 ITC Caslon No. 224 BT

Printed and bound in Singapore

Contents

Preface

Imagine yourself wanting to learn about a game or sport – one that's quite complicated and which you have never seen, let alone played! What do you need? You could read lots of newspaper reports on particular games or listen to a radio commentary of a live match; but all those many words would probably make very little sense. The best thing would be to actually go and watch a match, and have someone with you – ideally an experienced player – who before the match could give you a general explanation and then was alongside you throughout the match to explain particular details. What you need is a guide – both before and during the game.

This book is designed to be just such a guide – a guide for a book which has proved to be as dynamic and active as any sport, but which describes something far more important than a mere game. The Bible pulsates with energy, touches on all aspects of life, and is full of wisdom. Yet so often it remains a closed book, gathering dust – sometimes revered, sometimes dismissed – but frequently kept at a distance. 'It's just too big, it's all so ancient – I wouldn't know where to begin!'

If that's you, and you have a desire to read the Bible but feel daunted, I would love this *Guide* to help you. It has been written for you! It does not presume any prior knowledge; it is not seeking to be impressively complicated but, rather, intelligently simple; it tries to explain 'first things first' and not dazzle you with subtle debates which, at this stage, you don't need to know. Too often Bible scholars get immersed in ever deeper layers of detail – like children going further and further inside a maze – but we can too easily forget to come back to the maze's entrance, to guide people on the edge who are wanting to come in. This *Guide* is your 'entrance' into the world of the Bible and, as you enter the maze, you're allowed to keep it with you!

Speaking personally, writing this *Guide* has itself been rather daunting. 'How can I write about the whole Bible? After all, I may have some areas of special interest, but there are parts of the Bible (especially in the Old Testament) where I myself desperately need a guide!' Yet those feelings of inadequacy have themselves been useful prompts – keeping me focused on how best to guide others who likewise may be struggling. And, as I went into less familiar areas, I was freshly amazed by what I was discovering. For, in the task of reading each book of the Bible (making copious notes, trying to use my historical imagination to get back 'inside their skin', and then thinking how to explain this material simply), I was repeatedly confronted with their hidden depths. Books which I myself had slightly dismissed – for whatever reason – came back into fresh relief. In particular, the 'historical' books of the Old Testament, far from being ancient tales about a rather murky episode in human history, came across as vivid and authentic accounts of life as it really is – with a remarkably contemporary feel.

Writing such a book I have been acutely aware of the many people who – for more than thirty years – have guided me in my reading of the Bible. Ministering for four years in a local church, studying for three years at a world-class biblical research library (Tyndale House, Cambridge) and then teaching the Bible in a ministry-training college – these have all given me ample opportunities to keep on learning. More practically, I am, of course, so grateful to Paul Clifford at Lion Hudson for dreaming up this *Guide*, for encouraging me in difficult days, and then for Miranda Powell and Jonathan Roberts who have patiently worked with me on the complex design process – we've had lively debates over just about every page!

So my hope is that this *Guide* will prove to be your gateway into the Bible – a good book to dip into before reading a section of the Bible for yourself. That's the goal: that you should be enjoying the Bible for yourself and reading it with understanding and greater confidence. Yet, if this volume can get you started, then it will have served its purpose well.

Peter Walker
Wycliffe Hall
University of Oxford
1 December 2009

How best to read the Bible

Whenever we buy a book, it's worth asking ourselves: 'how can we best read it to get the most out of it?' This will obviously include making practical choices, which reflect our own personal circumstances and preferences – whether to read the book on holiday or perhaps each evening in bed. There are also more strategic choices, however, which closely reflect the nature of the book concerned. So, if our new book is a novel, it's clearly best to read it from the beginning to the end, but if it's a detailed textbook or a collection of essays, almost certainly that will not be the best strategy. In particular, reference books (like dictionaries) are evidently not best read from cover to cover! So what is the best strategy for reading the Bible?

At one important level the Bible is indeed a story, so there are good arguments for reading it as any other story book – starting at the beginning and tracing the plot line as it develops (see p. 17). Yet this is quite a mammoth task. Some of the Bible's most obscure sections come near its beginning, which can discourage the first-time reader. Moreover, the Bible's contents are not presented to us in a strictly chronological order, so it's hard to trace the storyline in an orderly way. We also soon find that the Bible is made up of quite diverse types of literature (history-writing, poems, rule-books, personal letters and so on). These different genres (or styles of writing) may call for different reading strategies. So how can one process this large, diverse body of material?

Probably the best way for the first-time reader is to focus on the New Testament and, in particular, the Gospel accounts describing the life of Jesus Christ. There are strong arguments for seeing Jesus as the central, pivotal character in the Bible's story: he is the focus of *all* the New Testament writings and is the figure towards whom much of the Old Testament points. Christians would go further and suggest that Jesus is the 'gateway' or access point into all the truths contained in the Bible. So to focus our first attention on the person and work of Christ will never be wasted; for the Bible itself commends him to us as the one in whom are 'hidden all the treasures of wisdom'; and he is the one, so it is claimed, who can lead us by his Spirit 'into all the truth'. So go first to the Gospels (Mark is the shortest, Matthew the most compact, Luke perhaps the most psychologically compelling, and John the most profound); then to the rest of the New Testament. And then, at some point, come back into the Old Testament. For it will be so much easier to read this larger 'first half' of the Bible, if you have some idea (indeed some convictions) about where this story is headed.

This raises the difficult, but important, point as to the best frame of mind with which to read the Bible. For I have just suggested that the best way to enjoy the Bible is from the perspective of having some convictions (or faith) about Jesus Christ. There is, inevitably, some circularity of argument at this point. The Bible, of course, positively welcomes the reader who comes to it with an inquisitive mind. Yet gradually it invites us to come ourselves inside the 'house of faith' and to adopt its own worldview – a worldview filled with faith in a living God who has acted and spoken (and who is himself calling people to respond to him in faith). So, after a while, if any readers persist in ignoring this invitation and deliberately place themselves in opposition to this worldview, the Bible can mysteriously become something of a closed book.

The Bible is thus a text – quite different from most other texts – which invites us to read it from the perspective of faith in the God whom it describes. We are still to read it intelligently, using our critical faculties, but we will get the most rewarding results from reading it sympathetically rather than antagonistically. More than that, this is a text which demands not just faith but other spiritual and personal qualities too: for example, patience (when we don't understand things) and even obedience (when presented with truths to believe or commands to follow). These are all part of the frame of mind we would do well to cultivate as we dig into the Bible's pages.

More practically, should we read it in large chunks or in tiny pieces? Both approaches have their merits and most people would do well to vary their diet at this point. This is a text which can, and should, be pored over in minute detail. At the same time, any such small section always needs to be set within the Bible's wider context, so becoming familiar with the whole story is also important. This means, almost certainly, reading larger sections of the Bible at a quicker pace – perhaps even taking in whole books at one sitting.

This is where this *Guide* may prove its value. To read the whole Bible is indeed a daunting task. This *Guide*, however, gives you a short digest of each biblical book, so you can get an overview of all the Bible's material. Yet it also gives you a flavour of each individual book and can steer you as you prepare to read that particular book for yourself. In addition, at the end of each chapter of the Old Testament, some verses from the Psalms have been included, which can, if desired, be used by the reader as a form of prayer and reflection. For each book of the Bible is not just to be studied, but also to be prayed through.

Finally, we want this *Guide* not to replace the Bible (of course!), but rather to send you back to this great book with increased understanding and an eager anticipation for what you yourself can discover there.

Chronology of events

The Bible's storyline spans a period of nearly 2,000 years. In this chart the events described in the Bible (on the beige background) can be seen alongside those events associated with surrounding nations in the Ancient Near East (on the green background). From this, one can sense that, although the stories in Genesis may appear incredibly ancient, they are quite *late* when compared with the civilizations that had been developing in the previous millennium: for example, when Jacob's family settled in Egypt (Genesis 37–50), the great pyramid had already been standing there for 800 years!

Establishing the dates of biblical events is never quite an exact science and involves elaborate comparison with dates suggested for events in the Ancient Near East (themselves based on such things as astronomical data or perhaps Assyrian 'annals'). Some of the most assured dates on this chart are: the start of Solomon's reign (970 BC), the battle of Carchemish (605 BC), Antiochus' desecration of the Temple (168 BC) and the Romans' destruction of Jerusalem (summer AD 70). The most disputed would be that of the Israelites' conquest of Canaan: here a later date (c. 1230 BC) is assumed (see p. 65), but all the dates for previous events would need to be put back by 180 years if the other commonly suggested date (c. 1407 BC) were correct. By comparison the uncertainties over dates in the New Testament are quite minor (on the issues relating to dating Jesus' birth and crucifixion, see p. 219).

Events in the Bible's story

FROM GENESIS TO KINGS

- c. 1990–c. 1815 Abraham (based on c. 1270 Exodus)
- c. 1730–c. 1620 Joseph
- 1447 Exo

Events in the Ancient Near East

MESOPOTAMIA

- 3100 Beginnings of writing in Mesopotamia and Egypt
- 2750–2371 Early Dynastic Period in Mesopotamia
- 2700 Gilgamesh
- 2600–2400 Royal Cemetery of Ur
- 2371–2230 Dynasty of Akkad
- 2371–2316 Sargon
- 2113–2006 Third Dynasty of Ur
- 2113–2096 Ur-Nammu
- 1894–1595 First Dynasty of Babylon
- 1792–1750 Hammurabi
- 1595–1171 Kassite Dynasty of Babylon

EGYPT

- 2700–2136 Old Kingdom
- 2691–2672 Djoser (Step pyramid)
- 2593–2570 Kheops (Khufu) (Great pyramid)
- c. 2136–2023 First Intermediate Period
- 2116–1795 Middle Kingdom
- 1900–1800 First examples of alphabetic writing in Egyp
- 1795–1630 Second Intermediate Period
- 1540–1070 New
- 1479–1

| 3100 BC | 3000 BC | 2900 BC | 2800 BC | 2700 BC | 2600 BC | 2500 BC | 2400 BC | 2300 BC | 2200 BC | 2100 BC | 2000 BC | 1900 BC | 1800 BC | 1700 BC | 1600 BC | 1500 BC | 1400 B |

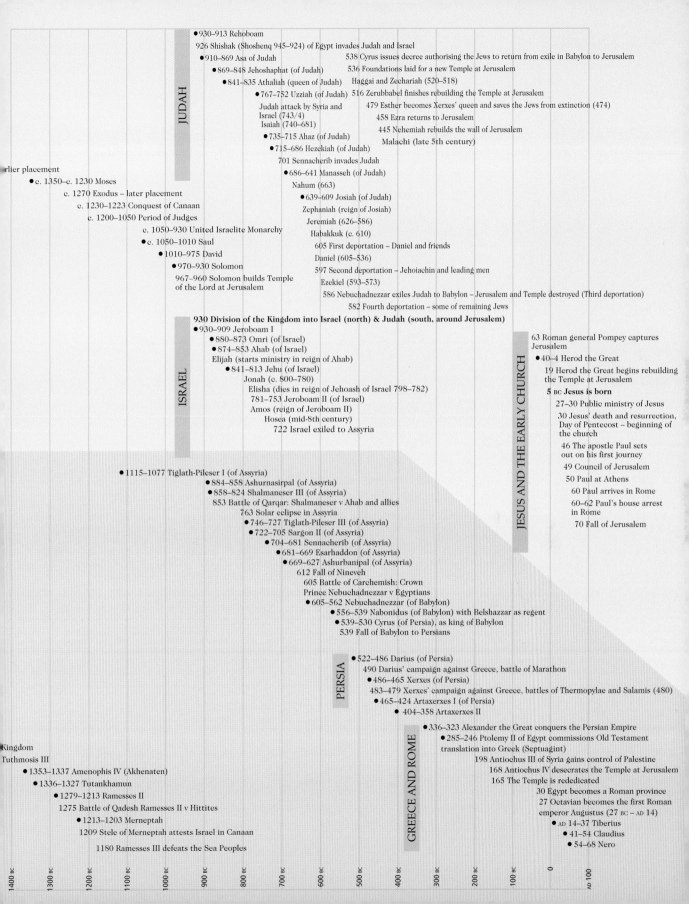

JUDAH

Earlier placement
- c. 1350–c. 1230 Moses
- c. 1270 Exodus – later placement
- c. 1230–1223 Conquest of Canaan
- c. 1200–1050 Period of Judges
- c. 1050–930 United Israelite Monarchy
- c. 1050–1010 Saul
- 1010–975 David
- 970–930 Solomon
- 967–960 Solomon builds Temple of the Lord at Jerusalem

- 930–913 Rehoboam
- 926 Shishak (Shoshenq 945–924) of Egypt invades Judah and Israel
- 910–869 Asa of Judah
- 869–848 Jehoshaphat (of Judah)
- 841–835 Athaliah (queen of Judah)
- 767–752 Uzziah (of Judah)
- Judah attack by Syria and Israel (743/4)
- Isaiah (740–681)
- 735–715 Ahaz (of Judah)
- 715–686 Hezekiah (of Judah)
- 701 Sennacherib invades Judah
- 686–641 Manasseh (of Judah)
- Nahum (663)
- 639–609 Josiah (of Judah)
- Zephaniah (reign of Josiah)
- Jeremiah (626–586)
- Habakkuk (c. 610)
- 605 First deportation – Daniel and friends
- Daniel (605–536)
- 597 Second deportation – Jehoiachin and leading men
- Ezekiel (593–573)
- 586 Nebuchadnezzar exiles Judah to Babylon – Jerusalem and Temple destroyed (Third deportation)
- 582 Fourth deportation – some of remaining Jews

- 538 Cyrus issues decree authorising the Jews to return from exile in Babylon to Jerusalem
- 536 Foundations laid for a new Temple at Jerusalem
- Haggai and Zechariah (520–518)
- 516 Zerubbabel finishes rebuilding the Temple at Jerusalem
- 479 Esther becomes Xerxes' queen and saves the Jews from extinction (474)
- 458 Ezra returns to Jerusalem
- 445 Nehemiah rebuilds the wall of Jerusalem
- Malachi (late 5th century)

ISRAEL

930 Division of the Kingdom into Israel (north) & Judah (south, around Jerusalem)
- 930–909 Jeroboam I
- 880–873 Omri (of Israel)
- 874–853 Ahab (of Israel)
- Elijah (starts ministry in reign of Ahab)
- 841–813 Jehu (of Israel)
- Jonah (c. 800–780)
- Elisha (dies in reign of Jehoash of Israel 798–782)
- 781–753 Jeroboam II (of Israel)
- Amos (reign of Jeroboam II)
- Hosea (mid-8th century)
- 722 Israel exiled to Assyria

- 1115–1077 Tiglath-Pileser I (of Assyria)
- 884–858 Ashurnasirpal (of Assyria)
- 858–824 Shalmaneser III (of Assyria)
- 853 Battle of Qarqar: Shalmaneser v Ahab and allies
- 763 Solar eclipse in Assyria
- 746–727 Tiglath-Pileser III (of Assyria)
- 722–705 Sargon II (of Assyria)
- 704–681 Sennacherib (of Assyria)
- 681–669 Esarhaddon (of Assyria)
- 669–627 Ashurbanipal (of Assyria)
- 612 Fall of Nineveh
- 605 Battle of Carchemish: Crown Prince Nebuchadnezzar v Egyptians
- 605–562 Nebuchadnezzar (of Babylon)
- 556–539 Nabonidus (of Babylon) with Belshazzar as regent
- 539–530 Cyrus (of Persia), as king of Babylon
- 539 Fall of Babylon to Persians

PERSIA
- 522–486 Darius (of Persia)
- 490 Darius' campaign against Greece, battle of Marathon
- 486–465 Xerxes (of Persia)
- 483–479 Xerxes' campaign against Greece, battles of Thermopylae and Salamis (480)
- 465–424 Artaxerxes I (of Persia)
- 404–358 Artaxerxes II

GREECE AND ROME
- 336–323 Alexander the Great conquers the Persian Empire
- 285–246 Ptolemy II of Egypt commissions Old Testament translation into Greek (Septuagint)
- 198 Antiochus III of Syria gains control of Palestine
- 168 Antiochus IV desecrates the Temple at Jerusalem
- 165 The Temple is rededicated
- 30 Egypt becomes a Roman province
- 27 Octavian becomes the first Roman emperor Augustus (27 BC – AD 14)
- AD 14–37 Tiberius
- 41–54 Claudius
- 54–68 Nero

JESUS AND THE EARLY CHURCH
- 63 Roman general Pompey captures Jerusalem
- 40–4 Herod the Great
- 19 Herod the Great begins rebuilding the Temple at Jerusalem
- **5 BC Jesus is born**
- 27–30 Public ministry of Jesus
- 30 Jesus' death and resurrection, Day of Pentecost – beginning of the church
- 46 The apostle Paul sets out on his first journey
- 49 Council of Jerusalem
- 50 Paul at Athens
- 60 Paul arrives in Rome
- 60–62 Paul's house arrest in Rome
- 70 Fall of Jerusalem

Kingdom
Tuthmosis III
- 1353–1337 Amenophis IV (Akhenaten)
- 1336–1327 Tutankhamun
- 1279–1213 Ramesses II
- 1275 Battle of Qadesh Ramesses II v Hittites
- 1213–1203 Merneptah
- 1209 Stele of Merneptah attests Israel in Canaan
- 1180 Ramesses III defeats the Sea Peoples

1400 BC | 1300 BC | 1200 BC | 1100 BC | 1000 BC | 900 BC | 800 BC | 700 BC | 600 BC | 500 BC | 400 BC | 300 BC | 200 BC | 100 BC | 0 | AD 100

The Bible's structure and themes

The Bible is not written in a straightforwardly chronological order. Instead its various books have been collated into sections that primarily reflect different styles of genres. There are four such sections in the Old Testament and another four (very similar) in the New Testament.

Old Testament

1. Law: an early history, focused on Israel's escape from Egypt, but with a substantial amount of instruction (known as 'Torah' in Hebrew, often translated as the 'Law'); these books (from Genesis to Deuteronomy) are also known as the five books of Moses (or the Pentateuch).

2. History: twelve historical narratives (from Joshua to Esther), taking forward the story of the people of Israel from their first arrival in the land through to their exile and return.

3. Wisdom: five more reflective books (from Job to Song of Songs), written in a poetic or proverbial style, passing on Israel's accumulated wisdom, together with its prayers and songs of worship.

4. Prophecy: seventeen books (from Isaiah to Malachi), most of which are completely given over to prophetic oracles.

New Testament

1. Gospels: four related but separate accounts (Matthew, Mark, Luke and John), which describe the life of Jesus and proclaim it as 'good news' (or 'gospel').

2. History: one book (the Acts of the Apostles), which tells some of the history of the early church (up until AD 62).

3. Letters: twenty-one letters or 'epistles' of varying length (from Romans to Jude), which are addressed to individuals or Christian congregations (thirteen written by Paul).

4. Apocalypse: one book (Revelation), which contains seven 'letters' from Christ to his church, followed by an extended unveiling (in Greek 'apo-calypse') of some dramatic scenes in heaven that culminate in a great finale (focused on a perfected new creation).

The *Guide* follows this long-established order and will introduce you to each of these major sections in turn. Within each section individual biblical books are also discussed in the order in which they appear in the Bible. There are two exceptions to this, however: the so-called 'minor prophets' are treated in their probable chronological order (see pp. 158–75); and Jude is discussed in a box within the chapter 1 and 2 Peter (see p. 282).

Finally, please note that this *Guide* does not cover the 'inter-testamental' writings (composed c. 300 BC to AD 70), because they have never been received by the Christian church as fully 'canonical' – that is, of having equal authority to the Old Testament (see pp. 176–77).

One book: many themes

For all its diversity of material, the Bible is remarkably coherent. Although it is made up of sixty-six separate books, these various books – despite being written over many centuries – come together to form a recognizably unified whole. It is important, therefore, for its readers not only to appreciate its enjoyable variety but also to look out for the underlying themes which foster its unity.

Perhaps, then, we should try to find a single theme which summarizes the whole. Yet isolating any one such thread will inevitably leave out other vital parts of the tapestry. So, although one obvious answer is that the Bible is all about God, others might equally argue that it is all about Christ, or God's people or God's purposes. And there are further key themes which we could add: for example, God's covenant promises, the manifestation of God's presence, or the revelation of his will. Yet further themes would include redemption or revelation; the renewal of creation or God's sovereignty; forgiveness or hope, love or grace… The list could go on!

A central theme: the kingdom of God

One helpful way to deal with this array of choices is to focus instead on the theme of God's kingdom, but ensuring that this is understood in quite a comprehensive way – as referring to God's kingly rule over God's people in God's chosen place (as represented in the diagram to the right). This accurately reflects the three-dimensional nature of the Bible's material. For this is no book of abstract theology (merely focused on a distant, transcendent God); rather it tells the story of a God in lively relationship with real people, who themselves have to live out their faithful response to God in the earthly here and now.

This triangular pattern can then be traced through different seasons within biblical history (see diagram overleaf). The essential pattern is established when God exercises his rule over Adam and Eve in the Garden of Eden. Then it is filled out (in Genesis 12)

15

when God enters into a covenant relationship with Abraham, which includes the promise of a place where they may serve him – namely the Promised Land. Hence the great tragedy when Israel finds itself removed from the land in exile: God's people are no longer in God's place.

	God's rule	God's people	God's place
Eden	God's Word	Adam and Eve	The Garden
Israel's History	Covenant Sinai Covenant Sinai Covenant	Abraham Israel under Moses Israel under monarchy	Canaan Promised Land, Jerusalem, Temple
Prophetic Vision	New Covenant written on the heart	Faithful remnant of Israel	Restored land, Jerusalem, Temple

JESUS CHRIST

	God's rule	God's people	God's place
New Testament/ Fulfilment	New Covenant – Christ's rule by his Word	Church – the Jews and Gentiles 'in Christ'	Whole world with a new temple where Christ dwells by his Spirit

The New Testament then reviews all this through the lens of Christ, who himself is the very embodiment of all three components: as we will see, Jesus is identified as God's king, who rules on God's behalf; he also embodies God's faithful people and is their true representative; yet he is also depicted as the true temple, the true 'holy place' where God dwells. Thus mysteriously he is the embodiment of God's rule, of his people and of his place – all in one! So the apostles will teach that after Christ a major shift has taken place: God's people now includes all people – both Jew and Gentile – who have faith in Christ; and God's place includes the whole inhabited world, not just the Promised Land. All nations are now invited to come under the rule of God's appointed king (Matthew 28).

Of course, matters are more complex than this simple schema would suggest. Yet this framework may prove helpful for readers as they set out on their long journey through the Old Testament. It also has the advantage that it reflects accurately the primary theme of Jesus' own teaching ministry – namely that the 'kingdom of God is at hand' (Mark 1:15). Jesus set out to announce – and indeed to inaugurate – God's kingly rule, and he did so precisely because this was the longing and hope of the Old Testament – that God's rule should properly be established over his faithful people. There are thus some good reasons for seeing God's kingdom as indeed one of the Bible's central themes.

Different eras: five main 'acts'

The schema also highlights for us that the Bible is a sequential story that moves through different eras, or epochapters. The diagram to the right conveys this same idea but in a slightly different way. It portrays how the Bible can helpfully be seen as a play in five Acts:

Act I: Creation and Fall
Act II: Israel
Act III: JESUS
Act IV: Church
Act V: New Creation

This reveals how the Bible is a story with a vital beginning and end: God is taking his world, despite the arrival of sin and evil through the Fall, towards a new destination – the renewal of creation. It highlights how Jesus' coming is the central event in the drama, the pivot on which the whole story turns. And it also helps us to see where we ourselves are located in the story – namely in Act IV (the era of the church).

   This can help us when reading the Old Testament (originally written for Act II), realizing that this material, though still authoritative and true, should only be read in the light of Act III (because Jesus has moved the story forwards into a new era). Finally, seeing ourselves as located in Act IV can help us also to sense our own responsibility as Bible readers: we are not just to read the play but also to live it out, in ways, of course, that are fully faithful to the script thus far, and that help move the story forwards towards God's revealed goal – the renewal of his creation, the time of peace and joy.

Possible dates for events described in the books of the Old Testament

Date	LAW	HISTORY	WISDOM (The date of any book's final written composition may be much later than any events described within it, particularly in the Wisdom literature).	PROPHECY
	Genesis 1–11			
2000 BC				
1950	Genesis 12–50 (start)			
1900				
1850				
1800				
1750				
1700				
1650			? Job (setting)	
1600	Genesis 12–50 (end)			
1550				
1500				
1450				
1400				
1350				
1300				
1270	Exodus			
1245	Numbers; Leviticus			
1230	Deuteronomy; Entrance into the Promised Land	Joshua		
1175		Judges		
1150				
1100				
1050		Ruth; 1 Samuel		
		1 Chronicles		
1010		2 Samuel		
1000			Psalms of David Proverbs of Solomon	
970		1 Kings; 2 Chronicles (start)		
950	DIVIDED MONARCHY:			
900	JUDAH & ISRAEL			
850		2 Kings (start)		
800				
760			?? Song of Songs	Amos
750				Jonah (ministry)
740				Hosea; Joel (earliest possible date)
720	FALL OF NORTHERN			Micah
710	KINGDOM (ISRAEL)			Isaiah (ministry in Jerusalem, until c. 680)
700				
662				Nahum (662–612)
650				
630				Zephaniah
628				Jeremiah (start of his ministry)
612				
605				Habakkuk
600				
592		2 Kings (end)		Ezekiel (first prophecies)
587				
580				Jeremiah (end); Obadiah
560				Daniel (setting)
587	FALL OF JERUSALEM:			
550	START OF EXILE			
539		2 Chronicles (end)		
520	FIRST RETURN: END OF EXILE	Ezra 1–6	?? Ecclesiastes Latest Psalms & Proverbs	Haggai; Zechariah (first prophecies)
500				
475		Esther		Malachi (earliest possible date)
450		Nehemiah		
400		Ezra 7–10		

THE
OLD TESTAMENT

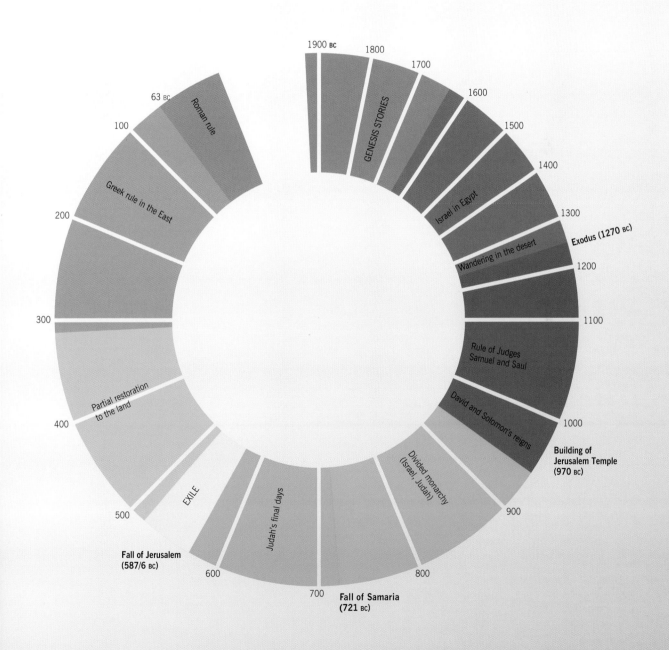

1900 BC
1800
1700
1600
1500
1400
1300
Exodus (1270 BC)
1200
1100
1000
Building of
Jerusalem Temple
(970 BC)
900
800
Fall of Samaria
(721 BC)
700
600
Fall of Jerusalem
(587/6 BC)
500
400
300
200
100
63 BC

GENESIS STORIES

Israel in Egypt

Wandering in the desert

Rule of Judges
Samuel and Saul

David and Solomon's reigns

Divided monarchy
(Israel, Judah)

Judah's final days

EXILE

Partial restoration
to the land

Greek rule in the East

Roman rule

The first five books of the Bible (from Genesis to Deuteronomy) are known as the Pentateuch (Greek for 'five books'). They are foundational to the whole Bible, introducing us to its great themes. After an opening primeval history (in Genesis 1–11), they tell the story of God's fulfilment of his promises made to Abraham – from the time of his first arrival in the Promised Land through to the moment (after many centuries spent in Egypt) when his descendants, the Israelites, are poised to enter the land.

Some parts are full of action, but there are two major sections where the narrative comes to a virtual standstill – when the Israelites are camped at Mount Sinai (Exodus 18 through to Numbers 10) and again in the desert plains across the River Jordan (Numbers 22 to Deuteronomy 34). These sections are filled with instructions for God's people, so the five books have often been referred to simply as 'the Law' (in Hebrew, *Torah*). However, these laws are set within the larger framework of this story of God's dealings with Abraham and Israel – focused around the life of their great leader, Moses. Since *Torah* may also be translated as 'instruction', it may be best, then, to see the Pentateuch as giving us *instruction through a narrative* – the narrative of which is told largely in the form of a biography of Moses.

This large body of material (comprising around 23 per cent of the Old Testament) had been divided up into its five books by at least the fifth century BC. However, its original date of compilation is hard to determine. There are several places in the text where Moses himself is described as committing things to writing, so the traditional view ascribed most of the Pentateuch to Moses' own hand – with subsequent editing producing a final version within a century of his death (i.e. some time back in the thirteenth or twelfth centuries BC: see p. 13). Modern scholarship, however, has produced an alternative account, known as the Documentary Hypothesis, which locates the original writing to much later. According to this hypothesis (formulated in the late nineteenth century), the Pentateuch is the merging of four originally separate documents or sources (now labelled: J, E, D and P).

Source name	Date originating from	Material
J-source ('Jahwist')	c. 950 BC	Consistently refers to God as 'Yahweh' (*Jahweh* in German).
E-source ('Elohist')	c. 850 BC	Refers to God as 'Elohim'.
D-source ('Deuteronomy')	Rediscovered by King Josiah in 622 BC (see p. 90)	Was the so-called 'book of the law'.
P-source ('Priestly')	c. 450 BC	Devoted to matters relating to priests.

It is thought that the J- and E-sources were combined around 750 BC. The D-source is thought to have been merged with the previous two documents. The final source, P, is thought to have been incorporated at a later stage (c. 450 BC).

This is many centuries after the events which the Pentateuch purports to describe. However, many of those who accepted these dates for the Pentateuch's written composition still argued that the narrative was an authentic witness to the events it relayed from the second millennium BC – this having been preserved through oral tradition. For them the date of composition was not the date of invention, but rather was the end-point of a long process of powerful memories faithfully preserved; so there was a substantial continuity between the books' storyline and the original history.

Since 1975 the Documentary Hypothesis itself has been subjected to major criticism. Overall, there is now far greater interest in reading the biblical books as literary units, respecting the final version of the text.

So, as you approach this ancient literature, watch out for its big themes. The pivotal turning point will be Genesis 12, as God establishes his rule over Abraham and promises him a land. From then on the Pentateuch will show us these covenant promises being successively fulfilled.

Yet, obviously, they are only fulfilled in part. If there were a complete fulfilment, the Bible's story would end at Deuteronomy! Instead the Pentateuch proves to be but the scene setting for a story that will run and run. And, because the divine promises to Abraham are portrayed as God's response to the *universal* problem of evil, it turns out to be a story which eventually involves us. Thus the Pentateuch is no longer just the history of a particular people in the Ancient Near East; it becomes the first chapter in *our* story, the true story – so it is claimed – of our contemporary world.

Genesis

Opening overture: creation (1:1 – 2:3)

'In the beginning God…' Genesis begins at the very beginning; the word 'Genesis' means 'beginning'. And it begins with *God*. This is a book all about God, focused on his power, character and actions. So throughout this opening chapter, the subject of almost every sentence is God himself: 'God said'; 'God made'; 'God called'… The writer's convictions are clear: behind the created world we see the powerful hand of the God who created the heavens and the earth out of nothing.

The account of creation is painted with a big brush and written in a stylized, memorable way. Having described the earth as 'formless and empty' (that is, without structure or content), the writer portrays the first three 'days' as introducing some *structure* (light, sky, land) and the next three 'days' as filling those three structures with *content* – namely the sun, moon and stars, the birds, and finally animals and humans (see diagram, p. 24). Other key points are also conveyed with great simplicity. God's word is powerful ('and God *said*, "Let there

'In the beginning God created the heavens and the earth. Now the earth was formless and empty, darkness was over the face of the deep, and the Spirit of God was hovering over the waters.'
Genesis 1:1–2

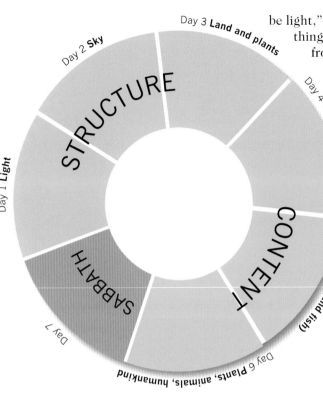

Day 1 Light
Day 2 Sky
Day 3 Land and plants
Day 4 Sun, moon and stars
Day 5 Birds (and fish)
Day 6 Plants, animals, humankind
Day 7

STRUCTURE
CONTENT
SABBATH

be light," and there was light'); his simple say-so can call things into existence. This God is also utterly separate from his creation; so creation is not itself divine, and created objects (like the sun and moon) must not be worshipped. Moreover creation is 'very good' – the result of a loving creator who delights in his work.

And the pinnacle of God's creation is humankind. Human beings are no mere afterthought. They may not be as impressive as the stars, but, unlike them, they have been made 'in God's image' – with a unique capacity to know God and to rule over God's creation on his behalf.

Yet if human beings are the climax of God's creation, they are not its goal. The ultimate purpose of creation is focused on the 'seventh day', the day of sabbath rest – a day for the goodness of creation to be celebrated. Creativity reflects God's image because creation is good.

Verse in Genesis	Hebrew title: 'These are the…'	Content
2:4	'… generations of the heavens and the earth' [**]	Story 1: Adam and his descendants
5:1	'… generations of Adam'	Genealogy: Adam to Noah
6:9	'… generations of Noah'	Story 2: Noah and the flood
10:1	'… generations of the sons of Noah'	'Table of nations' descended from Noah
11:10	'… generations of Shem'	Genealogy: Shem to Abraham
11:27	'… generations of Terah'	Story 3: Abraham and Sarah
25:12	'… generations of Ishmael'	Genealogy of Ishmael
25:19	'… generations of Isaac'	Story 4: Jacob and Esau
36:1, 9	'… generations of Esau'	Genealogy of Esau
37:2	'… generations of Jacob'	Story 5: Joseph and his brothers

** 'Generations' can refer either to a straightforward genealogy or to a narrative story about the persons involved. In 'stories' 3 to 5 this narrative focuses less on the person named and more on his children.

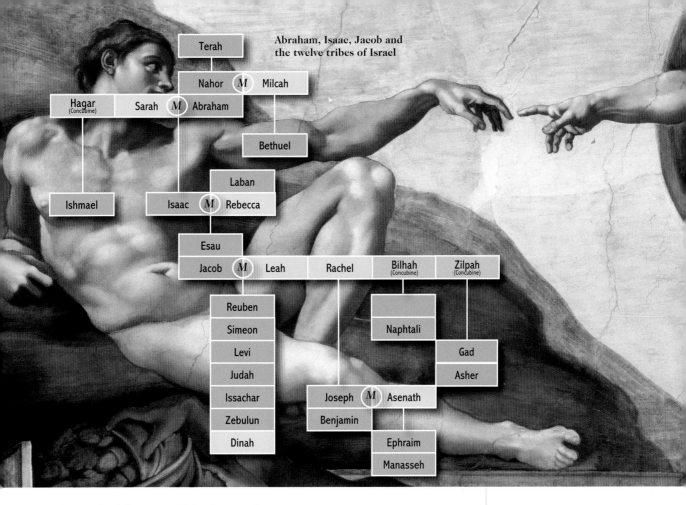

Abraham, Isaac, Jacob and the twelve tribes of Israel

Terah

Nahor — M — Milcah

Hagar (Concubine) — Sarah — M — Abraham

Bethuel

Laban

Ishmael — Isaac — M — Rebecca

Esau

Jacob — M — Leah — Rachel — Bilhah (Concubine) — Zilpah (Concubine)

Reuben
Simeon
Levi — Naphtali
Judah — Gad
Issachar — Asher
Zebulun — Joseph — M — Asenath
Dinah — Benjamin
Ephraim
Manasseh

Story 1: Adam and his descendants (2:4 – 6:8)

The narrator now back-tracks a little and then zooms in expressly on the story of humankind: we see the first man being created from the 'dust of the ground' and becoming a 'living being' through God's breathing into him the 'breath of life'; we see him located in the Garden of Eden and being presented with the other animals but 'no suitable helper' being found for him; and then we see the creation of woman, at which point the man bursts into a song of delight. It is a powerful picture of companionship and intimacy.

Yet it does not last. Adam (which simply means 'the man') and Eve (which means 'living') can enjoy the fruit of the garden with the exception of two trees – the tree of life and the tree of the knowledge of good and evil. Tempted by an evil serpent, Eve takes fruit from the second tree and shares it with Adam. Immediately they sense powerful new emotions – both of shame (realizing they are naked) and of guilt (hiding from God); they also start blaming one another. So God pronounces curses on the serpent, the woman and the man: enmity and tension will now appear in their relationships, and life will be tough. They are thrust out of the garden and the way back to the tree of life from now on is strictly guarded.

The Creation of Adam, by Michelangelo Buonarroti (1475–1564).

'So God created man in his own image... male and female he created them.'
Genesis 1:27

'This is now bone of my bones and flesh of my flesh.'
Genesis 2:23

The Fall in the garden

Genesis 3 is a key chapter within the Bible. In its artless way it brilliantly encapsulates human motivations: our dislike of being told what we cannot do; our desire not just to break rules but to *make* them – to be like God and in charge of our own destiny; the tendency to question God's words or to portray God's purposes as being malign; the temptation to follow what is pleasing to the eye rather than listening with our ears to what is right.

The consequences of human sin are equally vivid: defensiveness and passing the buck; blame and shame; friction between people, and tension between the sexes. Readers see here an echo of their own lives; it truly describes our disordered world.

Genesis 1–3 thus presents us with an important balance. Human beings are *both* created in God's image *and yet* fallen; our natures are neither totally good nor totally evil. Thus, what comes naturally to us may well be wrong; on the other hand, there is no human being who is worthless. So too the created world should be neither deified (treated as divine) nor discarded (treated as junk). Thus in the Bible we will see God not abandoning his creation, but working for its renewal.

The subsequent story of Adam and Eve's descendants is a sad decline – a continued departure from the lost paradise of Eden: their son Cain murders his brother Abel; death comes into the world with its crushing force. There are some notable exceptions (such as Enoch) but overall the picture is bleak, culminating in a tragic indictment of humanity: 'every inclination of the thoughts of the human heart was only evil all the time. The Lord regretted that he had made human beings on the earth, and his heart was deeply troubled' (Genesis 6:5).

Story 2: Noah and the flood
(6:9 – 11:26)

This is the prelude for the story of Noah and the flood. This act of devastation is seen as God's judgment on human sin. It is a kind of *de-creation* before God *re-creates* his world, giving it a fresh start. The key point is that righteous Noah had swum against the tide of sin, walking with God; so God prepares a means of escape for him (in the building of the ark – a large boat). It is thus a story of divine salvation (or rescue) in the face of divine judgment.

God also promises 'never again to curse the ground' and makes rainbows to be the clear guarantee of this promise. However heavy the rain in the future, Noah's descendants can be assured that this will never be the prelude to another total devastation: the sun *will* shine once more.

So the story continues, tracing Noah's descendants through his good sons (Shem and Japheth) and his evil son (Ham). At this point 'the whole world had one language and a common speech'. However, when some people plan to build a 'tower that reaches to the heavens' God responds by scattering them across the earth and confusing their language. They cannot complete their grandiose project. The story almost certainly parodies the great ziggurat built in Babylonia, the top of which was thought to reach into heaven. The narrator instead sees this as a classic instance of human folly and calls the tower 'Babel' – a word which sounds like the Hebrew for 'confused'. Human beings are reduced to speaking *babbling* nonsense.

The story thus encapsulates in pictorial form the issue of human pride and independence. Despite God's re-creation in the era of Noah, there is seemingly an endless clash between God and his creatures. There is now a universal, worldwide problem: has God got any solutions up his sleeve?

Story 3: Abraham and Sarah (11:27 – 25:11)

The answer is yes. God does have a solution to the problem of human sinfulness. He is going to call one man into a unique relationship with himself; and then, through him, he is going to build up a nation that will reflect his holiness and will produce (in due season) a key figure who will finally undo the curse of Adam's sinfulness. So we come to the call of Abram (later renamed Abraham), being told that in this one man and his descendants there lies the solution to the universal problem of

Left: Adam and Eve are depicted in *The Fall from Grace*, by Nicholas of Verdun (1181).

Below: The Elamite 'Ziggurat' (or temple-tower) in ancient Dur-Untash, Mesopotamia (c. 1250 BC): now called Choga Zanbil (Khuzestan, Iran).

NEW LIGHT ON GENESIS 1–11

Some remarkable parallels to Genesis 1–11 have been discovered from ancient Mesopotamia:

- a seventh-century BC cuneiform tablet from Nineveh, which refers to a devastating flood, from the *Epic of Gilgamesh* (originally composed c. 1700 BC);
- the *Atrahasis Epic*, which recounts world history from creation to the flood (for which King Atrahasis builds an ark);
- a similar account (known as the *Eridu Genesis*) emanating from Sumeria;
- a Sumerian king list (c. 1900 BC), listing eight kings before the flood, and then numerous ones after it.

Though some of the material in these accounts is rather bizarre, these were attempted early histories (proto-histories), explaining events along the historical timeline.

Genesis 1–11 is thus the Bible's own proto-history. There are some clear parallels as well as differences – both of detail and of perspective. Thus, instead of many gods, acting in immoral ways, Genesis portrays the one creator God who, being holy, is concerned about evil. Instead of humankind being seen as an accidental after-thought (and as a threat to the gods), men and women are portrayed as God's image-bearers and encouraged to multiply. And, in contrast to the optimistic idea that history was moving in a positive direction, Genesis emphasizes that things are getting worse because of human sin.

The Israelites may have consciously adapted these pagan stories at quite a late date, but arguably they could have preserved an alternative account from very early times.

All four texts refer to a devastating flood. This strongly suggests a memory of a real cataclysmic event. Some now identify this event with the end of the last Ice Age (c. 10000 BC); others with a series of floods in Mesopotamia (known to have occurred c. 3000 BC). Others, however, focus on the flooding of the area now covered by the Black Sea when the dam (where the Bosphorus is now) was breached around 5000 BC. These may not match the common understanding of a flood that covered the entire planet, but anyone seeing water now reaching to all four horizons might be forgiven for thinking the whole of their world had just been obliterated.

The genre of Genesis is thus perhaps best described as 'primeval history' – neither straightforward history nor pure myth. Nor was it intended to be scientific, for there are fairly clear hints that the act of creation was consciously being described in broad brush terms so that readers could be taught key theological insights (God's transcendence, his delight in his creation, the power of his word, and the importance of human beings within his purposes), all of which would have been missed by a merely scientific account. By contrast, it is remarkable how the biblical account conveys them so artlessly and so succinctly.

Cuneiform tablet (25 cm x 19.4 cm) with the Atrahasis Epic (c. 1650 BC): from Sippar, southern Iraq.

human sin: *Abram* is thus the divine response to *Adam*.

Abraham's father Terah had set out earlier from Ur of the Chaldees, travelling northwestwards to Haran. While there Abraham receives a dramatic call from God to 'Go... to the land I will show you;' God is promising to make him into a 'great nation', through which all peoples will be blessed. So Abraham courageously sets out towards the land of Canaan, accompanied by Sarah his wife and his nephew Lot.

The remainder of Abraham's story reveals how these incredible promises are fulfilled despite many setbacks. Above all, there is the key problem that Abraham has no children. Sarah suggests to Abraham a surrogate marriage with her slave-girl, Hagar (who gives birth to Ishmael), but this is not the solution God intends. Three mysterious visitors then announce that 'this time next year' Sarah will have a baby boy – at which ridiculous idea the elderly Sarah simply laughs! The prediction, however, comes true, and Isaac is born.

All eyes are now on Isaac, but in a seemingly bizarre episode Abraham receives a command from God to offer Isaac as a sacrifice. Abraham sets out with a heavy heart, but then God shows him a ram caught in a nearby bush and overturns the original command: and the child of promise survives. So Abraham's story finishes on a much happier note – with Isaac being married to Terah's great-granddaughter, Rebekah. Abraham's family line looks set to continue into the future. The whole story is told at some length, giving us fascinating

*'Is anything too hard
for the Lord?'*
Genesis 18:14

Abraham would have lived a nomadic existence (similar to modern Bedouin), so he greeted his mysterious visitors 'at the entrance to his tent' (Genesis 18:1).

The divine promises to Abraham

'Go... to the land I will show you. I will make you into a great nation... and all peoples on earth will be blessed through you.'
Genesis 12:1–3

This is the foundational promise in Genesis – and indeed in the whole Bible. It outlines the essential shape of God's kingdom (see p. 15) – God exercising his rule over a chosen people in a designated geographical place.

Within Genesis itself the promise is repeated often – both to Abraham and then to his descendants, Isaac and Jacob. It becomes clear that this is an 'everlasting covenant'; that circumcision is its outward sign; and that it is based simply on Abraham's faith – Abram 'believed the Lord, and he credited it to him as righteousness' (Genesis 15:6). Yet God is also evidently looking for obedience within the covenant. So when Abraham reveals his deep obedience with regard to Isaac (Genesis 22), the divine promise is confirmed even more strongly: 'all nations on earth will be blessed, because you have obeyed me'.

This long-term goal of bringing blessing to *all* nations is vital. The very name 'Abraham' mean the 'father of *many* nations'. Eventually his offspring (or 'seed') will outnumber the stars and will include 'nations and kings' – indeed a 'community of peoples'. So Paul will teach in Galatians that this promise has finally been fulfilled in Christ (the true 'seed' of Abraham) as people from all nations (both Jew and Gentile) come into the new worldwide people of God through their faith in Christ.

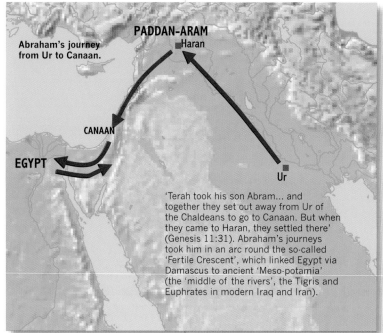

PADDAN-ARAM
Haran

Abraham's journey
from Ur to Canaan.

CANAAN

EGYPT

Ur

'Terah took his son Abram... and
together they set out away from Ur of
the Chaldeans to go to Canaan. But when
they came to Haran, they settled there'
(Genesis 11:31). Abraham's journeys
took him in an arc round the so-called
'Fertile Crescent', which linked Egypt via
Damascus to ancient 'Meso-potamia'
(the 'middle of the rivers', the Tigris and
Euphrates in modern Iraq and Iran).

Top right: Modern Bedouin
women can wear elaborate
jewellery. Sarah, Rebekah,
Leah and Rachel (the wives of
Abraham, Isaac and Jacob)
play a key role in the way their
family story develops.

insights into life in the early second
millennium BC: we see betrothal
and marriage customs; patterns of
hospitality outside nomadic tents;
treaties being brokered and land-
purchase agreements being discussed
at the city gate. Abraham emerges
as a real, imaginable character,
marked by some evident weaknesses. Yet Abraham's great faith in God
shines through, as he trusts God's promise about his descendants
(reiterated five times in different ways). On one occasion, Abraham is
given the sign that is to accompany this 'covenant'-promise – his male
descendants are to be circumcised. This then ensures that the divine
promise will not get lost in future generations because those to whom
the promise has been given will be identifiably different. So, when Isaac
is circumcised 'on the eighth day', we are witnessing the birth of the
chosen nation.

After his death Abraham is buried in the cave outside Hebron. This
family grave would be the only piece of land Abraham ever owned – a
tiny foothold in the land he had been promised.

Story 4: Jacob and Esau (25:19 – 35:29)

After a short interlude, which lists the descendants of Ishmael (the
child of Hagar), we come to the story of Isaac's twin sons Jacob and
Esau. It is a story of a long-running family feud that eventually reaches
a happy resolution. From the start, Isaac loves Esau; Rebekah loves
Jacob. Jacob (whose name effectively means 'grasping deceiver')
persuades Esau to give up his birthright as the first-born son and then
(helped by Rebekah) cheats his blind father into giving him, not Esau,
his death-bed blessing. Esau then plans to kill Jacob, at which point
Jacob flees far away to Rebekah's brother Laban.

Marrying into Laban's family, Jacob raises a large family of his own and eventually considers making his return. Jacob is understandably anxious about Esau's reaction and decides to send a string of gifts ahead of him – himself coming at the rear. Then he sees Esau in the distance – approaching with 400 men. Is Esau coming to kill him? But 'Esau ran to meet Jacob and embraced him.' It is a powerful moment of reconciliation. The sibling rivalry is over.

The whole story is shot through with fascinating detail and is carefully arranged in a 'chiastic' structure (see diagram, right), which highlights the central importance of the birth of Jacob's son Joseph.

This careful structure also reveals the importance of two key episodes in Jacob's life when he had powerful encounters with God. The first is when he is fleeing from the land: he has a dream, in which he sees a stairway to heaven and hears God encouraging him with an assurance of divine protection until his return.

'For to see your face is like seeing the face of God, now that you have received me favourably. Please accept the present, for God has been gracious to me.'
Genesis 33:10–11

25:19–34	First encounters of Jacob and Esau	A
26:1–33	Isaac and the Philistines	B
26:34 – 28:9	Jacob cheats Esau out of his blessing	C
28:10–22	Jacob meets God at Bethel	D
29:1–14	Jacob arrives at Laban's house	E
29:15–30	Jacob marries Rachel and Leah	F
29:31 – 30:24	Birth of Jacob's sons	G
30:25 – 31:1	Jacob outwits Laban	F'
31:2–55	Jacob leaves Laban	E'
32:1–2	Jacob meets angels of God at Mahanaim	D'
32:3 – 33:20	Jacob returns Esau's blessing	C'
34:1–31	Dinah and the Hivites	B'
35:1–29	Journey's end for Jacob and Esau	A'

The episode of Jacob wrestling with God comes when he is on his own, having sent his family across the River Jabbok (which flows from near Amman down into the Jordan).

Jacob names the place Bethel ('house of God') and vows his loyalty to God.

The second episode is when he returns to the land some twenty years later: Jacob has a mysterious encounter, wrestling through the night with a strange 'man', and emerging thereafter with a pronounced limp. The man, however, assumes a seemingly divine role – offering his blessing to Jacob and renaming him Israel (meaning 'he struggles with God'). In some strange way, then, Jacob has been struggling with God and he names the place Peniel ('face of God') – because he had survived seeing God face to face. It is a powerful experience, which marks Jacob for life (literally and metaphorically), but which also signals his being broken and remade by God. For, after a lifestyle marked by deceit, the trickster is himself outwitted by God. Yet he also finds his identity reshaped – his new name Israel highlighting how he had truly engaged with God.

This all happens on the night before Jacob meets Esau. So, for the narrator, their reconciliation is the result of God's powerful intervention. Despite their failings, this family is one in which God is at work. What will happen next?

Story 5: Joseph and his brothers (37:2 – 50:26)
After an interlude to describe the descendants of Esau (the older brother who, like Ishmael, is *not* the child of the promise), the story continues with an account of Jacob's children, focused especially on his son Joseph. This lengthy story has become justly famous. For it is a finely worked piece of writing, full of colour and deep emotions. It is also a story of God at work, bringing good out of evil and tenaciously fulfilling his promises.

Joseph, though only the eleventh of Jacob's twelve sons, has some precocious dreams in which he rules over his brothers. They become increasingly hostile to him, aware too that he is their father's favoured child. Eventually they sell him to some traders travelling down to Egypt. Joseph ends up in the household of Potiphar, an important man in Pharaoh's Egypt. When Potiphar's wife tries to seduce him, he flees but is then accused of initiating the seduction and is thrown into prison. There he languishes for several years until Pharaoh's butler remembers how this young Hebrew had correctly interpreted his dream (that he would be released from prison). He recommends him to Pharaoh, who has been troubled by some dreams. So Joseph is ushered into Pharaoh's presence and succeeds in explaining his dreams (that there would be seven years of plenty in Egypt followed by a severe famine). At this, Pharaoh appoints Joseph to be in charge of food reserves, effectively making him his prime minister.

So, when the famine strikes and Jacob's family comes down from Canaan to Egypt to buy grain, Joseph is the one responsible for selling

Joseph sold into Egypt, by William Brassey (1846–1917).

grain to his brothers. Joseph recognizes them immediately but they have no idea who this official is. Joseph accuses them of being spies and requires that they bring their youngest brother (Benjamin) back with them before he will sell them any grain. After they return with Benjamin, things get still worse, with Benjamin being arrested by Joseph for supposedly stealing a precious goblet. So do the brothers return to their father without Benjamin (almost certainly precipitating Jacob's death through grief) or do they risk Pharaoh's wrath by pleading Benjamin's innocence? Joseph has them hanging on a thread.

Then, in a remarkable act which reveals a deep change of heart, Judah steps forward – the brother who had suggested selling Joseph to the traders. Judah now offers to take the punishment instead of Benjamin, laying down his life vicariously on behalf of his brothers. At this Joseph bursts into tears and finally reveals his true identity. It is a truly dramatic moment. And so the final chapters are marked by incredible joy as Joseph asks them to bring back his ageing father, and as Jacob meets Joseph's children. The book closes with Jacob blessing his own children and ensuring that he and Joseph will have their bones carried back after their deaths to the Promised Land.

'I am your brother Joseph, the one you sold into Egypt! And now, do not be distressed and do not be angry with yourselves for selling me here, because it was to save lives that God sent me ahead of you... to preserve for you a remnant on earth and to save your lives by a great deliverance.'
Genesis 45:4–5, 7

* * *

The importance of Genesis, as the first book within the Bible's plot line, cannot be overstated. It introduces us to the story's chief character – God. We see his sovereignty, his holiness, his love for human beings, his being at work to bring good out of evil.

Yet the book also opens up the dramatic tension which the rest of the biblical story will seek to resolve: sin has entered into God's good world; human beings are now out of sorts with their creator and have been banished from the garden of God's presence.

Genesis 12 then marks the pivotal turning point in the Bible's storyline. It is the launch of God's rescue plan. In terms of the five-act play (outlined on p. 17), we have sat through the first Act in the biblical drama (the creation and the Fall) and are now being introduced to Act II: the calling into existence (through Abraham) of the nation that will come to be known as Israel.

We will be in Act II throughout the rest of the Old Testament. And, if ever we wonder why there is this seemingly narrow focus on the single nation of Israel, we should remind ourselves of the story's opening back here in Genesis: this nation is the one through whom *all* nations will be blessed and through whom God will deal with the *worldwide* problem revealed in Genesis 1–11. So the story, far from being very small and particular, ends up being a universal story – God's story for the world.

Once we come to the New Testament, we will discover that its writers are convinced that Jesus has inaugurated the next act in this drama. Jesus is the ultimate descendant of Abraham, says Paul, who has dealt with human sin and re-opened the way back into God's presence. Through him God's blessings can now go out to all nations, and those who display a faith like Abraham's will be welcomed into God's people. Thus the divine covenant outlined to Abraham, Isaac and Jacob has now been fulfilled and *all* people, not just the circumcised, may now share in its blessings.

There are many other ways in which the New Testament will look back to Genesis; for example Jesus himself quotes Genesis 2 as the basis for marriage; Peter compares Christian salvation to Noah's rescue from the flood; Revelation portrays heaven in terms reminiscent of the Garden of Eden.

The New Testament's own story also echoes Genesis: Abraham's willingness to offer his only son as a sacrifice turns out to reflect something of God's own activity in the event of Jesus' crucifixion – not sparing his only Son; and Joseph, like Jesus, becomes the means of saving those who have hated him.

Genesis thus proves to be not only a rich treasure trove but also the fundamental building block for the rest of the Bible. It reveals the Bible's essential framework – its worldview of creation, the Fall and God's rescue – and invites us then to find our own place within that world.

Come, let us sing for joy to the Lord...

For the Lord is the great God,
*   the great King above all gods.*

In his hand are the depths of the earth,
*   and the mountain peaks belong to him.*

The sea is his, for he made it,
*   and his hands formed the dry land.*

Come, let us bow down in worship,
*   let us kneel before the Lord our Maker.*

Psalm 95:1a, 3–6

Exodus

'The Israelites groaned in their slavery… God heard their groaning and he remembered his covenant with Abraham.'
Exodus 2:23–24

Will the people of Israel ever return to the Promised Land? The book of Exodus tells the story of how, several generations later, the God of Abraham indeed rescues his people, bringing them up to the land of Canaan, and reveals himself to them in awesome events in the Sinai desert. It is a book, as its title suggests, about a dramatic exit (or exodus, departure) – from slavery in Egypt to freedom in the Promised Land.

Prior to departure (chapters 1–11)

Exodus begins with a bleak picture. Over a period of nearly 400 years the people of Israel have expanded considerably, causing them to be viewed as unwelcome immigrants and a threat to Egypt's national security. The pharaohs try to impose population control (ordering baby boys to be killed) and force them into slave labour. But God is 'concerned about them' and has a plan.

The plan is focused on a Hebrew baby boy, hidden by his mother in a basket on the Nile. Pharaoh's daughter finds him and chooses to raise him as her own adopted son, giving him a quite common Egyptian name – Moses. Some years later Moses runs away from Pharaoh's court. He goes out into the Sinai desert, where in due course he marries a Midianite girl.

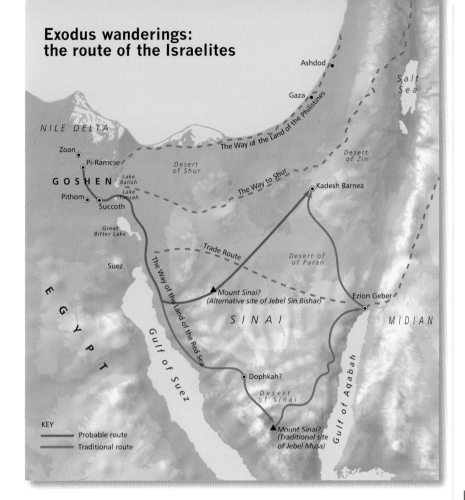

Exodus wanderings: the route of the Israelites

NILE DELTA

Ashdod

Gaza

Salt Sea

The Way of the Land of the Philistines

Zoan

Pi-Ramese

Desert of Shur

Desert of Zin

GOSHEN

Lake Ballah

The Way to Shur

Pithom

Lake Timsah

Kadesh Barnea

Succoth

Great Bitter Lake

Trade Route

Desert of of Paran

Suez

The Way of the Land of the Red Sea

EGYPT

Mount Sinai?
(Alternative site of Jebel Sin Bishar)

Ezion Geber

SINAI

MIDIAN

Gulf of Suez

Dophkah?

Desert of Sinai

Gulf of Aqabah

Mount Sinai?
(Traditional site of Jebel Musa)

KEY
— Probable route
— Traditional route

The Israelites fled across the 'Sea of Reeds' – quite probably to the area of the 'bitter lakes' which may have been joined up to the Red Sea (Gulf of Suez) in that period. Traditionally, Mount Sinai has been identified with Jebel Musa, quite far to the south, but recent scholarship has suggested the more northerly Jebel Sin Bishar. The events of Numbers 1–11 are set near Kadesh Barnea.

Christians in the 4th century identified this as the site of the burning bush. A small chapel was built over its roots and the area later brought within the Monastery of the Transfiguration. It is a rare species of the rose family called Rubus Sanctus, native to Sinai and extremely long-lived.

It is here in the desert that he has a profound encounter with God. He sees a bush, which strangely is in flames but is not being burned up. He also hears a voice calling him by name: 'I am... the God of Abraham... I am sending *you* to Pharaoh to bring my people the Israelites out of Egypt.' Moses responds with some bold questions: how can he, Moses, know that this is for real? And how can he persuade Pharaoh to set the Israelites free? So Moses is given some signs of God's miraculous power and is promised the help of his older brother Aaron. Above all, however, he is given the assurance of God's own unique identity: 'say to the Israelites: "I AM has sent me to you."' This name (in Hebrew script made up of the four letters *Y H W H*, now rendered as 'Yahweh' or translated as 'the Lord') can also mean 'I will be'; it thus speaks of God's eternal existence and his faithful constancy and reliability.

Moses then returns to Egypt and tells the Israelites what God has promised. The people initially are overjoyed; but then Pharaoh responds by making the Hebrews' working conditions even worse, and so the people turn on Moses and Aaron. Moses goes back to Yahweh to demand an explanation. And he hears in reply the same promise, only this time even stronger: 'I will redeem you... and I will bring you to a

Hieroglyphs from the temple in Edfu, built in the 3rd century BC. It is the best preserved temple in Egypt.

'I am the Lord, and I will bring you out from under the yoke of the Egyptians.'

Exodus 6:6

land flowing with milk and honey…' Yahweh is building a *relationship* with his people; and he will surely rescue them and give them a *place* where they can serve and worship him.

A contest between Pharaoh and Yahweh is then fought out through the famous sequence of ten plagues, which come on Egypt in response to Moses' predictions as given to him by Yahweh. The Nile tended to flood each September, so the first plague (the Nile being turned to blood) may have been caused by flagellates (micro-organisms) coming down the river and thus killing the fish. This led in turn to the frogs leaving the river; next the damp conditions led to a plague of mosquitoes and then dog flies. After that the dead frogs led to anthrax being carried by the flies to cattle and then humans. And then three regular hazards of Egyptian life (hail, locusts and darkness) hit the land – probably the result of a severe desert sandstorm.

So the first nine plagues, though particularly severe on this occasion, were perhaps not totally out of the ordinary. From Pharaoh's perspective they could thus be dismissed as just an unusually rapid sequence of previously experienced phenomena. From the perspective of the biblical narrator, however, this was the determined activity of Yahweh. And the tenth plague, when Yahweh 'passes over' the land in a judgment which results in the death of every first-born son in the land, is clearly no coincidence but demonstrates Yahweh's unique power.

The story is told with appropriate repetition, but each time there is a slight variant that builds up a real sense of tension and crescendo. Pharaoh, for example, begins to suggest that only the Israelite *men* need go, leaving behind the women and children; next, that *everyone* can go but they must leave behind their *animals*. Moses insists, however, that it is all or nothing – 'not a hoof is to be left behind'! Sometimes Pharaoh asks Moses for relief from the plague, sometimes he confesses he has been wrong; but each time he reneges on his promises. Pharaoh increasingly 'hardens his heart', reacting obstinately to this revelation of Yahweh's supreme power.

'I will take you as my own people and I will be your God.'
Exodus 6:7

The River Nile at sunrise.

From Egypt to Sinai (chapters 12–18)

Prior to the last plague, Moses had told the Israelites that they must slaughter a lamb or goat and then daub the door-lintel of their houses with the animal's blood: 'when the Lord goes through

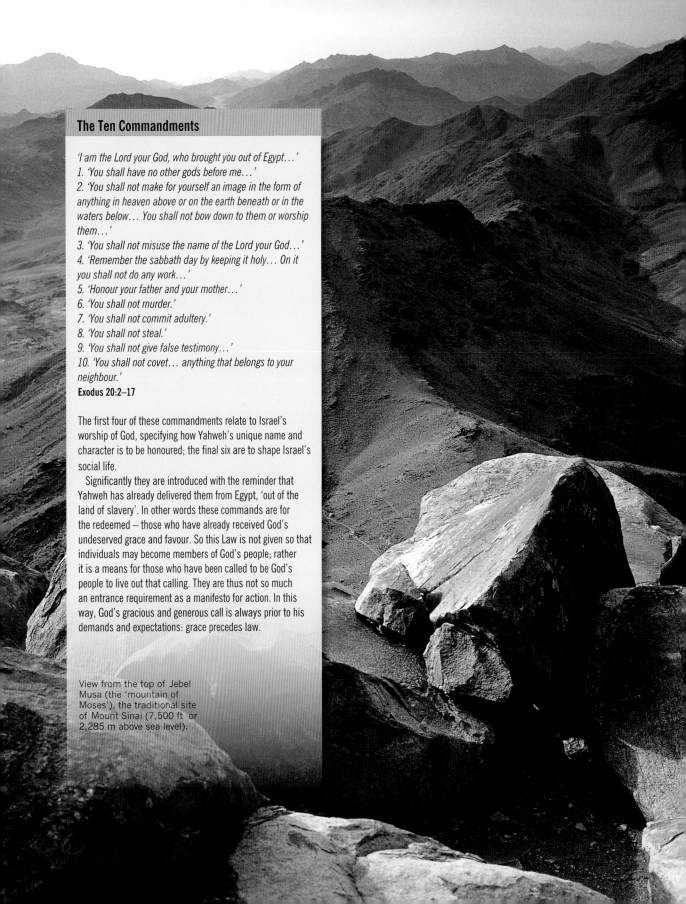

The Ten Commandments

'I am the Lord your God, who brought you out of Egypt…'
1. *'You shall have no other gods before me…'*
2. *'You shall not make for yourself an image in the form of anything in heaven above or on the earth beneath or in the waters below… You shall not bow down to them or worship them…'*
3. *'You shall not misuse the name of the Lord your God…'*
4. *'Remember the sabbath day by keeping it holy… On it you shall not do any work…'*
5. *'Honour your father and your mother…'*
6. *'You shall not murder.'*
7. *'You shall not commit adultery.'*
8. *'You shall not steal.'*
9. *'You shall not give false testimony…'*
10. *'You shall not covet… anything that belongs to your neighbour.'*

Exodus 20:2–17

The first four of these commandments relate to Israel's worship of God, specifying how Yahweh's unique name and character is to be honoured; the final six are to shape Israel's social life.

Significantly they are introduced with the reminder that Yahweh has already delivered them from Egypt, 'out of the land of slavery'. In other words these commands are for the redeemed – those who have already received God's undeserved grace and favour. So this Law is not given so that individuals may become members of God's people; rather it is a means for those who have been called to be God's people to live out that calling. They are thus not so much an entrance requirement as a manifesto for action. In this way, God's gracious and generous call is always prior to his demands and expectations: grace precedes law.

View from the top of Jebel Musa (the 'mountain of Moses'), the traditional site of Mount Sinai (7,500 ft or 2,285 m above sea level).

the land… he will see the blood… and *pass over* that doorway.' So Israel's first-born sons will be spared. And, sure enough, when the 'destroyer' *passes over*, only the Egyptians' houses have been struck.

At this, Pharaoh finally relents. So the Israelites set out eastwards, ready for a journey into the wild unknown. The Israelites are going *home* – to the land of their forefathers.

However, they are not yet completely safe. Pharaoh changes his mind and sends his troops out in hot pursuit. What are the Israelites to do as they approach the Sea of Reeds? The people panic, but Moses assures them that Yahweh will deliver them. Throughout the night there is a strong east wind, which enables all the Israelites to negotiate their way through the waters successfully. Towards morning, however, Moses stretches out his hand again, and the wind changes direction. Pharaoh's chariots are unable to get through and all his troops are drowned. On seeing this the Israelites burst into song (the so-called 'Song of Moses'), praising Yahweh for his great power.

After these two dramatic actions by Yahweh (first the Passover and now this passing through the waters) one might expect this stance of faith to last for some time. Instead, however, there follow three episodes where the Israelites grumble at Moses, not trusting Yahweh to provide for them: the water is too bitter; next there is no food; and, finally, the water supply runs out altogether. 'Why did you bring us up out of Egypt?' they complain, thereby challenging Yahweh's whole rescue plan. Yet Yahweh acts to provide for his people: he causes water to gush forth when Moses strikes a rock, he sends some quail for them to eat along with the mysterious manna (a bread-like substance that appears on the ground each morning except on the sabbath). Yahweh indeed provides for his people – despite their ingratitude and lack of faith.

The giving of the Law (chapters 19–24)

Six weeks after this escape, the Israelites arrive at the 'mountain of God' in the Sinai desert – the same place where Moses had earlier encountered Yahweh in the burning bush. This now becomes the scene for a unique revelation of Yahweh. In a dramatic spectacle marked by thunder, fire and trumpet-blasts, Yahweh manifests his divine presence. The mountain becomes a sacred space, with Moses alone being allowed up to the summit.

This then is the setting for Yahweh giving the essential ingredients of his divine Law – the Ten Commandments. These basic principles are to

Passover

Modern nations often celebrate key events in their founding with a special anniversary. So too ancient Israel would look back each year to the dramatic events of the Passover. Exodus thus includes instructions on this future celebration: there is to be a week-long festival of unleavened bread; the Passover meal is to be eaten by everyone in their households, but must exclude uncircumcised foreigners. And throughout the year all first-born sons are to be 'redeemed' soon after their birth – with special sacrifices offered as a reminder that it is only through God's mercy that they have been spared.

Passover was celebrated each spring throughout the Old Testament era. Some celebrations were particularly memorable (for example, those under Joshua, Hezekiah and Josiah). By the first century AD those who could travel to Jerusalem would celebrate the meal in extended family groups within the city walls. The meal would remind them of their affliction in Egypt – with a lamb (sacrificed earlier that afternoon in the Temple), with unleavened bread and bitter herbs, and with a mixture (*haroset*), that, though sweet to taste, looked like the mud from which they were forced to make bricks.

There was also a retelling of the Exodus story (the *Haggadah*) in which participants imagined themselves being rescued from Egypt. In the New Testament period – with the Jewish nation finding itself under Roman occupation – Passover was the season of renewed hopes that God would once again rescue his people. This would then make Jesus' dramatic words at his Last Supper with his disciples all the more shocking: his death at Passover would be his rescue of people by his own 'body' and 'blood'.

'The Lord is my strength
   and my defence;
      he has become my
         salvation…
The Lord is a warrior…
Pharaoh's chariots and
   his army
      he has hurled into the
         sea…
Who among the gods is
   like you…?
The Lord reigns for ever
   and ever.'
Exodus 15:2–4, 11, 18

undergird all that the Israelites do, colouring their public and private lives. If they obey these, Moses is told, they will truly be Yahweh's treasured possession, a holy nation and capable of acting in the face of other surrounding nations as a 'kingdom of priests' – that is, revealing Yahweh's character to those who have not been privileged to receive this unique revelation.

The Ten Commandments are followed by several chapters which give guidance on how these basic principles are to be worked out in a wide selection of circumstances (or what we might call 'cases'). Here there are rules about such things as: how are slaves to be treated? What compensations should there be for accidents? What is the right response to theft or dishonesty?

So there is a frank acknowledgment that the Israelites will *not* follow these commandments perfectly – hence the clear teaching on how imperfect situations can be brought back on track. Ideals will not always be maintained, but Yahweh still wants his people to be holy.

Moses then reads to the people this 'Book of the Covenant' (presumably both the Ten Commandments and the subsequent material); and they respond in a special ceremony with promises that they will worship God and obey his teaching. And so, in a fitting climax, the 'glory of the Lord' comes to settle on the mountain – appearing as a cloud to Moses but also (to the Israelites viewing from a distance) as a 'consuming fire'. It is a powerful theophany – an awesome manifestation of Yahweh's presence.

Disaster averted (chapters 32–34)

Yet a major crisis is just around the corner. Moses is up the mountain for forty days receiving further instructions from Yahweh. This is far too long for the people, who soon become restless. In an act of blatant disobedience, they persuade Aaron to set up for them an idol for worship in the form of a golden calf. *This*, they proclaim, is the god who had brought them out of Egypt.

This triggers the greatest crisis in divine–human relations since the flood (p. 26). Moses walks down the mountain, carrying some stone tablets on which have been written the Ten Commandments,

'You yourselves saw what I did to Egypt, and how I carried you on eagles' wings and brought you to myself.'
Exodus 19:4

and immediately smashes them. The covenant, so recently agreed, now lies in pieces. And Yahweh threatens to destroy this 'stiff-necked' and 'corrupt' people, sending them on their way without his presence.

At this Moses pleads with God to turn from his wrath and to forgive his people. He offers to have his own name struck out of the 'book of life' if only Yahweh will spare his people. And Yahweh responds in grace, relenting from his threatened judgment and revealing to Moses more about his glorious name. So Moses returns once more from the mountain, carrying two freshly rewritten tablets of the Law, and relays to the people what he has seen and heard. And his face, we read, 'was radiant because he had spoken with the Lord'. For Yahweh had spoken to Moses 'face to face, as one speaks to a friend'.

There are clearly lessons to be learned. From now on the Israelites should understand that being Yahweh's people is no trifling matter. Evidently they are his people not because of their own intrinsic worth but because of his gracious calling – for they turn to idolatry at a moment's notice. Moreover, this inherent sin within them will then always require God's forgiveness – needing to be removed from his sight (or atoned for).

The tabernacle: Yahweh's presence and atonement
(chapters 25–31; 35–40)
This need for atonement and forgiveness explains why so much space is given in the final chapters of Exodus to the construction of the tabernacle. This is effectively a portable tent, which the Israelites are to take with them through the desert. It is also called the 'tent of meeting', the place where they will meet with Yahweh. Essentially it is to contain two key components: an altar for sacrifices and an inner sanctuary known as the Most Holy Place (or the Holy of Holies). These two features will then highlight the two basic truths which Israel is being taught in the desert – this urgent need for atonement from their sins and the reality of Yahweh's presence among them. They cannot have the latter without the former; only if their sins are 'covered' can they enjoy his dwelling among them. Despite Israel's idolatry, Yahweh still graciously offers to be the king who dwells with his people.

So the book ends on a climactic note. When the tabernacle has been built in accordance with Yahweh's instructions, the 'cloud of the glory of the Lord fills the tabernacle'; so God's

'The Lord, the compassionate and gracious God, slow to anger, abounding in love and faithfulness, maintaining love to thousands, and forgiving rebellion, wickedness and sin. Yet he does not leave the guilty unpunished.'
Exodus 34:6–7

'Then I will dwell among the Israelites and be their God.'
Exodus 29:45

Bronze-gilded bull, from the temple of Baalat-Gebal, Byblos, Lebanon. Dating from c. 1800 BC, it would have been used as a votive offering to the pagan god Baal.

presence will now be 'in the sight of all the house of Israel during all their travels'. Yahweh is truly travelling with his people.

***

The book of Exodus moves the Bible's plotline forwards in some dramatic ways:

- The family, through whom God is going to combat sin in his creation, has expanded from just one individual, Abraham, and now comprises a large nation.

- God is beginning to restore his rule over a disobedient world through giving this nation his Law.

- And, if after the Fall human beings had been banished from God's presence (see p. 25), the Israelites are now being given – through the tabernacle – a taster of a restored Paradise and the means of enjoying God's presence.

Exodus also introduces us to the big theme of redemption: the Israelites are rescued by God, brought out from slavery into freedom and transferred from the harsh service of Pharaoh into a new kind of service – namely, worshipping Yahweh and living as *his* people. All that happens to Israel will now have to be seen against this background of redemption – they have been 'purchased' by God's undeserved grace. So later biblical writers will look back to this Exodus redemption as the defining moment in their national life and long for God to perform a new exodus.

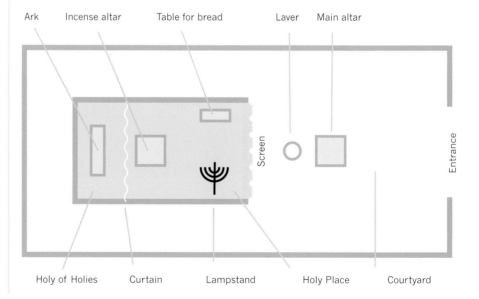

Plan of the Tabernacle (or 'Tent of Meeting'), as described in Exodus 25–31 and 35–40.

Ark   Incense altar   Table for bread   Laver   Main altar

Screen

Entrance

Holy of Holies   Curtain   Lampstand   Holy Place   Courtyard

moment in their national life and long for God to perform a new exodus.

The New Testament writers will then teach that, in Jesus, Israel's God has indeed performed this new exodus. In Luke's Gospel, Jesus' death and resurrection are explicitly referred to as an *exodus*. God is redeeming all people at a new and deeper level – from 'slavery to sin' – and Christian believers are described as those who have been brought out from slavery into freedom.

At the heart of this redemption is the event of Passover. This too is seen in the New Testament as dramatically fulfilled by Jesus in his death. At his Last Supper, Jesus indicates that his death will be like that of the Passover lamb – a death which causes God's judgment to 'pass over' those who are 'covered' by his blood. The book of Exodus thus proves to be a vital, essential instalment in the Bible's story.

Your ways, God, are holy.
What god is as great as our God?

You are the God who performs miracles;
you display your power among the peoples.

With your mighty arm you redeemed your people,
the descendants of Jacob and Joseph.

The waters saw you, God,
the waters saw you and writhed;
the very depths were convulsed.

Your thunder was heard in the whirlwind,
your lightning lit up the world;
the earth trembled and quaked.

Your path led through the sea,
your way through the mighty waters,
though your footprints were not seen.

You led your people like a flock
by the hand of Moses and Aaron.

Psalm 77:13–20

Leviticus

Leviticus is not the easiest book to read. It has no stories and virtually no action. Instead it is almost entirely a long list of instructions given by Yahweh to Moses. It reads like an official rulebook, dealing with minutiae; and the subject matter is, to modern readers, remote and even bizarre.

Yet, if we take ourselves back into the mindset of ancient Israel, Leviticus reveals some rich treasures. Thus one very positive theme is that Israel's God is the God of *vibrant life*. That's why things which showed signs of not enjoying 'fullness of life' (maimed animals, or people who had been touching corpses) were not to be brought into his presence. And that is also why he gave his laws to his people – because these commands would lead to fullness of life.

'Keep my decrees, for the person who obeys them will find life by them.'
Leviticus 18:5

Name of sacrifice	Purpose	Types of animal	Hand-laying	Use of blood	Priestly portions	Lay portions
Burnt	Not to be eaten by anyone (priest or lay) because its purpose is to offer the whole animal to Yahweh as an act of devotion and dedication (poorer people can offer a grain or cereal offering instead).	Cattle, sheep, goats, birds	Yes	Poured on altar sides	No	No
Peace (or fellowship offering)	The worshipper is allowed to have a good share of the meat – precisely because this offering is one where a family is having a meat meal (quite a rarity!) to celebrate or give thanks for something.	Cattle, sheep, goats	Yes	Poured on altar sides	Yes	Yes
Sin	The blood is smeared onto the altar in order to effect the worshipper's forgiveness and to protect the holiness of the altar.	Cattle, sheep, goats, birds	Yes	Smeared on altar, sprinkled inside tent	Yes, usually	No
Guilt	This offering is somewhat rarer, in response to unintended sacrilege but especially to being caught stealing. It involves the worshippers restoring what they have stolen, offering a ram and making an extra monetary payment (20 per cent of the value of either the ram or the item stolen).	Rams	Probably	Poured on altar sides	Yes	No

Table 1: Procedures for different sacrifices.

Laws on sacrifice and the ordination of Aaron's family
(chapters 1–10)

The opening chapters spell out procedures for a series of different sacrifices. Underneath the four main types of sacrifice there is a common pattern (with hands being laid on the animal, its blood being used liturgically and then its meat being eaten), but there are also important variants (see table above).

There is then a short narrative describing Aaron's ordination as high priest. This is in some ways the centrepiece of the book. After Aaron's disobedience in the episode of the golden calf (see p. 42), the reader might wonder whether Moses will ever ordain Aaron. Yet, because of God's grace, he does.

So, one week later, Aaron offers sacrifices himself and blesses the people. When Moses and Aaron emerge from the Tent of Meeting, Yahweh reveals his presence. Two of Aaron's sons, however, having somehow offered 'unauthorized fire', are consumed by Yahweh's fire, causing Moses to remind Aaron sternly of Yahweh's words: 'Among those who approach me I will be proved holy.' This is no game. Yahweh may be good, but he is not 'safe'.

One of the main tasks of the priests would be to face towards this holy God, offering sacrifices on behalf of the people – acting as

A limestone altar (30 cm square top; 67 cm high) used for burning incense – not animal sacrifices. From Megiddo, northern Israel (c. 1050 BC).

'The glory of the Lord appeared... when all the people saw it, they shouted for joy and fell face down.'
Leviticus 9:24

Human Beings	Animals	Birds	Fish
Priests	Sacrificial animals (cattle, sheep, etc.)	Sacrificial birds (doves, pigeons, etc.)	
Israel	Clean animals (cloven-hooved, cud-chewers)	Clean birds (all except birds of prey)	Fish with fins and scales
Other nations	Unclean animals	Unclean birds	Water creatures without fins and scales

Table 2: The grades of holiness.

intermediaries between them. Yet, they would also have responsibilities towards the people: teaching them God's rules and preserving the distinction between the 'holy and the common'. This then explains two final sections of Leviticus – with their focus on what is unclean and what Yahweh wills for Israelite society.

Treating the unclean (chapters 11–16)

Two key insights may help us appreciate the focus of Leviticus here on the unclean:

- **The language of cleanness is being used in a primarily religious sense** – describing that which is 'fit for worship'. Uncleanness is that which might defile Yahweh's dwelling-place. As noted above, this particularly rules out things which in some way signify death rather than abundant life (for example, birds of prey are unclean). It may also rule out people who are temporarily unclean – not because they are somehow sinful, but simply because they need to observe basic procedures of hygiene before attending worship.

- **Israel's dietary laws reflected the nation's sense of being called by Yahweh to be his special people.** Thus, just as Yahweh, when faced with all the nations of the world, had restricted his choice to Israel, so his people had to limit their food intake to that which was clean. Table 2 (above) explains how the food they offered in sacrifice was to reflect their own calling as God's clean people in the world – fit for worship.

The section closes with regulations for the annual Day of Atonement (Yom Kippur), designed to cleanse the Tent of Meeting of any contamination and procuring atonement for the sins of Israel. On this unique day, the high priest was to go alone into the Most Holy Place to smear the 'atonement cover over the ark' with sacrificial blood. The high priest would also lay his hand on a goat, confessing the Israelites' 'wickedness'; the goat, known as the scapegoat, would then be escorted from the precincts and released somewhere far away in the desert.

Holiness in practice – the 'holiness code' (chapters 17–27)

This final section tackles the worst kind of uncleanness – that moral corruption which could contaminate even the land itself. For several times here the Israelites are warned that the Promised Land may 'vomit' them out if they pursue various 'detestable' practices.

In chapters 18–20 we find clear commands on a range of matters: killing one's children in sacrifices to other gods; consorting with mediums; and cursing one's parents. Illicit forms of sexual relationship are also ruled out – some because they are adulterous (one of the parties being married), others because they are a form of incest (the parties being close relatives); further categories that are also forbidden include homosexuality and bestiality.

Overall these practices are described as 'detestable' and 'defiling', for they do not lead to true and abundant life. Yahweh wants his people to be different: 'I am the Lord your God, who has set you apart from the nations… to be my own.' Evidently, in contrast to those nations, there is a better way of being human.

The book closes with further instructions, some relating to the sanctuary (on priests, religious festivals and fulfilling vows: see table 3, above), others relating to social issues. Here Leviticus mentions two important principles:

1. If there is a need for restitution between people, then the offending person(s) should pay back what they have taken (or suffer what they have inflicted), but it should be directly proportionate and not excessive (the so-called *lex talionis*: 'an eye for an eye, a tooth for a tooth').

2. Every seventh sabbath year (that is, every fifty years) there was to be a Jubilee, when surrendered property was to be returned to its original owner and hired servants given their freedom. No Israelite was to be permanently disenfranchised, losing their stake in the land, or kept in servitude forever.

Festival	Date	Modern time of year	Reference
Passover	14th–21st of first month	Easter	23:4–14
Weeks	1st of third month	Pentecost	23:15–21
Trumpets	1st of seventh month	Late September	23:24–25
Day of Atonement	10th of seventh month	September/October	23:27–32
Booths	15th–22nd of seventh month	October	23:34–43

Table 3: The year's festivals.

Leviticus 19: Love, Holiness and Justice

The second most important commandment (summarized as neighbourly love by Jesus in Matthew 22:39) appears within a long list of instructions in Leviticus 19:

'Be holy because I, the Lord your God, am holy.
Each of you must respect your parents, and you must observe my sabbaths… Do not turn to idols or make metal gods…
When you reap the harvest, do not reap to the very edges of your field; leave them for the poor and the foreigner.
Do not steal. Do not lie. Do not deceive one another. Do not swear falsely…
Do not defraud your neighbours or rob them. Do not hold back the wages of a hired worker overnight…
Do not go about spreading slander among you. Do not do anything that endangers your neighbour's life. Do not hate a fellow Israelite. Do not seek revenge… but love your neighbour as yourself.
Stand up in the presence of the aged…
When foreigners reside in your land, do not mistreat them… Love them as yourself, for you were foreigners in Egypt.'

The list is framed by a revelation of God's holiness and a reminder of his gracious act of redemption; so these are ethical guidelines for God's redeemed people. Yet this blueprint for authentic and meaningful life may have remarkable relevance for all societies. For, if Israel's society was to reflect the values of an eternal creator, then these ancient commands, far from being primitive, may contain within them the recipe for a 'civilized' society in any age.

*Ascribe to the Lord the
    glory due his name;
bring an offering and
    come into his courts.*

*Worship the Lord in the
    splendour of his
    holiness;
tremble before him,
    all the earth.*

Psalm 96:8–9

The book concludes with a list of blessings and curses. These decrees, if followed, will bring life; but, if not, disobedience will lead to death and calamity.

* * *

Leviticus has proved remarkably influential. Its ideal of neighbourly love was upheld by Jesus as the second greatest command. Its vision of a Jubilee year has in recent years inspired international campaigns to release poorer nations from debt. And Leviticus has left many with a profound sense of God's holiness.

Christian interpreters have also seen it as enshrining a key principle that explains Jesus' death – namely, that true atonement comes about through means of a divinely sanctioned sacrificial death. Though perhaps bizarre to modern ears, Jesus affirmed this principle and the writer of Hebrews sees Jesus' death as the one true 'sacrifice for sins'. Indeed, in Hebrews, Jesus is both the ultimate sacrificial victim and also the true high priest who offers his own blood 'once and for all' (see further pp. 275–76). As a result, the sacrificial requirements of Leviticus become redundant because of Christ's death. Yet they permanently illustrate the key point – that a holy God can only be approached through an atoning death.

Not all of Leviticus, however, can be seen in this light. In addition to these sacrificial regulations (often termed 'ceremonial' or 'cultic' laws), there are laws of both a moral and civil kind. By and large, the New Testament writers are clear that these *moral* requirements continue in force, as seen, for example, in 1 Peter 2 (below, p. 281).

With regard to the *civil* laws, however, the issue is less clear cut. On the one hand, regulations that perpetuate the distinction between Israel and the other nations are generally seen as redundant within the New Testament era. Now that Jew and Gentile are joined in one new people of God, such things as circumcision and strict dietary laws are outdated. Thus, when Jesus deliberately touched people who were unclean and stated that what people eat cannot make them unclean (see Mark 1:40–45; 7:14–23), he was signalling an end to these civic laws.

On the other hand, there remain parts of Leviticus' civil law that have a potentially international application – for example, the Jubilee laws. In these mandates for Israelite society we sense a divine pattern for the health and well-being of *all* nations. So those responsible for public policy, even in quite different cultures, may well find in Leviticus some key biblical principles for human flourishing.

*'The land must not be sold
permanently, because the
land is mine and you reside
in my land as foreigners and
strangers.'*
Leviticus 25:23

*'For the life of the creature is
in the blood, and I have given
it to you to make atonement
for yourselves... it is the
blood that makes atonement
for one's life.'*
Leviticus 7:11

Numbers

The book of Numbers sounds as though it is going to be all about maths. In fact – apart from two censuses – the book is all about the Israelites' wanderings in the desert. 'Wanderings' is indeed the key word, because the journey from Mount Sinai (where the Israelites are for the first third of the book) to the plains of Moab (where they are for the book's last third) should only have taken a few weeks. Instead the journey takes forty years!

For, in response to the Israelites' grumbling, Yahweh announces that none of the original generation will set foot in the Promised Land. They are poised to enter, but never do. Literally, so near and yet so far. Yet great lessons were learned here in the heat of the desert; Israel's national character was forged in this crucible of waiting. For here the Israelites discovered their dependence on God's provision, his utter holiness, and the strength of his promise.

Key chapters in Numbers

The Aaronic blessing (chapter 6)

Spies' visit to Canaan (chapter 13)

Korah's rebellion (chapter 16)

Water from the rock (chapter 20)

Balaam's prophecies
(chapters 22–23)

In the Sinai and Negev deserts, through which the Israelites wandered, there are some surprising springs of water: this is the spring near Avdat.

'The Lord bless you
and keep you;
the Lord make his face
shine on you
and be gracious to you;
the Lord turn his face
towards you
and give you peace.'

Numbers 6:24–26

The final months at Mount Sinai (1:1 – 10:10)

The opening chapters are given over to the census, which Moses conducts to see how many men over twenty are able to serve in the army. The total emerges as 603,550 (on this, see box, below). This figure, however, excludes the Levites, who are not to fight because they are responsible for 'caring for the tabernacle of the Testimony'.

Much of the subsequent instruction is similar to Leviticus: for example, clarifying procedures for those who become unclean and dealing with suspected cases of marital unfaithfulness. It describes the ceremonies for the Levites' consecration and the tabernacle's dedication. It also contains the famous Aaronic blessing.

From Sinai to Kadesh Barnea (10:11 – 20:21)

Then, at last, some thirteen months after they first left Egypt, the cloud of God's presence (which by night 'looked like fire') 'lifted from above the tabernacle'. This was God's signal to leave – they must now follow wherever the cloud leads.

Problems with Numbers

The two censuses in Numbers give the total number of men over twenty as 603,550 and 601,730; this suggests a total population of around 2 million. Although Jacob's family might have multiplied to this extent over the four centuries spent in Egypt, these figures remain extraordinarily high.

These figures have been questioned for three reasons:

• If the number of first-born males was 22,273 (Numbers 3:42), the average family unit would have contained over thirty-five male children.

• The Israelites were normally able to find enough water, and were all close enough to see various things in the camp centre (for example, Moses going into the tent or the bronze serpent). Moreover, they are described as the 'fewest of all peoples'. Overall it is hard to imagine 2 million people surviving in the desert, or 600,000 men storming Jericho.

• Archaeology suggests that the first settlements in Palestine had populations in the hundreds, not thousands.

Perhaps, then, the biblical writers have either exaggerated or given numbers belonging to a later period? Arguably, however, the numbers were originally recorded using an alphabetical system, later misunderstood. There are also known instances where the Hebrew word for 'thousand' refers instead to a smaller unit or clan; it may also have referred to a 'captain of 1,000' (just as a centurion supposedly looked after a hundred men). Both these meanings may have occurred in the census figures and later become confused in copying. A more likely figure is around 20,000 fighting men (with a total population of 75,000).

Returning from Canaan, the Israelite spies 'cut off a branch bearing a single cluster of grapes; two of them carried it on a pole between them, along with some pomegranates and figs' (Numbers 13:23). Here we see something similar in a relief of an Assyrian procession: Nineveh (c. 700 BC).

They set out in good heart. Three days later, however, they are complaining about their monotonous diet of manna. Egypt begins to look rosy by comparison: 'We remember the fish we ate in Egypt... the cucumbers, melons, leeks, onions and garlic.' So the same old negative behaviours are seen again now as they leave.

Yet this time things turn out even worse. Yahweh again sends some quail for them to eat, but this time a plague breaks out. Moses again strikes a rock to produce water, but this time Yahweh senses something wrong in Moses' attitude and announces that he and Aaron will never enter the Promised Land. And when the Israelites are again attacked by the Amalekites, this time they are defeated. Yahweh seemingly now expects the Israelites to have a new trust in him – presumably because of the awesome revelations recently given at Sinai.

Yet the people prove instead to be ungrateful and unfaithful: they simply do not trust Yahweh to provide for them. Hence their response to the report brought back by the spies sent into Canaan. Two of them, Joshua and Caleb, are upbeat about the land and are confident that Yahweh will help them. The majority, however, paint a negative picture, saying they felt 'like grasshoppers' when compared with Canaan's inhabitants. The people immediately panic and want to choose a leader to take them back to Egypt.

Yahweh sees this as a contemptuous failure to trust him despite the many miraculous signs they have witnessed. Once again Yahweh's threatened destruction is only averted through Moses' intervention, as he prays for Yahweh to remember his great love and forgive the people who now bear his name. In the end the Israelites are told that only Joshua and Caleb will enter the land; everyone else in that generation will die in the desert.

The last straw is a defiant mutiny. Korah, Dathan and Abiram lead an uprising against Moses and Aaron. In a series of dramatic events – including the ground opening up to swallow the three ringleaders and their families – Moses and Aaron are vindicated by Yahweh. In particular the Levites learn that, despite their own particular privileges, they are not allowed to be priests. That prerogative belongs only to Aaron's family.

From Kadesh Barnea to the Plains of Moab (20:21 – 36:13)

So the Israelites set out, going back southwards to the desert. At this point Aaron dies and is succeeded by his son Eleazar. Some time later venomous snakes also invade their camp; Moses responds by holding up

The Israelites circled around to the eastern side of the Dead Sea, travelling through the territory of the Moabites (in modern Jordan). This early morning view from near Mount Nebo looks south-westwards across the northern end of the Dead Sea towards the hill-country of southern Judah.

a bronze snake, which brings healing to those who look at it.

The big issue, however, is this: how are the wandering Israelites to engage with the various people groups around them? For to those watching its movements, this vast nomadic tribe poses a real threat. The Israelites send messages of peace to the Edomites (descendants of Jacob's brother Esau) but are threatened with attack. They move on northwards to the area ruled by Sihon, king of the Amorites, and Og, king of Bashan. Here they are drawn into battle and emerge victorious. They then return to the plains of Moab, where the Moabites fear that these invaders will 'lick up everything' around them.

So the Moabite king, Balak, summons a Mesopotamian seer called Balaam to look down over the Israelites camped below in the plain, hoping he will pronounce a curse over them. Balaam, however, is constrained by Yahweh to speak only *his* words: out from Balaam's mouth come five oracles which serve only to confirm Yahweh's promises.

So powerful oracles are being uttered at the top of the hill. However, down below (as at Sinai) there are problems. A number of Israelite men are having sex with the nearby Moabite women and worshipping their god – the Baal of Peor. Aaron's grandson, Phinehas, kills one of the leading culprits, and Moses, for the first and only time, is commanded to conduct a 'holy war' against the Moabites. The Israelites are successful, but their warriors are treated as unclean. War, though necessary, is still an evil that needs cleansing.

By now Moses has conducted his second census. This time he is working out the different sizes of the tribes for the time when the Promised Land will be apportioned. For there is a real optimism in

'How can I curse those whom God has not cursed?'
Numbers 23:8

'A ruler will come out of Jacob...'
Numbers 24:19

these final chapters that the land will soon be theirs, with Yahweh giving new instructions for their life in the land – the land where he himself will be present.

The book of Numbers thus ends on a positive note. Despite Israel's many failures and Yahweh's judgments, the covenant promise will surely be fulfilled. Only one dark cloud hangs over the narrative. Moses knows he himself will never enter the land. In preparation for this, fearing the people would be left as 'sheep without a shepherd', Moses has already been instructed to appoint Joshua as his successor. But, after all the challenges to Moses' own leadership, how will this transition work?

Today, if only you would hear his voice,

'Do not harden your hearts as you did…
in the wilderness,

where your ancestors tested me…

For forty years I was angry with that generation;
I said, "They are a people whose hearts go astray…"

So I declared on oath…
"They shall never enter my rest."'

Psalm 95:7–11

* * *

The book of Numbers demonstrates how Israel, despite the revelations at Sinai, was slow to learn its lessons. So the book gives us an extended primer in what it means to belong to Yahweh's people. What the Israelites learned in harsh reality, we can learn by proxy from their example: God is holy, God is faithful, so his people must avoid unbelief, idolatry and immorality, and, if they wish to enjoy his presence, they must approach him on his terms, not their own.

What was true for the Israelites back then has been equally true for individual believers ever since – hence the frequent references back to Numbers made by Paul and others in the New Testament. For here the apostles saw important principles to be heeded by all God's people in Christ as they travel towards the new Promised Land. So, in the words of a famous Welsh hymn ('Guide Me, O Thou Great Redeemer'), this book encourages believers to see themselves travelling as 'pilgrims through this barren land' and asking God to guide them until they arrive safely 'on Canaan's side'.

'Do not defile the land where I dwell, for I dwell among the Israelites.'
Numbers 35:34

A plateau in the Moabite hills, with the Dead Sea rift valley visible in the distance beyond.

Deuteronomy

In Deuteronomy we listen to the final words of Moses – his last will and testament before his death. The book is therefore poignant, full of accumulated wisdom, but also full of vision – as Moses' words provide a foundational charter for Israel's future existence as a nation. Here, then, we will find the essential DNA of ancient Israel.

Although Deuteronomy literally means a 'second law' (based on the Greek translation of 17:18), the book is more strictly a reinforcement of the *original* Law given at Mount Sinai. Deuteronomy is thus an extended exposition of that Law, seeking to motivate God's people to be faithful to God's covenant. As they stand on the threshold with new responsibilities, how will they respond to this challenging agenda for their future?

Some of the earliest evidence for writing is of pictographs used by temple administrators, recording the storage of goods. This Sumerian clay tablet (c. 3100–2900 BC) predates the era of Moses by at least 1,500 years.

Moses' first speech (1:1 – 4:43)

The bulk of Deuteronomy is made up of three speeches given by Moses. The first speech begins with a review of the Israelites' recent history – as seen in Exodus and Numbers. There is then a powerful call to obedience in the hope that the surrounding nations will note Israel's wisdom and comment on Yahweh's closeness to his people. Israel is evidently meant to be a shop window on God's character, a missionary bridge head within the world – pointing others to the reality of its righteous God. This call, however, is underpinned by severe warnings against idolatry; if the Israelites succumb to idol worship, they will be scattered among the nations. Even so, Yahweh will never forget the covenant he made with their forefathers. Israel's God thus exhibits both severe judgment and profound mercy.

The speech closes with some reminders that Israel's experience has been unique: hearing the living God, being called by him to be his people, being 'brought out of Egypt by his Presence and great strength'.

Verses	Deuteronomy's structure	Compared with ancient treaties
1:1 – 4:43	Moses' first speech ('these are the words': recapitulation)	Preamble (listing parties involved) and historical prologue (recent events)
4:44 – 28:68	Moses' second speech ('this is the law': exposition)	General stipulations and more detailed stipulations
29:1 – 30:20	Moses' third speech ('these are the terms': exhortation)	Blessings/curses (sanctions) and 'witnesses'
31:1 – 32:47	Final instructions and the 'Song of Moses'	
32:48 – 34:12	Moses blesses the tribes of Israel, climbs Mount Nebo and dies	

The covenant

The Old Testament is, literally, the Old Covenant. Its authors are telling the story of God's covenant promises. In the Bible God makes covenants on several occasions (with Noah, with Israel at Mount Sinai, with King David) but arguably these are all related to one main stream of covenant promises – made originally to Abraham (see p. 29) and then confirmed by Jesus in the days of the 'new' (or 'renewed') covenant.

A covenant was a solemn agreement between two parties, involving commitments on both sides. It was similar to a business contract, but it went deeper, emphasizing more personal aspects of the parties' relationship; hence 'covenant' language was used to express the commitments of marriage. The Old Testament's conviction is that, amazingly, Israel's God wants to enter into such a personal commitment with his people; he plays, as it were, the role of a loving bridegroom (an image picked up by Hosea, who portrays Israel acting like an unfaithful bride: see p. 161). In Deuteronomy, we thus see great emphasis on

Yahweh's covenant with the Israelites being based on his loving-kindness; and they are to love him with 'all their heart'.

Yet the book also suggests a comparison with the 'vassal-treaties', which were drawn up in the Ancient Near East between rulers and their subjugated peoples. For Yahweh is also Israel's authoritative king. Such treaties regularly contained blessings and curses, encouraging people not to break this solemn agreement. Deuteronomy follows this pattern, with some of its closing chapters (27–28) acting as a severe warning against disobeying Yahweh. Yet the book also adapts the pattern, highlighting how Yahweh, though Israel's king, is also the God of abundant grace, providing for his people.

They are therefore to 'keep his decrees' so that they 'may live long in the land the Lord gives them'.

Moses' second speech (4:44 – 28:68)

Moses' second speech is the main heartbeat of the book. It begins by repeating the Ten Commandments (see p. 40). Obeying these will mean that the Israelites 'enjoy long life' and 'increase greatly in a land flowing with milk and honey'. There then follows the famous *Shema* (Hebrew for the opening command, 'hear'):

Hear, O Israel: The Lord your God, the Lord is one.
Love the Lord your God with all your heart
and with all your soul and with all your strength.

Deuteronomy 6:4–5

This overarching principle then colours the following chapters (6–11). The Israelites are not to become proud, but must take every opportunity to explain these commands to their children. They are not to be contaminated by the idolatry of the Canaanites (see further p. 70). However, when the Israelites witness Yahweh's help in conquering the land, they should not start trusting in their own righteousness, but recognize that they are a 'stiff-necked' people who had to be humbled and tested in the desert. God has chosen them not because of any merit but simply because of his great love; so they must treasure his words,

'Has any other people heard the voice of God speaking out of fire…? Has any god ever tried to take for himself one nation out of another nation, by testings, by signs and wonders, by war, by a mighty hand and an outstretched arm?'
Deuteronomy 4:33–34

'For you are a people holy to the Lord your God… [who] has chosen you out of all the peoples on the face of the earth to be his people, his treasured possession.'
Deuteronomy 7:6

and never forget his love and grace. They are to 'circumcise their hearts', to 'fear the Lord and serve him', to 'hold fast to him'. For 'he is their praise' and he is giving them a 'covenant of love'.

From chapter 12 onwards the focus becomes more specific, with detailed instructions in the Promised Land. In essence the Ten Commandments (with their focus on true worship and on life in society) are simply being fleshed out here in more detail.

An ancient set of rules from the Hittite empire (c. 1400–1200 BC), laid out in the form of a treaty or agreement – similar to the format used in Deuteronomy between God and his people.

Moses looks across from Mount Nebo, seeing the land of Canaan, but dies before entering it himself: this is the view north-westwards from Mount Nebo towards the Promised Land beyond the river Jordan.

True worship

- Radical action must be taken to purge away the evil of idolatry (including its custom of child sacrifices).

- Tithing is to be practised (with priests and Levites being properly catered for).

- Unclean foods must be avoided and the *kosher* principle followed of avoiding meat and milk in the same meal (14:21).

- Sorcery and witchcraft are to be detested.

Lawsuits

- Judges must not accept bribes and there must always be two or three witnesses. Any 'false witnesses' are to be punished in direct proportion to the evil they had inflicted on the innocent party – a 'tooth for a tooth'.

- There are procedures for dealing with unsolved murders and the provision of several 'cities of refuge' for those needing asylum after accidentally committing manslaughter (to prevent an endless cycle of revenge).

- Intentional murder, however, is a capital offence, as is adultery (even with a person only *engaged* to be married); as a result, there are some criteria for distinguishing between innocent and complicit victims of rape.

Other guidelines

- Inheritance issues are discussed.
- Among fellow Israelites there is to be no usury and every seventh year their debts are to be cancelled. Loans and pledges need to be carefully controlled, preventing abuse of the poor.
- Proper procedures are to be observed in times of war.

The speech then draws to a close by outlining a future ceremony in which the Israelites will pronounce a series of blessings and curses; these effectively summarize the preceding laws in a more liturgical form. In chapter 28, however, these are spelled out in minute detail – which makes for some chilling reading.

Moses' final speech and death (29:1 – 32:48)

In the final speech Moses again summons all Israel to him, and then calls them to 'enter into a covenant with the Lord your God this day' – a covenant which will confirm them as his people; he warns them again that abandoning this covenant will lead to divine judgment, but repentance to God's blessing. He finishes with a rousing appeal:

> *See, I set before you life and prosperity, death and destruction… This day I call heaven and earth as witnesses against you… Now choose life, so that you and your children may live and that you may love the Lord your God, listen to his voice, and hold fast to him. For the Lord is your life, and he will give you many years in the land he swore to give to your fathers, Abraham, Isaac and Jacob.*

Deuteronomy 30:15, 19–20

'All these curses… will pursue you and overtake you… You who were as numerous as the stars in the sky, you will be left but few in number… the Lord will scatter you among the nations… There… you will find no repose [but have] an anxious mind, eyes weary with longing, and a despairing heart.'
Deuteronomy 28:45, 62, 64–5

'The Lord your God will circumcise your hearts… so that you may love him with all your heart and with all your soul, and live… The Lord will again delight in you and make you prosperous.'
Deuteronomy 30:6, 9

*'Is this the way you repay
  the Lord,
    you foolish and unwise
    people?
Is he not your Father,
    your creator,
  who made you and
    formed you?*

*Remember the days of old;
    consider the generations
    long past.*

  *Ask your father and he will
    tell you,
  your elders, and they will
    explain to you.*

*When the Most High gave the
  nations their inheritance,
when he divided all the
  human race,
he set up boundaries for
    the peoples
  according to the number of
  the sons of Israel.'*

Deuteronomy 32:6–8

These climactic words take us to the heart of the book's purpose: the call to obedience to the Lord in the land, an obedience which will prove to be truly life-giving. Yet the narrative climax, which readers are prepared for in various ways, is yet to come – the death of Moses. After reciting the famous 'Song of Moses', which will serve as an indictment of this faithless people, Moses climbs Mount Nebo, where he sees the Promised Land, and then dies.

These final chapters prove incredibly powerful as the drama moves towards its predicted close. The theme of Moses' certain death is interwoven tightly with the other theme – the *uncertain* destiny of Israel. What more can Moses possibly do to ensure his people are faithful to the Lord after he has gone? He has preached to them at length and called them to covenant renewal, outlining the covenant's blessings and curses; he has left them a song to recite and pronounced his own parting blessing. The book's readers, in this moment of solemn respect for the dying Moses, are being prevailed upon by every possible means to pledge their own loyalty to the God whom Moses served and knew face to face. But will they?

* * *

So ends the Pentateuch, the so-called 'books of Moses'. In terms of the Bible's developing plotline the key foundations are now clearly in place. And the reader has been left with a key question to be asking as the story unfolds: will Israel prove faithful to Yahweh or not? For the blessings and curses pronounced in Deuteronomy hang like a cloud over all that follows: will they experience God's blessing in the land or will they be sent into exile?

Deuteronomy is thus strategic within the Bible's developing story. It has also proved indispensable within later Christian thought. The New Testament sees Jesus, who himself quoted from Deuteronomy more than any other book (for example in his period in the desert: see pp. 193–94), as the 'prophet like Moses' predicted in Deuteronomy 18. And Paul draws upon it quite heavily when outlining the fulfilment of God's covenant faithfulness in Christ (see p. 234).

In Deuteronomy we see two great truths. First, we see the covenantal nature of God's grace: having redeemed his people, God brings them into a covenant relationship of grace and love. He is a God of committed, faithful relationship who gives good things to his people – gifts such as forgiveness, belonging to God's people and knowing his presence in their lives. And these gifts are precisely gifts – undeserved expressions of divine generosity, given to those whom God has already graciously redeemed.

Thus *what Israel is called to do* (chapter 12 and following) is only spelled out after we have heard *what God has done for them*

*We will tell the next generation
  the praiseworthy deeds of the Lord…*

*He decreed statutes for Jacob
  and established the law in Israel,
  which he commanded our ancestors
  to teach their children…*

*Then they would put their trust in God
  and would not forget his deeds
  but would keep his commands.*

Psalm 78:4–5, 7

God's people were to treasure 'every word that comes from the mouth of the Lord' (Deuteronomy 8:3). Over the centuries Deuteronomy and the rest of the Pentateuch were carefully preserved on 'Torah scrolls'.

(chapters 1–11). Their communal life is a response to God's prior self-revelation. In this profound way, grace actually *precedes* the law.

Deuteronomy thus challenges its readers to respond in gratitude to the God of grace, turning away from alternative modes of worship and coming to love him with all their heart and soul.

Second, Deuteronomy offers a compelling vision that the whole of human life is to be brought under the sphere of God's rule and be sanctified by his values. So it contains some remarkable principles which can be applied to all societies: the sanctity of human life; the value of community relationships; the importance of people not being separated from a means of livelihood; and the priority of showing kindness to the disadvantaged and the alien in one's midst. Such principles, which were placed in Israel's foundation charter, can provide a powerful blueprint for other societies to enshrine within their common life.

'[The Lord] defends the cause of the fatherless and the widow, and loves the foreigners residing among you, giving them food and clothing. And you are to love those who are foreigners, for you yourselves were foreigners in Egypt.'
Deuteronomy 10:18–19

History

The twelve 'historical books' cover a period of over 800 years: from the Israelites' first arrival in the Promised Land to the period of their exile in Babylon and eventual return. These books contain many different styles of writing: memoirs, building descriptions, laws, prayers, battle accounts, public speeches and so on. They give a fascinating insight into the world of ancient Israel and, though hotly contested, there are good grounds for seeing them as conveying accurate historical information. The writers indeed have a theological view of history (bringing their God into the story), but this does not make their writings non-historical (see further p. 69); nor does the lack of corroborating evidence from outside the Bible, for there is always an 'argument from silence'. Instead the events described here fit remarkably well with the general setting established from archaeology.

Their location within the Old Testament
Although the Hebrew Bible has these books in a different order, modern translations reflect the order established in the Greek translation of the Hebrew Bible (the so-called Septuagint, from the third century BC). Yet this alternative arrangement does not affect the books' interpretation and accurately conveys that these twelve books, unlike any other Old Testament books, are all historical *narratives*. They therefore provide the historical backbone to the Old Testament and explain the context in which the prophetic books were written. For this reason alone there is real merit in readers becoming familiar with the storyline at this point, since it will greatly help those seeking to understand the Old Testament's subsequent sections.

Issues of history and dating
When exactly were these books written? The final edition of 2 Kings cannot precede 562 BC (referred to in its final verses). So some scholars suggest that much of the material from Joshua onwards was written up for the first time in this exilic period. Moreover, the discovery of the 'book of the Law' during the reign of Josiah (see p. 90) probably refers to the book of Deuteronomy. Although some see this as a veiled hint that Deuteronomy was *first composed* at this time, others argue that this was the time when some scribes (the so-called Deuteronomistic historian[s]) were inspired by Deuteronomy's rediscovery to compose the books of Joshua to Samuel. Yet, quite feasibly, these earlier works were first drafted much closer to the events described; some scholars therefore see Judges 4–5 as some of the earliest texts in the Old Testament. These earlier historical books could then simply have been *re-edited* by the Deuteronomistic historian and/or the final editors of 1 and 2 Kings in the exilic period.

Meanwhile, Chronicles, Ezra, Nehemiah and Esther all describe *post*-exilic events. Since both Ezra and Nehemiah contain material written in the first person by these two individuals, Ezra and Nehemiah themselves may have composed the first drafts. Yet the close overlap which exists between them (and between the end of Chronicles and the start of Ezra) indicates that their *final* edition probably coincides with that of Chronicles (itself perhaps influenced by Ezra the priest). So these four books may have been published in their present form around 400 BC (see p. 18). Meanwhile Esther describes events around 475 BC, presumably being written down soon afterwards.

One particular historical issue concerns the dating of Israel's arrival in the Promised Land under Joshua. If Solomon began building the Temple in 967 BC (as commonly supposed), and if this was indeed 480 years after the Exodus (see 1 Kings 6:1), then that suggests a date of 1447 BC for the Exodus and 1407 for the conquest. However, this is problematic since Canaan was very much under Egyptian control during the fifteenth century BC. Joshua and Judges give no hint of such Egyptian control (indeed, quite the reverse!). Egyptian control, however, waned late in the thirteenth century, creating a power vacuum which would make the Israelites' conquest a possibility.

Most scholars therefore argue for a later dating, with the conquest being c. 1230 BC. Other supporting arguments include:

- The earliest Egyptian reference to the Israelites existing in Canaan is found on the Merneptah stele (late thirteenth century).

- The Amarna letters (c. 1360–1330 BC), which include references to cities such as Hazor and Shechem, make no reference to the events mentioned in Judges but presume that Pharaoh should be informed of local developments.

- There is clear archaeological evidence that Hazor was destroyed by fire in the late thirteenth century (which fits with Joshua 11:13) and that Israelite occupation of various Canaanite villages had begun by the period known as Iron Age I (early twelfth century).

So the reference to 480 years might best be understood as referring to a period going back twelve 'generations' ('generation' being a notional period of forty years); in historical reality the time gap of these twelve generations might be c. 325–350 years. This means the dates assigned to the different judges must contain some overlap (see p. 70); and Jephthah's claim that Israel had occupied the land 'for 300 years' (Judges 11:26) was either a known exaggeration or based on ignorance.

Granite stone stele from the mortuary tomb of Pharaoh Merneptah (1236–1217 BC), which details his military victories: 'Canaan is captive with all woe. Ashkelon is conquered; Israel is wasted, bare of seed...' Set up by his successor in 1208 BC, it is the oldest reference outside the Bible to 'Israel' as a nation. This stele (318 cm by 163 cm) was discovered in 1896 by Flinders Petrie.

Jericho, the first town conquered by Joshua, is the oldest city in the world (its first walls were built c. 6850 BC); it lies in an oasis below the hills of the Judean desert.

Joshua, Judges and Ruth

The first historical books are remarkable for their raw, unedited, colour. This is no whitewash with everything being neat and tidy. On the contrary, we are introduced to primitive tribal politics – with all its machinations and intrigue. Here we find scenes of deception and trickery; there are disputes over territory and savage reprisals. We read of military manoeuvres, of all-night marches and successful ambushes. We see good promises broken, but immoral vows kept. And we see in a character like Samson the combination of incredible strength and utter stupidity. So to read these books requires something of a strong stomach!

The birth of a nation is seldom straightforward – as seen in numerous parts of the world in our recent history (such as Bosnia, Rwanda or Zimbabwe). Such transitions are never squeaky clean. So the books' authors knew that many events which they described were far from ideal, some downright evil. Yet they recorded them so that the mistakes of history might not be repeated. These episodes became thus a lesson book for Israel about how *not* to be God's people.

Through it all, however, the authors were convinced that Israel's God was still at work. This God was not aloof – having nothing to do with imperfect people – but instead was seemingly determined to stick with his covenant people through thick and thin. This, then, is the story of the biblical God, involved with real people – even during their darkest hours.

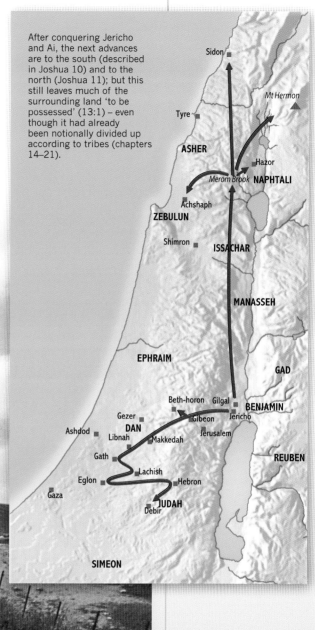

After conquering Jericho and Ai, the next advances are to the south (described in Joshua 10) and to the north (Joshua 11); but this still leaves much of the surrounding land 'to be possessed' (13:1) – even though it had already been notionally divided up according to tribes (chapters 14–21).

'*Keep this Book of the Law always on your lips; meditate on it day and night… Be strong and courageous… the Lord your God will be with you wherever you go.*'
Joshua 1:8–9

Above: 'When Joshua had spoken to the people, the seven priests carrying the seven trumpets before the Lord went forward, blowing their trumpets' (Joshua 6:8).

Above right: Bible translations which speak of 'cities' and 'kings' can give the wrong impression; instead many of the places mentioned in Joshua would have been small villages, with mud-brick houses, ruled by tribal chieftains.

Joshua

The book of Joshua begins with God's promise to be with Joshua as he had been with Moses. The whole book then serves to illustrate this. In Israel's successful crossing of the River Jordan on foot, in the famous collapse of Jericho's walls, in the conquest of Ai and the establishment of their headquarters at Gilgal, we are to see signs of God's faithfulness. Chapter 12 acts as a summary of this first phase of Joshua's campaign, giving a total of thirty-one tribal 'kings' defeated because of God's guiding presence. So 'the land had rest from war'.

There are also other key stories here: Rahab sheltering Israel's spies in Jericho and thus being spared in the eventual attack; the deception of Achan (keeping for himself some of Jericho's plunder when it was supposed to be offered to Yahweh), which led to his being stoned to death; and the Israelites' brave rescue of some Gibeonites, despite having been lured into a treaty with them on false pretences. Overall there is a strong sense of Israel's obedience and consecration to Yahweh, and of *his* active commitment to *them*. This then culminates in a covenant renewal ceremony led by Joshua on Mount Ebal.

Israel's conquest of the Promised Land

How reliable is Joshua historically? Even if the conquest is dated to the thirteenth century (see p. 65), there appears to be no archaeological evidence of Jericho or Ai being inhabited during this period. So some see the conquest narrative as fiction: perhaps the Israelites' ancestors were really indigenous Canaanites, or wandering nomads who settled gradually?

Yet since 1967 archaeologists in the land's central highlands have found over 250 villages that were occupied c. 1200 BC; among their remains, intriguingly, there are no religious shrines and no pig bones. This matches Joshua's account, which suggests that the Israelites (after the initial whirlwind campaign) settled the hill country quite gradually. Joshua only mentions three towns (Jericho, Ai and Hazor) that were razed to the ground; the normal procedure was to drive out the inhabitants, take over their property and then farm the land using local techniques. So we should not be looking for signs of dramatic destruction or massive cultural shifts.

At Jericho, the remains may simply have suffered erosion; at Ai the fortifications, abandoned c. 2200 BC, may have been reused as an outpost by the citizens of neighbouring Bethel. More positively, Joshua's references to the Philistines' 'iron chariots' authentically reflect this new feature of the dawning Iron Age.

With chapter 13, however, we are introduced to Joshua as now 'old and well advanced in years'. What follows then relates to a later period and summarizes what has *not* been achieved during that entire first generation. There are thus lists of the cities that still need to be taken; six cities are designated as 'cities of refuge' (see p. 60); and the tribe of Levi (who are not allocated any land but whose inheritance is the Lord himself) are given as compensation a total of forty-eight towns.

The book closes with a farewell speech from Joshua, in which he rehearses God's faithfulness and warns them not to 'violate the covenant' through idolatry. The author comments that the Israelites had 'rest on every side' – a sure sign that 'not one of the Lord's good promises had failed'. These themes are then expanded in a final covenant renewal ceremony at Shechem with Joshua's resounding appeal that they choose to follow the Lord. When the people promise to serve Yahweh, a large stone is set up as a witness.

Israel's conquest of Canaan poses an urgent and difficult moral problem. What are we to make of the divine command to kill the land's occupants? Is this a form of genocide or ethnic cleansing?

The word used for this killing is *herem* (often translated as 'devotion to destruction') and reflects a concept well known in the ancient world. The full implementation of this *herem* policy, however, was quite limited (only at Jericho and Ai), with inhabitants elsewhere simply abandoning their homes. The numbers of those killed through *herem* was thus quite small.

Even so, the biblical writers see this *herem* as an appropriate punishment for the sin of the Canaanites – not least their child sacrifices. So this judgment falls, not because they were occupying the Israelites' territory, nor because of their race *per se*, but because of their sin. The conquest reveals God's judgment against evil – a reality which in the Old Testament was seen in historical events, but which now (in the light of the New Testament's teaching about resurrection) is manifested primarily after death.

Christians also see this 'holy war' as strictly unique within salvation-history – necessary for the establishment of Israel as a nation. The narrative pattern of the book of Acts suggests we should see this conquest (where Yahweh established his rule in the promised land under Joshua) as now fulfilled in the way God establishes his rule throughout the world under Jesus. Jesus' disciples are to go to the ends of the earth to implement his kingly rule –but not by force of arms.

Judges

The book of Judges receives its name because it tells the next phase of Israel's life as a story gathered around twelve named judges (or rulers) who came to prominence at different points in the next 150 years: Othniel, Ehud, Shamgar, Deborah (with Barak), Gideon, Tola, Jair, Jephthah, Ibzan, Elon, Abdon and, finally, Samson. Precisely because the unified leadership under Joshua came to an end, these judges never ruled over the whole land, but were short-term focal points of leadership among their own (and neighbouring) tribes. They were dotted around the land, and some of them would have been ruling at the same time as each other.

Some of the twelve are only mentioned in passing, but the exploits of others are given in some detail:

- Deborah, who defeats the armies of Hazor under Sisera in the strategic plain of Jezreel;

- Gideon, who defeats the nomadic Midianites with a reduced army of just 300 men;

- and, above all, Samson, the man with enormous strength, who endlessly provokes the Philistines living on the coast. Samson eventually dies in Gaza – when he pushes apart the wooden pillars of the Philistines' temple – thus killing 'many more when he died than while he lived'.

From chapter 2 onwards the narrators give the reader a clear signal about how to interpret what is going on. They sense a cyclical pattern: the Israelites forgot Yahweh, practised idolatry, and experienced military defeat; they then cried out to Yahweh, so in his compassion he sent them a judge who turned things back in their favour. These were generations who 'neither knew the Lord nor what he had done for Israel' and who therefore 'violated the covenant'; in response Yahweh used the surrounding nations to 'test' them to see whether they would 'walk in the way of the Lord'.

Later a key editorial comment is added, repeated in the very last verse: 'In those days Israel had no king; everyone did as they saw fit.' In other words this story is not just about how a highly disunited nation is struggling to find good central leadership; it is also about how God's people are losing their way spiritually. Politically this was a time of messy, even if necessary, transition; spiritually, however, the mess was not strictly necessary. It could have been managed differently if only God's people had been following him more closely. The narrators thus set up an appropriate critical distance from what they are reporting.

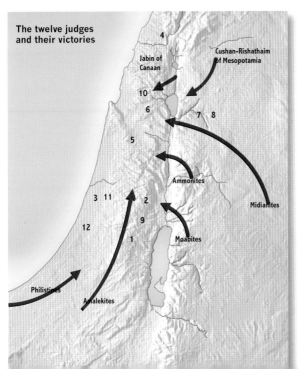

The twelve judges and their victories

1. **Othniel** of Judah (3:10): victory against Cushan-Rishathaim.
2. **Ehud** of Benjamin (3:15): victory against Eglon of Moab.
3. **Shamgar** (3:31): victory against the Philistines.
4. **Deborah** (Ephraim) and Barak (Naphtali) (4:4-6): victory over Jabin and Sisera.
5. **Gideon** of Manasseh (6:11): victory over the Midianites and Amalekites.
6. **Tola** of Issachar (10:1).
7. **Jair** of Gilead (10:3).
8. **Jephthah** of Gilead (11:11): victory over the Ammonites.
9. **Ibzan** of Bethlehem (12:8).
10. **Elon** of Zebulun (12:11).
11. **Abdon** of Ephraim (12:13).
12. **Samson** of Dan (15:20): victory against the Philistines.

Above: The plain of Jezreel (or the Esdraelon Plain) was a fertile area for crops, often contested by armies: Deborah encourages Barak to muster 10,000 men on Mount Tabor, who swoop down upon Sisera's troops.

71

Their perspective hangs like a cloud over the narrative, teaching us that this is precisely *not* Israel as it should be.

So Judges is a sorry chapter of mistakes. Some of the events described must be seen in this light:

- Gideon setting up an idol in his retirement home, which becomes a snare for his family.

- Abimelech murdering Gideon's seventy sons and attacking the city of Shechem in mischievous ways.

- Jephthah vowing to sacrifice to Yahweh whatever first came out of his house to greet him – only to end up sacrificing his only child, his daughter.

- Above all, perhaps, the Benjamites' gang-rape and killing of some guests staying in Gibeah, leading to savage reprisals by all the other Israelite tribes.

There are many brave and heroic episodes; but, mixed up inextricably among them, are such moments and seasons of madness and stupidity.

Yet in this mess there is also Yahweh himself. When Samson's parents rightly question their son's demand to marry a Philistine woman, we read that 'his parents did not know that this was from the Lord'. Bizarrely this was going to be the means by which Israel would have an opportunity to confront the Philistines. So, as we read of Samson's provocative acts against the Philistines (some caused by his love affairs with some of their women), we are meant to see somewhere in this the hand of Yahweh. There are also explicitly times when 'the spirit of the Lord' comes upon characters such as Samson and Gideon; and both their lives are preceded by an appearance of a mysterious 'angel' (or 'man of God'), who indicates that Yahweh will do some amazing things through them. In the darkness, there are thus also some glimmers of light.

Ruth

This beautiful short story, set 'in the days when the judges ruled', could easily have been included within the book of Judges, but at some point it was given a focus all of its own. And rightly so – it is a gem.

The story is simply told. Bethlehem (the town associated with both David and Jesus in later years) is experiencing a famine. So a man called Elimelech migrates some 50 miles east, travelling to the land of Moab, and taking with him his wife, Naomi, and their two sons. The sons marry Moabite wives, but within ten years all the men in the family have died. So Naomi proposes to return to Bethlehem, leaving behind her two daughters-in-law. One agrees to stay, but the other, Ruth, clings to Naomi with the famous words: 'Where you go, I will go... Your people will be my people and your God my God.'

On arriving in Bethlehem, Ruth goes into the fields, following the harvesters, working hard to pick up any left-over grain (as encouraged in Mosaic law). The field she works in turns out to belong to a man called Boaz. When Ruth mentions his name to Naomi, Naomi is overjoyed at Yahweh's kindness: for this Boaz is a distant relative of her deceased husband. As such he was potentially what was known as a kinsman-redeemer. When a man died without sons, Israel's law encouraged a relative to marry his widow, so that a new heir could continue the family name. This was the role Boaz could fulfil!

So Naomi encourages Ruth to ask Boaz to be her kinsman-redeemer, to protect her and to marry her. Boaz agrees to the proposal in principle. But he chooses to act properly and warns her that there is another man who is her closer relative and who therefore has what we would call first refusal. The next morning, surrounded by the town's elders at the city gate, Boaz discusses the issue with this other man, who eventually decides he will not act as the kinsman-redeemer. So Boaz buys the land that had belonged to Elimelech and marries Ruth 'in order to

In ancient Israel the barley was normally harvested in April, the wheat in May: Ruth thus arrived in Bethlehem in April.

The city-gate (left) at Shechem was built in the 11th century BC around the time of Abimilech (Judges 9, see p. 72); to deter attackers, city gates were often constructed in a zig-zag shape, surrounded by guard-rooms, but at other times were a natural meeting-place for the town's elders (Ruth 4; Psalm 127:5).

maintain the name of the dead with his property, so that his name will not disappear from among his family or from his hometown'. The book then ends with Naomi's delight in caring for her grandson, Obed, the child born to Ruth and Boaz. Naomi's earlier bitterness has been transformed into profound joy.

The book of Ruth is a beautiful story, full of charm and vivid colour, and giving us a precious window into life in a rural town. Yet it also gives us an enduring example of human faithfulness in adversity, and of family loyalties being embraced even when the way ahead is bleak. Moreover, it also presents us with a story of the faithfulness of Yahweh – bringing good out of evil and using ordinary people to fulfil his longer-term purposes of salvation.

For, just before the end of the story, we are told the punch line – Ruth's baby, Obed, would be the grandfather of Israel's later great king, David. Suddenly we see how Yahweh has used the plucky determination of this young Moabitess, weaving her colourful thread into the larger tapestry of his purposes. We also perhaps begin to wonder what will happen when this same God finally sends the ultimate king – a descendant of David born similarly in Bethlehem. Will this be the moment when Gentile people, like Ruth, can at last be ushered into God's family?

* * *

These three books have moved the Bible's storyline forward through one of its darkest patches. Any initial euphoria on entering the land has evaporated in the hard reality of struggling to survive as a cluster of clans surrounded by hostile neighbours. Yet the Israelites have survived, despite their failings – through their God being faithful to his promises.

In particular, the book of Ruth, coming as a voice of sanity after the madness seen in Judges, speaks a calm word that Yahweh has not abandoned his people. In life's dark valleys – whether those of an individual like Naomi or those of the whole people, languishing under the unruly rule of their so-called 'judges' – God is at work, bringing good out of evil, order out of the chaos.

> *O God, do not remain silent...*
>   *do not stand aloof, O God.*
> *See how your enemies...*
>   *rear their heads.*
> *With cunning they conspire against your people...*
> *'Come,' they say, 'let us destroy them as a nation...'*
> *Do to them as you did to Midian,*
>   *as you did to Sisera and Jabin at the river Kishon.*
> *Let them know...*
>   *that you alone are the Most High over all the earth.*
>
> **Psalm 83:1–4, 9–10, 18**

1 and 2 Samuel

The books of 1 and 2 Samuel continue to describe the complex birth pangs of Israel as a nation. Israel's tribes have now settled and expanded, but how will they be kept together? How will their corporate national identity be preserved? If a single ruler is required, from which tribe should he be chosen, and should this be in strict rotation thereafter? And then there's the question of a suitable capital city: where could one find a site, acceptable to all, which would offer a focus for unity?

In the wider political context there was something of a power vacuum in this period, with no major power (like Egypt) asserting control over the Promised Land. There was thus a window of opportunity for Israel to establish itself on the political map. Indeed in 2 Samuel David's kingdom has expanded rapidly (see map, right). Yet none of this came about without fierce competition with other local tribes – who probably had similar expansionist agendas and would go out to fight each springtime. So throughout these books there are frequent raids from Israel's warring neighbours.

The Israelite tribes thus faced critical issues on all fronts: their foreign policy needed to be tough simply to survive in the wider political jungle; but there were also these internal issues that needed resolution. Yet the biblical writers maintained their conviction that, somewhere in the midst of this disorder, the God of Israel was also at work, moving his purposes forward.

Samuel and Saul (1:1 – 15:35)

The book of 1 Samuel begins with the same gentle feel we found in Ruth: it appears a quiet, rural scene, but something momentous is stirring. When visiting the sanctuary at Shiloh (the new location for the ark of the covenant), a poor woman called Hannah prays for a child in the presence of Eli the priest. Her prayer is answered and the next year she joyfully hands over her baby to Eli so that the child can serve full time at the sanctuary. The child is Samuel – the one who will grow up to be the key priest, prophet and judge in the next stage of Israel's life.

Some time later Samuel experiences a distinct calling from Yahweh and is immediately given the difficult task of prophesying to Eli that judgment is coming against his family because of the wicked actions of his two sons. In due course these sons are killed in battle; and, when he hears the bad news, Eli himself falls off his chair and also dies. Worse still, the Philistines have captured the ark of the covenant. Israel is at its lowest ebb. The name of Eli's grandson, Ichabod, is truly apt: for, both literally and metaphorically, Israel's 'glory has departed'.

The books of Samuel tell how this dire situation was gradually turned around over the next century. This begins with the ark being returned; and with Israel experiencing some peace with its neighbours under Samuel's leadership.

At this point, however, the Israelites ask Samuel to appoint a king. Samuel sees this as a rejection – both of himself and indeed of Yahweh – and warns them

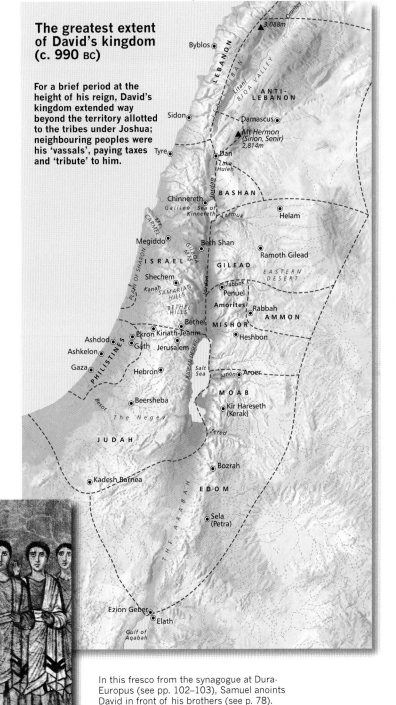

The greatest extent of David's kingdom (c. 990 BC)

For a brief period at the height of his reign, David's kingdom extended way beyond the territory allotted to the tribes under Joshua; neighbouring peoples were his 'vassals', paying taxes and 'tribute' to him.

In this fresco from the synagogue at Dura-Europus (see pp. 102–103), Samuel anoints David in front of his brothers (see p. 78).

Short sword and dagger from Ancient Mesopotamia.

'Then we shall be like all the other nations, with a king to fight our battles.'
1 Samuel 8:20

'The Lord has torn the kingdom of Israel from you and given it to one of your neighbours – to one better than you.'
1 Samuel 15:28

of the disadvantages of monarchy; but eventually he gives in to their request. He anoints with oil an 'impressive young man' called Saul, who is a 'head taller' than anyone else. Soon afterwards Saul leads a daring rescue operation on the besieged town of Jabesh-Gilead. His position, despite some detractors, is effectively confirmed.

Some years later there are renewed Philistine attacks, in which Saul's son Jonathan comes to the fore as remarkably brave. Saul, however, fails to follow Samuel's clear instructions to subject the Amalekites to *herem* (a total destruction). Samuel responds by announcing that this disobedience will mean the end of his kingship: 'The Lord has sought out a man after his own heart.'

Saul and David (chapters 16–31)

Enter David. Although he is the youngest of Jesse's eight sons, Samuel anoints him as Israel's future king. In due course he serves in Saul's court as a young musician, but famously comes to the fore in his dramatic encounter with Goliath. This Philistine champion daily taunts the Israelites to a duel; not daunted, David takes on the challenge, asking, 'Who is this uncircumcised Philistine that he should defy the armies of the living God?' So, equipped only with his sling and stones, David delivers Goliath a knockout blow and cuts off the Philistine's head with his own sword.

Israel now has a new hero in its midst. Responding to popular pressure Saul gives David a high rank in the army, where he proves incredibly successful; but this only provokes Saul to paranoia. Twice he tries to pin him to the wall with his spear. Then he tries to arrest him, but David flees to Samuel. Remarkably Saul's son, Jonathan (who might have expected to inherit the throne) recognizes David as Israel's anointed leader and acts on David's behalf – sounding out his

David flees into the desert, to a place called Wildgoats' Rocks near the springs of En Gedi (1 Samuel 24). He is hiding with his men in one of the caves near here when Saul, his pursuer, stands at the cave's entrance.

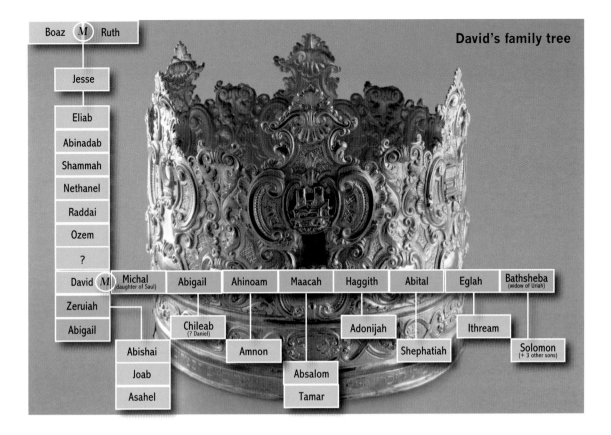

David's family tree

Boaz M Ruth
Jesse
Eliab
Abinadab
Shammah
Nethanel
Raddai
Ozem
?
David M Michal (daughter of Saul) | Abigail | Ahinoam | Maacah | Haggith | Abital | Eglah | Bathsheba (widow of Uriah)
Zeruiah
Abigail
Chileab (? Daniel)
Abishai
Amnon
Adonijah
Ithream
Joab
Shephatiah
Solomon (+ 3 other sons)
Asahel
Absalom
Tamar

father's intentions and warning David when flight is best.

David flees to various other places. Twice he has the opportunity to kill Saul privately, but he refuses to kill the 'Lord's anointed'; and Saul is suitably ashamed. Eventually the safest place for David to hide is among the Philistines.

Meanwhile Saul, fearful of a new attack from the Philistines, tries to consult the now deceased Samuel through a medium – only to receive the dire warning that he will die in battle the next day. Sure enough, the Israelites are defeated, three of Saul's sons (including Jonathan) are killed, and Saul commits suicide. Saul's life thus ends in shame, and Israel's first attempt at kingship comes to its sorry, ambiguous close.

David as king (2 Samuel 1–7)

The second book of Samuel begins with David hearing this tragic news and lamenting for Saul and Jonathan: 'Your glory, O Israel, lies slain on your heights. How the mighty have fallen!' Jonathan's death particularly affects him since the two of them had sworn a covenant of friendship together. These royal deaths, however, inevitably open the

King David

David's reign is a high point in the biblical narrative. Despite initial hesitations as to whether Israel (being ruled by God) should have a king, David shows how a good king can be a blessing. So, although God's kingdom has previously been seen in terms of God's *rule* over God's *people* in God's *place* (see Introduction, p. 16), there is now another ingredient: this divine rule can be administered through God's appointed king. In 1 and 2 Samuel, David is portrayed as a 'man after God's own heart', yet his sins are also quite apparent; so evidently God's call was due to his divine grace, not David's merit.

In 2 Samuel 7 God confirms David's kingship: the 'house of David' will be a key feature in the future of God's people. Yet this will cause considerable heartache when, 400 years later, the kings of Judah (David's successors) are taken into exile – never to return (see p. 91). What has happened to God's kingly rule? Disobedience has led to disaster, but are those promises to David now abandoned *entirely*?

'Messianic' hopes then develop: when will God anoint another David and restore Israel's kingship? These are burning questions in Jesus' day, and the New Testament is adamant that Jesus is indeed God's answer to them: the true king of God's kingdom has been revealed.

Many of the psalms celebrate Israel's king, portraying him in almost divine terms as the one through whom God is ruling. The New Testament endorses this 'messianic' reading and sees these texts as prophesying God's ultimate king, who would prove to be both human and divine.

way for David to return to Israel and launch his bid for the throne.

David is initially crowned king in Hebron by the tribe of Judah, but the northern tribes are loyal to a surviving son of Saul, Ish-Bosheth, promoted by Saul's army chief, Abner. Civil war breaks out, but when Ish-Bosheth is murdered, the northern tribes endorse David's kingship. So David now establishes a new capital closer to the centre of the land – on a small hill previously occupied by the Jebusites. Jerusalem thus becomes the City of David, the centre of his new regime – uniting the southern and northern tribes like a capstone bringing together two sides of an arch. And soon he arranges for the ark – that important symbol at the heart of all Israel – to be brought into his new city. The glory is returning.

At this point, David wonders if he should build a permanent temple to house the ark, but is told through the prophet Nathan that this will be done by one of his sons. Instead Yahweh is promising to build *him*, David, a house – that is, a dynasty through his descendants: 'Your house and your kingdom will endure for ever before me.' David is moved to humble praise of God for his grace.

David's family: the seeds of decline (chapters 8–24)

This marks the high point of David's reign: we are told of his numerous victories and the extent of his kingdom (see map p. 77). But then, walking on the roof of his palace, David notices the beautiful Bathsheba, the wife of Uriah. He commits adultery with her, and then,

when she falls pregnant, he tries various strategies to avoid blame, eventually engineering Uriah's death on the front-line. 'But the thing David had done displeased the Lord.'

So the prophet Nathan returns, but this time with a word of judgment, warning that the child will die. Moreover, Yahweh warns: 'Out of your own household I am going to bring calamity on you.' Although David repents (and Bathsheba bears another child who will be his successor, Solomon), the rest of the book is the sorry tale of how this prophetic word comes true. Great King David, though powerful on foreign fields, experiences havoc at home.

First, his son Amnon rapes his half-sister Tamar and is killed in revenge by Tamar's brother Absalom; Absalom is eventually allowed to return to Jerusalem, but for two years David refuses him an audience. Next, Absalom plots against his father and has himself proclaimed king in Hebron. David flees over the Mount of Olives into the desert and crosses over the Jordan. Absalom then fights David's troops and loses. He flees on his mule but, with his famously long hair, he gets entangled in the

View south-westwards from the Temple steps (right) down towards the Ophel Ridge (off left), which was the heart of David's Jerusalem. This 'city of David', though very small, was an ideal location – being surrounded by valleys on three sides and with accessible water-springs. David's son Solomon would then build the Temple to the north (off right) on what had been the 'threshing floor of Araunah' (2 Samuel 24:18).

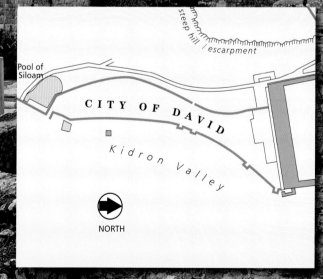

Pool of Siloam

steep hill / escarpment

CITY OF DAVID

Kidron Valley

NORTH

David flees Jerusalem, going up over the Mount of Olives and into the desert. The so-called tombs of Absalom and Zechariah (foreground left and right), built out of the natural rock, were built much later (c. 300 BC). Jesus would use a similar route, but in reverse, as the crowds welcome him into the city shouting 'Hosanna to the son of David!' (Matthew 21:9).

branches of an oak tree – the mule disappearing from under him. Joab, one of David's generals, despite David's orders to the contrary, kills Absalom. Once again David mourns for the death of his enemy; but Joab warns that David's supporters will desert him if he continues, seemingly, to love his enemies more than his friends. David takes the point and makes his way back to Jerusalem. It is a 'return of the king' – marked by generous amnesties to those who had taken Absalom's side.

The monarchy is thereby restored but David's position is still weak – with Joab having to put down a rebellion in the north. The last four

chapters then contain a miscellany of material: a psalm of David (virtually identical to Psalm 18); a list of his mighty men and some of their exploits; and the episode of David's calling of a census which, according to the prophet Gad, is contrary to Yahweh's will. This triggers an episode of divine judgment in the form of a plague; but Gad then instructs David to build an altar on the threshing-floor of Araunah the Jebusite. The discerning reader knows this is the place where Solomon's Temple will soon be built, and so has the incentive to read on into 1 Kings. Yet at just this point the book comes to an abrupt end: 'then the Lord answered prayer, and the plague was stopped'.

* * *

This powerful story is told very vividly. The characters of Saul and David are finely drawn. Saul is seen as full of promise, but perhaps marked by an inferiority complex, and he ends up knowing he has played the fool. David starts as a less likely leader, but rises quickly to the challenge and, at least initially, hardly sets a foot wrong. Yet moving from opposition to government is never easy and he gradually begins to abuse his power. Sexual temptation takes its toll and his complex family situation begins to unravel before his eyes.

Moreover, to maintain his control as others jostle for supremacy, David has to act tough. Frequently, however, he prefers the soft option, allowing his enemies on one occasion to curse him in public. At one level this may be a sign of David's humility after his own failures – or perhaps his weariness of revenge after a lifetime of fighting? Yet one also wonders if there is an implied critique here of the very nature of kingship. Perhaps it can only be maintained at the cost of some brutality, or through asking others (such as Joab) to do your dirty work for you.

The biblical writers are therefore presenting us with unresolved issues about human characters and about the government of human society. One of the story's most fascinating features is this explicit ambiguity about kingship – something which weakens the ideal of Israel's being a theocracy (ruled by God alone) and yet which is used by God to forward his purposes. Despite their failures, Saul and then David are offering a necessary leadership within God's people; and David becomes an icon for the ideal way in which God will one day rule his people by an anointed king.

In later biblical thought this becomes the key legacy of 1 and 2 Samuel. With the arrival of David's kingdom we reach the high-water point of the kingdom of God (see pp. 16–17).

I will sing of the Lord's great love forever...

You said, 'I have made a covenant with my chosen one,
I have sworn to David my servant,

"I will...
make your throne firm through all generations..."

I have found David my servant;
with my sacred oil I have anointed him...

surely my arm will strengthen him.

He will call out to me, "You are my Father,
my God, the Rock my Saviour."

And I will appoint him to be...
the most exalted of the kings of the earth...

My covenant with him will never fail.

I will establish his line forever,
his throne as long as the heavens endure.'

Psalm 89:1, 3–4, 20–21, 26–29

In David we have a sneak preview of how God will rule over his people – through a righteous king. Centuries later Israel would hope for the restoration of this Davidic kingship and the arrival of a Messiah (the 'anointed king'). The New Testament then expressly picks up the words of Nathan's prophecy and says that Mary's child will 'reign over the house of his father David' and that 'his kingdom will never end' (Luke 1:32–33). Jesus is thus the long-awaited Davidic king, who rules perfectly over God's people. David thus foreshadows the Messiah and so proves to be a vital element, despite his failings, in the gradual revelation of God's purposes.

1 and 2 Kings

The books of 1 and 2 Kings cover the period from c. 975 BC to
c. 560 BC – from the death of David to the death of his kingdom.
During these 400 years the Ancient Near East was going through
some turbulent times. Initially Israel had to contend with local
political rivals, but eventually new 'super-powers' emerged in the
region (Assyria and then Babylon). Building a kingdom on this
stretch of land was like building a bird's nest on a busy motorway!
Even so, David's kingdom would have fared much better if it had not
been riven with internal discord. The Israelites held together during
the long reign of his son Solomon, but the nation then divided into
two. The southern kingdom (named Judah) retained Jerusalem as its
capital but was made up of only two of the twelve tribes (Judah and
Benjamin). The majority of tribes formed an alternative kingdom to
the north and took with them the name of Israel. Despite its larger
size the northern kingdom was eventually overrun by the Assyrians
– leaving Judah, despite ominous threats, unscathed. In 597 BC,
however, the southern kingdom would be invaded by the Babylonians
and Jerusalem itself eventually destroyed.

The books make references to official 'annals' in the royal
archives (which may have given largely positive accounts of each
king's exploits), but the narrators themselves see this instead as a
sad story of division and decline – largely due to idolatry. They see
the eventual disappearance of both kingdoms in theological terms
– as an outworking of Yahweh's judgment upon his own people for
forsaking him. This tragedy was not a sign of Yahweh's weakness,
but a sign of *their* faithfulness and *his* awesome power. The books
of 1 and 2 Kings are therefore remarkably self-critical books – quite
unlike histories of other ancient nations – and give us a perceptive
angle on this nation's history. Thus, although the overall storyline
is faintly depressing, the underlying tone is one of hope and faithful
determination: for in this act of self-criticism and painful reflection
lay the long-term seeds of the nation's ultimate renewal.

The united kingdom (1 Kings 1–11)
The narrators in this opening section focus on Solomon; and they are
full of praise. They describe how he establishes his power and builds
up an impressive administrative team to run the country; they relate
how he prays for wisdom. Solomon's wisdom becomes legendary,
leading to the inquisitive visit of a queen from distant Sheba (in
modern-day Yemen).

'The king made silver as common in Jerusalem as stones, and cedar as plentiful as sycamore-fig trees.'
1 Kings 10:27

'But will God really dwell on earth? The heavens, even the highest heaven, cannot contain you. How much less this temple I have built!'
1 Kings 8:27

He is also rich. Under Solomon the nation enjoys an unparalleled prosperity, and there is enough money to finance some impressive building projects. Indeed Solomon builds a fleet that sails every three years from Elath (modern Eilat) on trading expeditions, bringing back exotic treasures.

The crowning glory is the building of Jerusalem's Temple (970–954 BC), constructed with massive stones and furnished in bronze and gold. The climax of the elaborate dedication festival is when the ark of the covenant is brought up triumphantly from the city of David and taken into the Holy Place. At this point a cloud fills the Temple preventing the priests from performing their duties because of 'the glory of the Lord'. Recalling God's promises to David, Solomon offers a lengthy prayer and dedication, asking that Yahweh would hear the prayers of all those who humbly turn towards this Temple.

This is the high point of the story, and indeed of the much longer biblical story – the apex in the fulfilment of God's purposes. After all the nation's struggles, Solomon can conclude:

Praise be to the Lord, who has given rest to his people Israel… Not one

The Queen of Sheba with King Solomon, by Bonifazio 'Veronese' de Pitali (1487–1553).

word has failed of all his good promises… may he never forsake us. May he turn our hearts to him to walk in obedience….

1 Kings 8:56–58

Yet it was not to be. Solomon's own heart turns away from Yahweh. The narrators attribute this chiefly to his love for the 'many foreign women' in his vast harem. Solomon also builds 'high places' around Jerusalem for foreign deities, but Yahweh responds: 'I will most certainly tear the kingdom away from you…'

The divided kingdom (1 Kings 12–16)

This divine wrath then works itself out in bitter practice over the next centuries. During the reign of Solomon's son, Rehoboam, there is a revolt led by Jeroboam, who establishes an alternative kingdom. He builds a new capital (initially at Shechem) and some new cult centres (at Dan and Bethel), where the deity is portrayed as a golden calf. The narrators see this as Jeroboam's defining 'sin' and refer back to it repeatedly when describing his like-minded successors. They mention prophecies of judgment, which come to pass in due course.

Judah in the south fares little better. Rehoboam establishes 'high places... on every high hill and under every spreading tree. There were even male shrine prostitutes in the land...' However, his grandson, Asa, removes some of these offensive cultic practices. So Judah experiences ups and downs. Yet, in a repeated phrase, the narrators speak of Yahweh's preserving a lamp in Jerusalem; for the sake of David 'the Lord was not willing to destroy Judah'. In the enveloping darkness, a small wick is being kindled, which will not be snuffed out.

Elijah and Elisha (1 Kings 17 – 2 Kings 8:15)

After various coups and counter-plots we come to the reign of Ahab (874–853 BC) – the era of the great Elijah and Elisha. We enjoy extended accounts of their various exploits:

- During a severe famine Elijah is fed by ravens and helps a widow in Zarephath (near Sidon) with a continual supply of oil; he also restores her dead son to life.

- He challenges 450 prophets of Baal, associated with Ahab and his wife (Jezebel), to a showdown on Mount Carmel; Yahweh vindicates Elijah, sending fire on his altar. Elijah then flees to Mount Horeb, there to be recommissioned by Yahweh with words spoken in a 'still, small voice'.

- Later Elijah prophesies against Ahab and Jezebel for their treatment of Naboth, whose vineyard they wanted but whom they murdered when he refused to sell.

- Elijah is eventually 'taken up to heaven' in a whirlwind with 'chariots of fire', leaving Elisha to pick up his mantle (both literally and metaphorically). Elisha is recognized as Elijah's successor, performing similar miracles such as the continual supply of a widow's oil and raising the dead son of his kind hostess in Shunem.

- When an Aramaean army officer called Naaman daringly comes seeking a cure for his skin disease, Elisha instructs him to wash seven times in the Jordan. Despite proud protestations, Naaman eventually agrees and returns home healed.

- And in a dramatic story, when the city of Samaria is being besieged by the Aramaeans (even causing cannibalism),

A relief found in Samaria of the god Hah (surrounded by two 'Ankh' signs, the symbol for 'life' in Egyptian mythology) shows the dominance of paganism in this central city within the Northern Kingdom of Israel.

Elijah Resuscitating the Son of the Widow of Zarephath, by Louis Hersent (1777–1860).

Elisha predicts that within twenty-four hours food prices will have dropped to nothing. Sure enough, the enemy forces (hearing chariots and fearing a major attack) flee during the night. The next morning some lepers discover the deserted campsite, replete with all its provisions.

The divided kingdom, continued (2 Kings 8:16 – 17:41)

The narrators now resume their catalogue of kings, and things continue on their relentless downward spiral. There is some rapprochement between the kings of Judah and Israel during this period – a sign of which is Joram, the king of Judah, marrying one of Ahab's daughters, Athaliah. In the next generation, however, when Joram's son dies, Athaliah seizes power as the queen mother and proceeds to murder all the remaining princes in Judah. Except one, that is – who is successfully smuggled into the Temple courts and raised there in hiding for seven years. This young Joash is then crowned king by his uncle one Friday evening. So, Judah's royal line survives – but only just. Joash proves to be a good king, ensuring that Solomon's Temple (now 150 years old) is suitably repaired.

Discovering the 'book of the Law'

2 Kings 22 tells of how when King Josiah gives instructions in 622 BC for Jerusalem's Temple to be redecorated and restored, he is in for a surprise. An ancient text containing God's Law is discovered. This is often identified with what we now know as Deuteronomy (the so-called 'second Law').

Josiah has the book read out to him and immediately 'tears his robes', sensing how much God's people have disobeyed its instructions. He then consults Huldah, a prophetess, who confirms that God has been provoked to anger by Israel's idols and will bring judgment upon 'this place'. However, she says that Josiah's own repentance has been noted, so Josiah himself will not see this judgment during his own lifetime.

It shows the powerful effect on God's people when they rediscover God's words. This has been repeated countless times – both in individuals' lives and within the church's corporate life (for example, in the Reformation period, when people started reading the Bible in their own language).

In Josiah's day it led to his summoning Israel's leaders to hear the book's words and to renew their covenant before God. It may also have inspired a Deuteronomistic school of editors to re-edit Israel's earlier histories in the light of Deuteronomy's important emphasis on obedience (see p. 62). Yet such responses were too little, too late. Jeremiah (who also began his ministry in the 620s BC) announced that judgment was inevitable. In due course Josiah would die in 609 BC, and Jerusalem was completely destroyed in 587/6 BC.

Meanwhile, back in the north, there has been a bloodbath. Around 841 BC Jehu takes the throne, and proceeds to kill all Ahab's descendants and the queen mother, Jezebel; he also slaughters all surviving prophets of Baal. However, it is prophesied that Jehu's dynasty will last only four generations, during which time Israel concedes much territory to the Aramaeans in Damascus.

Around fifty years later, however, a new threat looms over the horizon: the Assyrians. At one point, Ahaz, the king of Judah, appeals for help from the Assyrian emperor Tiglath-Pileser III; but this high-level politics is a dangerous game. The Assyrians are expanding their empire and the next emperor, Shalmaneser, is soon at the city gates of Samaria. After three years he captures it and immediately deports the Israelites back to Assyria (722 BC).

This is a major tragedy – the loss of the ten northern tribes. The narrators are convinced that 'all this took place because the Israelites had sinned against the Lord'. Their territory is repopulated with foreigners, so any Israelite worship is severely compromised. Outright idolatry and confused syncretism become rampant.

Relief from the ruins of Assyria's capital, Nineveh, carved during the reign of Sennacherib (704–681 BC).

The solitary kingdom (2 Kings 18–25)

The tragic fate of the northern kingdom then hangs like a cloud over Jerusalem for the next 150 years. One of the darkest moments occurs in 701 BC, when Shalmaneser's successor Sennacherib reaches Lachish (to the west of Jerusalem). In this crisis (recounted also in Isaiah 36–39), the prophet Isaiah predicts that Sennacherib will return home, where he will be assassinated: 'he will not enter this city, declares the Lord. I will defend this city and save it, for my sake and for the sake of David my servant.' Sure enough, the Assyrian army is decimated by a plague. Zion has survived once more; the 'lamp' is still burning.

Jerusalem's king at this time, Hezekiah, is humble and prayerful; but he also shows off his treasury to some visitors from an upstart nation centred on Babylon. So Isaiah prophesies that these same treasures will be carried off to Babylon and some of Hezekiah's descendants will be deported there. This prophecy too then hangs over the narrative.

Jerusalem then experiences major ups and downs: there is the idolatrous rule of King Manasseh conducting horrendous child sacrifices; but there is the reforming zeal of King Josiah as he purifies Jerusalem's worship – in response to some teaching found in a long-lost 'Book of the Covenant' discovered in the Temple (see box opposite). Yet these reforms are not sufficient for Yahweh to 'turn away from the heat of his fierce anger'.

The stage is thus set for the sad finale. After Josiah's death in battle in 609 BC, Pharaoh Neco chooses one of Josiah's sons (Jehoiachim) to be his puppet-king in Jerusalem. The Egyptians, however, are themselves defeated at Carchemish in 605 BC by the Babylonians, who attack Jerusalem and deport some of its inhabitants. Later the city is besieged and eventually capitulates (586/7 BC). The Babylonians burn the Temple, smash the city walls, plunder the Temple furnishings and deport most of its citizens. Many officials are brought before Nebuchadnezzar and sentenced to death. Judah's king (Zedekiah), however, is blinded and led off in shackles to Babylon.

It is a devastating spectacle. What has happened to those divine promises relating to David's kingdom? Surely the 'lamp' has finally gone out, never to be rekindled? Yet 2 Kings ends with a flicker of hope: King Jehoiachin (the Davidic king exiled during the first deportation, back in 597 BC) is released from prison. After thirty-seven years in a Babylonian jail, a new emperor (Evil-Merodach) honours him at his table and gives him a daily allowance. There is hope. The royal line, even if in exile, has not completely perished. The lamp flickers on.

'... I will reject Jerusalem, the city I chose, and this temple, about which I said, "There shall my Name be."'
2 Kings 23:27

This black limestone obelisk (198 cm high) was erected in 825 BC and depicts the victories of Shalmaneser III (858–824 BC) over various rulers, including King Jehu of Israel: 'the tribute of Jehu, son of Omri: I received from him silver, gold, a golden bowl... golden tumblers, tin, spears...'

Historical colour

These ancient books make fascinating reading from a merely historical point of view. We see society moving from the Bronze Age into the Iron Age. We see the management of a major building project (the Temple), involving an international consortium of craftsmen who need to be properly paid. We see an expanded governmental bureaucracy funded through extra taxes. We even see a tourist trade with international visitors fascinated to see Solomon's Jerusalem.

Then there are the political complexities. We see trade agreements, peace pacts and arms deals. Judah and Israel sometimes fight on the same side; at other times one of them teams up with a

Detail from the 'Ishtar gate', built c. 575 BC on the north side of Babylon during the reign of Nebuchadnezzar II (c. 605–562 BC).

third party to attack the other. The super-powers jostle for position, and their emperors demand annual tribute, leaving the Temple (which functioned also as a treasury or bank) stripped of its assets. So warfare is a constant threat, with kings regularly needing to go to war in the spring to settle boundary issues.

A Babylonian piece of pottery, bearing an account of the capture of Jerusalem in March 597 BC. 'In the seventh year, in the month of Kislev, the Babylonian king besieged the city of Judah, and on the second day of the month of Adar took the city and captured the king. He appointed therein a king of his own choice, received its heavy tribute and sent (them) to Babylon.'

Some lessons from history

Yet the narrators, though concerned with history, want to go further. First, they repeatedly highlight the role of prophecy; hence the extended focus on Elijah and Elisha. This powerful season of prophetic ministry thus confirms for the narrators that Yahweh is not only the God of revelation and kingly rule (as seen with Moses and David), but also the God of prophetic power. Unlike the gods of other nations, Israel's God is the living God, powerful in action, able to communicate his will through prophecy.

Second, the narrators focus on Jerusalem's Temple. This is not just a national landmark, but rather the place of the divine name and of God's mysterious presence. So the narrators rejoice at its dedication but grieve when it is contaminated by idolatrous worship and eventually destroyed, for this must signal in some way the departure of Yahweh from among his people (as made explicit by Ezekiel: see p. 147).

Third, they focus on the Davidic kingship – the dynasty endorsed by explicit divine promises. So there is the repeated insistence that Yahweh longs to spare his people 'for the sake of his servant David'. Yet the narrators know these promises are conditional. If God's gifts are abused (gifts such as the kingship, the land and even the Temple), then they could all be taken away. The rest of 1 and 2 Kings is recounted as the outworking of this warning.

* * *

So 1 and 2 Kings are history books written with a moral and a purpose. We are being taught about divine sovereignty and human responsibility; and about the importance of obeying God's words. This was the era when the young Israelite nation still needed to be trained in obedience. In the narrators' view, obedience led to blessing; disobedience to discord and disaster. Though exceptions to this rule might be learned later, this was a necessary first lesson for the young nation to grasp, but it signally failed to do so.

And, in terms of the overall plot line of the Bible, we are seeing how the pinnacle of God's purposes attained under Solomon was gradually unpicked through human sin. Yet it leaves us with the

1 AND 2 CHRONICLES

The books of 1 and 2 Chronicles cover the same historical period as that covered in 1 and 2 Kings. In 1 Chronicles 9 seven further generations of the Davidic kingship are listed after the exiled Jehoiachin – indicating these books were written after 450 BC (perhaps even as late as 325 BC). This would explain why the chronicler overlooks the history of the northern kingdom (that territory now being occupied by the Samaritans). It also makes sense of his greater emphasis on the Davidic kingship and the Temple – for the Jewish nation was now much smaller, clustered around Jerusalem, and the Temple was its central heartbeat. Hence the chronicler's interest in the Temple's liturgy and music, and in the reforms of its worship by Hezekiah and Josiah; hence the selective accounts concerning David and Solomon, which focus mainly on their plans for the Temple; and hence too the inclusion of faith-stirring stories, such as King Jehoshaphat's defeat of the Moabites after his earnest prayer in the Temple or King Hezekiah's faith when facing Sennacherib's attack ('There is a greater power with us than with him; with us is the Lord our God!').

Although there are some small details where Chronicles and Kings differ from each other, the two accounts are remarkably complementary – perhaps intentionally so. The chronicler, however, wishes to add more editorial comment, noting when people 'prostituted themselves' with idolatry or failed to 'seek the Lord'. Eventually both king and people became 'hard-hearted' and 'stiff-necked', until there was 'no remedy'. A particular low point was reached with the murder of Zechariah, a priest, in the Temple.

The chronicler gives greater space to Judah's kings, enabling his account to be more nuanced; thus we see the good and bad sides of Rehoboam, Asa, Jehoshaphat and even Manasseh. Even so, he omits many of David's failures and is silent about Solomon's apostasy. This is because the chronicler, though equally concerned with real history, is writing with a different purpose. The narrators of Kings had been concerned to explain the tragedy of the exile, but this is not now necessary for the chronicler. What is needed instead is a review of the nation's more glorious past – to encourage God's people even though they are a small entity within the Persian empire. It was also important to encourage the Levites and other Temple officials to learn from their predecessors in those posts.

History writing is never a final science, but each generation looks back on important events to draw out new significance for the present. Hence the value of the chronicler's alternative account – both for the original audience and for ourselves – encouraging us to look at the past with fresh eyes.

'We have no power to face this vast army; we do not know what to do, but our eyes are upon you.'
Jehoshaphat in 2 Chronicles 20:12

'The eyes of the Lord range throughout the earth to strengthen those whose hearts are fully committed to him.'
2 Chronicles 16:9

But you have rejected…
  your anointed one.

You have renounced the covenant with your servant
  and have defiled his crown in the dust.

You have broken through all his walls
  and reduced his strongholds to ruins.

All who pass by have plundered him…

You have put an end to his splendour
  and cast his throne to the ground…

How long, Lord? Will you hide yourself forever?
  How long will your wrath burn like fire…?

Lord, where is your former great love,
  which in your faithfulness you swore to David?

Remember, Lord, how your servant has been mocked…

  the taunts with which your enemies
  have mocked every step of your anointed one.

Praise be to the Lord forever!
  Amen and Amen.

Psalm 89:38–41, 46, 49–52

definitive model of what the kingdom of God might eventually look like: God's king over God's people in God's place. The New Testament will therefore compare Jesus to both Solomon and David, and claim that the long-vacated Davidic throne has once more been filled with a worthy, royal claimant.

Ezra, Nehemiah and Esther

The three books of Ezra, Nehemiah and Esther cover a period of just over 100 years (see p. 18). Ezra and Nehemiah both include sections written in the first person by these two individuals; but Esther is written by a brilliant story teller who is now unknown to us. Confusingly, Esther now appears in our Bibles *after* Ezra/Nehemiah, but the events it relates belong to the generation *before* Ezra and Nehemiah made their visits to Jerusalem – in other words, it falls in the time gap between the earlier events (of 539–516 BC) related in Ezra 1–6 and the moment of Ezra's own arrival (in 458 BC), as described in Ezra 7–10.

No attempt is made in these books to give a comprehensive account. The focus instead is on the preservation in precarious circumstances of Yahweh's people (now known as the 'people of Judah' or the 'Judeans'/'Jews'). We are seeing how they survived their exile – initially under the Babylonians but then under the Persians. It is a remarkable story of survival in the face of extreme odds. What made them cling on?

The answer may have much to do with Jeremiah (see p. 143), who had prophesied that Jerusalem's fall would be a sign of Yahweh's wrath but that they would return from their exile after seventy years. So, as we read these three books, we see Jeremiah's prophecy of restoration being fulfilled.

Ezra

While 2 Kings had finished with God's people tragically deported to Babylon, Ezra, by contrast, begins with an amazing reversal: God's people, several generations later, are coming home! Ezra 1–6 focuses on the first return made to Jerusalem (c. 539 BC). In response to the proclamation of Cyrus the Persian, some 'family heads of Judah and

---

Key chapters in Ezra, Nehemiah and Esther

Rededication of the Temple (Ezra 6)

Ezra confronts intermarriage (Ezra 9–10)

Nehemiah rebuilds Jerusalem's walls (Nehemiah 2–6)

Ezra reads out the Law (Nehemiah 7)

Esther's daring request (Esther 5)

Feast of Purim celebrated (Esther 9)

Much of the book of Esther is set in Susa (in modern Iran). The impressive palace had been built during the earlier reign of Darius I the Great (522–486 BC). After Esther's time it was destroyed by fire during the reign of Artaxerxes I (465–24/23) but gradually restored, being completed during the reign of his grandson Artaxerxes II (404–358).

Benjamin' together with 'priests and Levites' and 'everyone whose heart God had moved' return to Jerusalem, carrying with them many of the Temple's treasures. The number of returnees is around 40,000 and includes Zerubbabel (the grandson of Judah's King Jehoiachin).

They arrive safely, but those now living in the land vehemently oppose the people's rebuilding of the Temple, thereby delaying it for twenty years. Eventually the Persian governor asks Cyrus' successor, Darius I, to check the royal archives for any record of Cyrus' proclamation. The decree is duly found, so Darius orders the Temple's rebuilding to be resumed. Inspired by the prophecies of Haggai and Zechariah (see pp. 170–71) the exiles complete the Temple within four years (516 BC). There is then an elaborate dedication festival and a joyful celebration of Passover.

Ezra 7–10, however, focuses on events seventy years later. Ezra, a priest, obtains permission from King Artaxerxes to go to Jerusalem to see how the Jewish Law is being implemented. He travels with many exiles and, because of God's 'gracious hand', they too arrive

Terracotta vessel, decorated with ibex, from ancient Susa (c. 3500 BC).

safely. However, Ezra soon becomes aware that some of the Jewish population have been intermarrying with the local residents. Ezra is appalled. He can see history repeating itself here – with religious compromise being the inevitable result. So Ezra prays a long, impassioned prayer of confession: Yahweh has graciously given Judah 'new life', but now this small 'remnant' stands in danger of being completely destroyed. This soon leads to a public act of confession and (two months later) a list is drawn up of those who have intermarried.

The book ends with an unclear phrase, which almost certainly indicates that those found guilty had to divorce their partners. For at this point in the biblical story (unlike the days of the New Testament) Israel's historic faith could not be securely preserved except behind national and racial boundaries.

Nehemiah

The book of Nehemiah picks up the story about a decade later. Nehemiah, a Jew working in the court of this same Artaxerxes, hears the depressing news of how Jerusalem's walls have been broken down. After praying, he dares to ask the king's permission to return and rebuild the walls. Given that Artaxerxes in the intervening years had been persuaded that Jerusalem had a history of being a 'place of rebellion and sedition' (according to Ezra 4:18–22), this is indeed a daring request. But, because of the 'gracious hand of God', it is granted.

So Nehemiah arrives in Jerusalem as its governor. He inspects the city wall, and then allocates a vast array of people to work on its different sections. Again there is opposition from neighbouring groups, including the Samaritans. These enemies try every tactic: after ridiculing the project, they try to lure Nehemiah away for a meeting, and finally use death-threats and intimidating letters. Yet the work is completed in a remarkably short time (fifty-two days). Jerusalem's historic walls have been rebuilt, and its people can now live there secure. The book's highlight is thus the joyful dedication of the walls – complete with two choirs processing around on top of the walls!

Before that great day, however, the people listen to a reading of the Law. Standing on a platform, Ezra reads from Israel's scriptures. Then the Levites explain its meaning, 'helping the people to understand'. (These are the first references in the Bible to 'preaching' and what might be called 'interpretation'.) The people are moved to tears. They acknowledge Yahweh's great 'covenant of love' – despite their continuously 'stiff-necked' nature, often putting his Law 'behind their backs'. Eventually they make a solemn agreement that they will observe God's Law: avoiding intermarriage and sabbath trading; financing the Temple's worship and giving the required 'first-fruits' of their harvests.

It is a powerful moment in Israel's history – the nation gathering behind secure walls to hear God's word and responding in confession and commitment. There continue to be lapses and Nehemiah still has some reforming work to do, but the book ends with a sense that Nehemiah has fulfilled a vital task at a critical time in the nation's life.

'Do not grieve, for the joy of the Lord is your strength.'
Nehemiah 8:10

'But you are a forgiving God, gracious and compassionate, slow to anger and abounding in love. Therefore you did not desert them.'
Nehemiah 9:17

The Samaritans today are a small sect (c. 700 people) who trace their descent from the northern tribes of ancient Israel, mostly living near Mount Gerizim (above modern Nablus): here they process at the festival of *Shavuot*, celebrating the giving of the Torah at Mount Sinai.

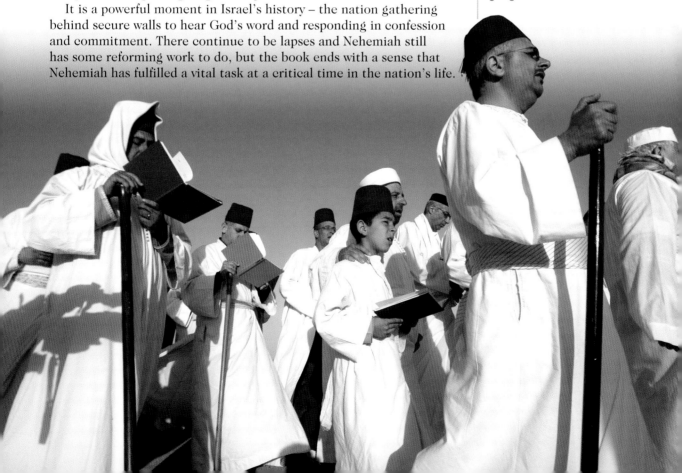

Esther

The book of Esther breathes a very different air. It is set some 700 miles east of Jerusalem in Susa, the winter palace of King Xerxes (or King Ahasuerus in some biblical translations). It tells the story of how Esther, though a young Jewish orphan raised by her cousin Mordecai, rises through the ranks of the harem to become Xerxes' favoured queen.

Mordecai is loyal to the king, yet he refuses to acknowledge the authority of Haman, a man whom Xerxes has appointed as his second-in-command. When Haman takes offence at this and persuades Xerxes in retaliation to issue an edict to massacre *all* the empire's Jewish exiles on a certain date, Mordecai pleads with Esther (through a third party) to use her influence to get the edict over-ruled. After three days of fasting she dares to come before Xerxes without having been appropriately 'summoned' – an action for which the potential punishment was death.

Xerxes, however, not only welcomes her but offers her up to half of his kingdom. Cannily she does not answer straightaway, but instead teasingly invites Xerxes and Haman to a private banquet on each of the next two days. Xerxes agrees and Haman, on receiving the invitation, feels dutifully honoured. Eventually Xerxes can stand it no more, so Esther whispers in his ear: 'If I have found favour with you, Your Majesty... grant me my life... And spare my people. For I and my people have been sold to be destroyed.'

Xerxes asks who is responsible for this alarming scenario, only to be told that it is the other person at the table – 'this vile Haman'. Xerxes is enraged – and even more so when he comes back from the garden to find Haman pleading with Esther for his life in a manner that could be misconstrued as rape. So Haman is immediately sentenced to death – hung on the very gallows which he had just built for Mordecai.

Mordecai is now introduced to Xerxes as Esther's cousin and is rewarded with the king's signet ring, effectively replacing Haman. Esther then demands that an edict be sent out which will give the Jewish exiles the right to defend themselves from any attack on the date specified in Haman's edict. When the long-awaited day comes, fighting indeed breaks out throughout the empire, with some savage slaughter, but the Jewish exiles are victorious and all Haman's sons are executed.

As a result Mordecai and Esther send a letter to their fellow nationals, encouraging them to remember this whole event in the future with an annual time of celebration – an anniversary known as Purim.

Individuals in the 'hand' of God

These three brief cameos give us a glimpse into Israel's life in exile. Here we are now in a very different world – the world of Persian kings, with their courtiers and perfumed harem, their garden palaces and lavish banquets, their political brutalities and powerful edicts. Yet Ezra, Nehemiah and Esther all succeed in maintaining their faith in Israel's God.

The books are designed to teach us more than good examples, however. Instead the ultimate focus is on God. Thus in the books of Ezra and Nehemiah there is the repeated refrain that 'the hand of God' was upon them. And the same is true in Esther – even though this book never mentions God by name! For the writer evidently sees this preservation of God's people as a miracle that came about through God's providential hand – hence the long sequence of apparent coincidences: God had been at work throughout Esther's life to bring her to that strategic moment when her people's destiny turned on her carefully chosen words.

Ezra, Nehemiah and Esther *all* find themselves, at certain critical points, standing solitary and vulnerable before a Persian potentate – moments when the whole future of God's people, as it were, hung by a single thread. The providence of God can be sensed: God is surely at work, not, in this season, through overt miracles, but rather through the apparently normal events of human history – as he uses the aptitudes of faithful individuals and fashions their circumstances, both large and small, to bring about his purposes.

A partial restoration from exile

In the books of Ezra and Nehemiah we also see how God's people adapted to their new circumstances. While in exile, far away from Judea and the Temple, there was almost inevitably an increasing emphasis on

Esther as history *and* literature?

Esther reads very differently from the other Old Testament books: it is a finely worked literary tale, so perhaps it is a 'historicized fiction'? Should we read it as a legendary account – designed to give meaning to the Jewish feast of Purim?

Its author, however, gives clear signals that it is to be received as a historical account of real events. Moreover, there are numerous points where its material is consonant with sources from outside the Bible:

- Inscriptions affirm the popularity of the name 'Mordecai' (related to the Babylonian god Marduk); much of the book's terminology reflects the language of the 'late Persian' period.

- Archaeological excavations of the palace at Susa match the account, showing how it was burnt down some thirty years after the time of Esther.

- The Persian empire was famous for its efficient postal service and witnessed other instances of anti-Semitism.

- Ancient historians (such as Herodotus and Diodorus Siculus) note how Persian rulers could not easily retract their edicts.

Herodotus in his *Histories* (Book VII: 14, 61, 113–114) calls Xerxes' queen Amestris, whereas in Esther chapter 1 she is called Vashti; yet analysis of how complex Persian names were translated into Greek and Hebrew script suggests these could well both be transliterations of the same original name. Indeed, using Herodotus' account, the date of the banquet (in Esther chapter 1) would be 483 BC, with Xerxes returning to Susa (in Esther chapter 2) after his being defeated by the Greeks at the battle of Salamis (in 480 BC). So Esther would have become queen in 479 BC.

such things as sabbath observance, food laws and avoiding racial intermarriage. For, if there were no *political* boundaries, the nation had to erect instead these boundary markers of *lifestyle* – to keep their identity visible and distinct. So these three books begin to use terms that will become frequent in the days of the New Testament – such as 'Jews', 'Samaritans' and 'Gentiles'. The boundary lines are being carefully drawn.

And, once they returned to the land, there continued to be new questions: for example, the Temple had been rebuilt, but had Yahweh returned there to dwell? And would it ever be possible, while under Persian rule, to restore the Davidic kingship? Zerubbabel, the rightful heir to the throne, had returned to Jerusalem but there was no coronation. It was a delicately balanced situation. The nation had indeed experienced a remarkable restoration to its land, yet it was only partial. So, in one sense the exile was over; in another sense, it was not. This ambiguity is caught brilliantly when Ezra and the people speak of themselves as still being slaves, even though they are back 'in the land' (Ezra 9:9; Nehemiah 9:36).

All these ambiguities would then rumble on, unresolved, for the next 500 years. Was there going to be a new and better Temple? Was Yahweh ever truly going to return and dwell among his people? And would there ever again be, as promised long ago, a king seated on David's throne?

> *Your name, Lord, endures forever,*
> *your renown, Lord, through all generations.*
>
> *For the Lord will vindicate his people*
> *and relent concerning his servants.*
>
> **Psalm 135:13–14**

Old Testament scenes depicted on the walls of the ancient synagogue at Dura-Europus (eastern Syria), completed in 240s AD.

Wisdom

The next five biblical books are quite distinct: Job, Psalms, Proverbs, Ecclesiastes and the Song of Songs. All of them include large amounts of poetry, and three of them (Job, Proverbs and Ecclesiastes) are the classic examples of what is known as 'wisdom literature'.

One key aspect of such wisdom literature is that it makes very little reference to the distinctively religious life of ancient Israel (thus there are no references to the Sinai covenant, the Davidic monarchy or the Jerusalem Temple, and the focus is on wise people, not priests or prophets). This makes it hard to date with any precision (see p. 18). It also begs the question as to whether this material is a foreign import. Thus some key parallels can be found with texts from Egypt and Mesopotamia. Did the Israelite 'sages' simply borrow from this stock of ancient wisdom?

Yet, if they did, this should hardly be a surprise. After all, these were common issues facing *all* human beings. Moreover, all truth was God's truth and (as Jesus himself would later teach) the wisdom of those outside God's people could sometimes be greater than that of the faithful. The important thing was to test the truth in practice (whatever its original source) and then to bring such wise insights into the service of Yahweh. So quite probably there were wisdom schools associated with Jerusalem's royal court where such sayings were collected and tested – and then passed on as part of Israel's *own* wisdom tradition.

Traditionally this wisdom movement was associated with King Solomon himself – the one whose wisdom, given by God, won him an international reputation (1 Kings 3; see p. 85). Being married to Pharaoh's daughter and developing a bureaucracy (perhaps patterned on that of Egypt), Solomon would have been ideally situated to 'plunder' the wisdom of Egypt or other neighbouring nations.

However, modern scholarship has questioned whether this wisdom literature is so ancient. Instead the final compilation for these three books is often attributed to the post-exilic period (fifth to third century BC). Even so, there are numerous sayings that could be very ancient indeed. Moreover, by the nature of things, they are quite timeless. So there may instead have been a gradual and steady accumulation of wisdom. Like a snowball gathering size and momentum as it travels downhill, so the wisdom literature comes to us with the power of a long journey. This is wisdom that has been tested over the generations and found to be true.

This means that, when Proverbs and Ecclesiastes open with references to Solomon, this may indicate that they only have an *affinity* with Solomon – standing in the literary tradition that he established. The same is true for the Song of Songs – though here the link with Solomon is connected to his reputation as a lover of women. The Song of Songs, however, is clearly set within the borders of Israel (hence the references to several local place names). So once again, even if its love poems have parallels with love poetry from elsewhere, this is an example of the Israelites bringing their distinctive views to bear on matters of broad human interest.

Something similarly 'universal' is found in the book of Job. The problem of suffering was not limited to Israel. So this may then explain the book's dramatic setting, which is in far-away Mesopotamia and in the days of the patriarchs (presumably some time well before Moses). In this way the book is set on a much broader canvas than just Israel and has the capacity to speak to people of all cultures. The book may be rooted in a historical person called Job, but it ends up having a timeless, eternal reach.

This also may explain why there are some parallels to Job in other ancient literature (for example, the early fifth-century BC *Prometheus Bound* story in Greek tragedy). It also allows us to compare Job as a literary achievement with other ancient musings on this universal problem. A concluding remark on this from commentator F. I. Andersen may then help us to appreciate Job as a masterpiece of ancient literature:

> *Job stands far above its nearest competitors, in the coherence of its sustained treatment of the theme of human misery, in the scope of its many-sided examination of the problem, in the strength and clarity of its defiant moral monotheism… in its dramatic impact, and in the intellectual integrity with which it faces the 'unintelligible burden' of human existence… Comparison only serves to enhance the solitary greatness of the book of Job.*

F. I. Andersen, in *Tyndale Old Testament Commentary*

Finally, the Psalms stand out as quite different in some ways from other wisdom literature – inasmuch as they are so clearly the prayer book of Israel (see p. 112). Even so, they have proved remarkably universal in their appeal, because they touch so directly on the emotional aspect of life that affects us all.

Thus these five books, located in the heart of the Old Testament, take us indeed by various different routes to matters of the heart. They enjoy a timeless air, speaking directly across the centuries to our shared human condition, giving key insight into the matters of everyday life – whether how to deal with suffering or despair, how to pray, or how best to enjoy true worship, fruitful business or good sex.

Job

Job focuses on the problem of innocent suffering. The Bible continuously presents us with an active and faithful God. Of course, if such a God does *not* exist, then the suffering of the innocent is a sign of that unpleasant arbitrariness which you would expect in a godless world. If this God *does* exist, why, as the Bible insists, is there so much suffering in his world?

The problem of suffering, however, for ancient Israel was yet more acute, because in biblical teaching obedience

Job, by Leon Bonnat (1833–1922).

Chapter	
1–2	Introduction (prose prologue)
3	Job's opening lament
4–31	Job's dialogues with his three friends (see below)
32–37	Elihu's monologue
38 – 42:6	Yahweh speaks out of the whirlwind
42:7–17	Finale (prose epilogue)

The structure of the dialogue cycles is as follows:

First	Second	Third
Eliphaz (4–5)	Eliphaz (15)	Eliphaz (22)
Job (6–7)	Job (16–17)	Job (23–24)
Bildad (8)	Bildad (18)	Bildad (25)
Job (9–10)	Job (19)	Job (26:1 – 27:12)
Zophar (11)	Zophar (20)	Zophar (27:13–23)*
Job (12–14)	Job (21)	Job (28–31)**

* These verses, which summarize the position of retribution theology, should almost certainly be assigned not to Job but to Zophar (who otherwise does not speak in the third cycle).

** Job's final speech begins with a poem on divine Wisdom.

to God brings blessing. For example, the historical books teach that Israel's exile was due to its sin. So is not suffering a clear sign of divine judgment?

Yet such 'prosperity' or 'retribution' theology patently does not fit the observable facts – either then or now. Good people can suffer severe testing and senseless tragedies.

Within the storyline of the Bible, the book of Job therefore acts as a vital mid-course correction – a moment to pause and to acknowledge that life is not quite so simple. And ever since, people in pain and grief have found comfort here, being able to identify in different ways with Job as he broods over his loss, searching for answers that do not come.

Job: the outline story

The plotline structure of the book of Job is reasonably clear and simple (see the diagram on the left). The main section, which is poetic in form throughout, is topped and tailed by two prose sections. In the opening sequence, Satan asks Yahweh if he may plague Job with various calamities in order to establish whether – if stripped of these blessings – he will start to curse God. Job responds without falling into any such cursing. He is then joined by three 'friends' or counsellors (Eliphaz, Bildad and Zophar) who sit beside him for an entire week without saying a word. Only when Job opens his mouth to 'curse the day of his birth' do they then respond.

The poetic central section then contains three lengthy cycles of dialogue in which Job responds to the various perspectives of his friends – as well as to some advice from a young impetuous man called Elihu. Suddenly Yahweh himself speaks 'out of the storm', reminding Job forcefully of his unique power – as seen in his act of creation. Job confesses that he spoke of things he did not understand: 'Therefore I despise myself and repent in dust and ashes.'

In the final (short) sequence, Yahweh chides Job's three friends (Elihu is disdainfully ignored!) for 'not speaking of me what is right, as my servant Job has'. They effectively apologize to Job, who prays for them, at which point Job experiences a restoration in his fortunes, beginning to build up his business again and eventually having ten more children. 'And so he died, old and full of years.'

'The Lord gave and the Lord has taken away; may the name of the Lord be praised.'
Job's words in Job 1:21

The powerful narrative

Despite being quite long, the book is remarkably powerful for its sheer drama. Partly this is helped by the dramatic irony whereby the reader knows from the very outset what Job's friends (and Job himself) do not know – namely that Yahweh has been commending Job as 'blameless' and that these calamities result from Satan's desire to test him. The participants struggle in the dark, while the readers are in the light;

'My feet have closely followed
   his steps;
I have kept to his way
   without turning aside.
I have not departed from the
   commands of his lips;
I have treasured the words
   of his mouth more than my
   daily bread.'
Job 23:11–12

'… I will not deny my
   integrity.
I will maintain my
   innocence…
my conscience will not
   reproach me…'
Job 27:5–6

eventually the tension becomes almost unbearable.

The dramatic force is also seen in the increasing sense of desperation. Initially Job's friends speak quite calmly. Gradually, however, as the impasse of understanding remains unresolved, their accusations become more blunt. Job's retorts also become stronger. He chides them for their insensitivity, and for their claims to unique wisdom, when in fact they are building mere 'defences of clay'; he describes them as 'miserable comforters' who pile on the agony and add insult to injury.

Who will break first? Not Job. Despite his counsellors' exasperation, Job does not budge on a key point – he swears his fundamental innocence. He is not claiming to be totally sinless – only that he has not committed some gross sin worthy of these severe punishments. Thus he has not 'shaken his fist' at God, but has rather remained prayerful, appropriately fearing God's judgment. Indeed Job's life is marked by a fundamental attitude of ongoing repentant humility, readily confessing his sin and knowing his need of God's mercy: 'Though I were innocent [of great transgression]… I could only plead with my Judge for mercy.'

So Job sticks resolutely to his claim, and his counsellors begin to back away. This is when the young upstart, Elihu, interrupts, being unable to contain his frustration and anger any longer. So he launches into a monologue, becoming ever more shrill and opinionated. It is at this moment – when Elihu is in full throttle – that suddenly Yahweh speaks, effectively interrupting this blathering hot-head! The effect on the reader is thus also one of sheer relief. At last this barrage of pointless words has been stopped; now at last the truth will out.

The impasse is caused by Job's four interlocutors all espousing a

kind of retribution theology. Moving on from the biblical premise that those who sin will suffer the consequences, they have reversed this to 'those who suffer must have sinned.' 'He repays people for what they have done,' asserts Elihu. There is no room in their scheme for any suffering that is plainly disproportionate to the sin. And Job's difficulty is that *on some levels*, he agrees with them, acknowledging that God does punish sin. Eventually, his counsellors fall back on the possibility that Job's particular sin is precisely the fact that he is arguing with God: 'To his sin he adds rebellion... and multiplies his words against God.'

The argument is clearly going nowhere fast. In his final speech Job continues to protest his innocence, going through all aspects of his life with a fine-tooth comb. If in his earlier speeches Job has been filled with despair, the tone at the end is more one of adamant forthrightness – desiring to meet God and argue his case. Job has thus moved through bewilderment and despair to a point of anger. It is into this anger – this frustration at having no answer – that God, at long last, speaks.

***

There are no easy answers. While never abandoning its condemnation of moral evil and sinful behaviour, the book of Job demonstrates that any naïve retribution theology is plainly inadequate: there will be many instances of apparently innocent suffering that cannot be explained. Those who suffer, however, can learn three key things from the revelation given to Job:

- Allowance must be made for the evil work of Satan, as well as for the permissive will of God (allowing evil things to happen).

- Suffering can be a means of testing what is in a person's heart.

- Above all, trusting God is always the path of wisdom, while cursing God is inappropriate; he is the almighty Creator before whom humility is required.

So, as summarized at the end of Job's poem to Wisdom: 'the fear of the Lord, that is wisdom; and to shun evil, that is understanding'.

Yet within the Bible as a whole this is decidedly not the last word on the problem of suffering. Job takes us as far as any Old Testament writer could. The New Testament, written in the light of Jesus' resurrection, will take us considerably further: it will present us with a Jesus who walked on the path of the uniquely innocent sufferer (like Job but far more so); and it will claim that, in Jesus, Israel's God was *himself* experiencing suffering 'from the inside'. Yahweh thus turns out to be no stranger to the suffering in his world, but tastes it fully in Jesus – supremely at the cross.

How long, Lord? Will you forget me forever?
How long will you hide your face from me?

How long must I wrestle with my thoughts
and day after day have sorrow in my heart?
How long will my enemy triumph over me?

Look on me and answer, Lord my God.
Give light to my eyes, or I will sleep in death...

But I trust in your unfailing love;
my heart rejoices in your salvation.

I will sing the Lord's praise,
for he has been good to me.

Psalm 13:1–3, 5–6

Seen in this light, it is no surprise that Christians have often come back to the book of Job with fresh eyes. And they note with interest those brief moments when Job longs for an advocate who will speak in his defence and when, just for an instant, he catches a glimpse of life beyond the grave. So Job's words (familiar from the aria in Handel's *Messiah*) have run down the years as words of hope to many in the encompassing gloom: 'I know that my redeemer lives, and that in the end he will stand on the earth. And after my skin has been destroyed, yet in my flesh I will see God.'

Psalms

*Blessed are those
    who do not walk in step with the wicked…
    but who delight in the law of the Lord…*

*They are like a tree planted by streams of water…
    and whose leaf does not wither –*

*For the Lord watches over the way of the righteous,
    but the way of the wicked will be destroyed.*

Psalm 1:1–3, 6

Some favourite psalms

'The heavens declare the glory of God'
(Psalm 19)

'The Lord is my light and my salvation'
(Psalm 27)

'As the deer pants for streams of water'
(Psalm 42)

'How lovely is your dwelling place'
(Psalm 84)

'Praise the Lord, O my soul'
(Psalm 103)

'I lift up my eyes to the hills'
(Psalm 121)

'By the rivers of Babylon'
(Psalm 137)

'Praise the Lord, O my soul, and forget not all his benefits – who forgives all your sins and heal all your diseases, who crowns you with love and compassion… The Lord is compassionate and gracious, slow to anger and abounding in love.'

Psalms 103:2–4, 8

The book of Psalms is unique within the Bible. Here are 150 songs and prayers, composed at various times in Israel's life and now gathered together into five short books:

Book 1:   Psalms 1–41
Book 2:   Psalms 42–72
Book 3:   Psalms 73–89
Book 4:   Psalms 90–106
Book 5:   Psalms 107–150

These five smaller collections have some recognizably distinct themes (for example, almost all the psalms in Book 1 are attributed to David), but overall, the book of Psalms exhibits an astonishing variety. In one psalm the writer is grieving over some personal misfortune; in the next the writer is praising God for his blessings to all his people. This very variety gives the psalms their lasting appeal: there is something for everyone, in every circumstance of life. And those who read through the psalms regularly encounter a bewildering array of emotions and situations. Life's rich tapestry is here being explored in the presence of God.

The psalms begin by noting the blessings of the upright, who 'delight in the law of the Lord and meditate on it day and night' (Psalm 1); these five books will demand careful attention and practical obedience. They close with a resounding note of universal praise: 'Let everything that has breath praise the Lord!' (Psalm 150); so the book of Psalms should lead its readers into new depths of worship.

The psalms take us right inside the faith of ancient Israel. Other Old Testament books describe the nation's history and its laws, or preserve its proverbs and prophecies, but here we are taken into its life of prayer and praise – what it *really* meant on the ground to live one's life before God as a member of his people.

Moreover, as a collection of prayers, it is best for people not so much to *read* the book of Psalms as to *pray* through it. For each psalm is an invitation for the reader to start joining in its language of prayer; and many of them are expressly a summons to worship: 'Come, let us sing for joy to the Lord… let us bow down in worship… before the Lord our Maker…' (Psalm 95). The psalm verses mentioned at the end of each Old Testament chapter in this *Guide* can be used in this way (see p. 11).

Focusing first on the psalms designed for public use, let us note some of the different issues they address:

1. Public worship. Many of the psalms would have been sung by worshippers gathered in Jerusalem's Temple: the worshippers often use the liturgical refrain 'Give thanks to the Lord, for he is good!' Occasionally there are references to processions or other liturgical actions. Frequently there is a rejoicing in God's presence as experienced in his 'house' (i.e. the Temple). (See Psalms 24, 26, 68, 84, 118, 135, 136.)

2. Pilgrimage. A related category focuses on pilgrims going up to Jerusalem's Temple. The so-called 'Psalms of Ascents' (Psalms 120–134) were probably written for those making their 'ascent' up to Jerusalem. Other psalms celebrate Jerusalem as the 'city of God'. (See Psalms 46, 48, 87.)

3. Israel's life as a nation. In other psalms we encounter the joys of success in battle, or extended laments after military defeat. Some celebrate God's provision in a fruitful harvest; others cry out for justice in the face of prevalent evils in society. Several reflect on Israel's relationship with God, rehearsing the nation's history – presumably to encourage faithfulness in the next generation. Some are clearly written in the exile – with the nation mourning its loss. (See Psalms 74, 79, 89.)

4. Israel's king. Some focus expressly on Israel's king, rejoicing in his strength, and praying for him to exercise God's rule well. Some will have been composed for state occasions (for example, a royal wedding) and are coloured with the language of the royal court. (See Psalms 20, 45, 72.)

This then links in to those psalms written by individuals, for many of these are attributed to one of Israel's kings, namely David. So in these psalms we are not reading words *about* the king, so much as *from* the king. Some are tied to episodes in David's life in more specific ways: when he was hiding from King Saul (Psalms 57 and 59); or when confessing his adultery with Bathsheba and the murder of her husband (Psalm 51; as told in 2 Samuel 11: see pp. 80–81).

Many other psalms are not linked explicitly to a specific person, but take us into the individual experience of the (anonymous) psalmist. Here we see some raw honesty as the writers wrestle with life's tough situations:

- being opposed by enemies or being betrayed by friends;
- disliking the advance of old age or reflecting on the follies of one's youth;
- feeling worthless and lonely; suffering from evident depression or being spiritually dry and in a 'desert place';
- voicing frustration at seemingly unanswered prayer;
- asking for God's mercy and forgiveness in the light of recognized sin or folly.

'The Lord is my shepherd,
I lack nothing…

he leads me beside quiet
waters…

Even though I walk
through the darkest valley,
I will fear no evil…

Surely your goodness and
love will follow me
all the days of my life,
and I will dwell in the house
of the Lord forever.'

Psalms 23:1–2, 4, 6

Some psalms end without the matter having been resolved: the negative feelings remain. Yet a good number of the psalms show signs of resolution, as the psalmist moves from earnest prayer to joyful praise. For modern readers, therefore, praying through the Psalms can be more than just a comfort (allowing them to express negative thoughts constructively before God, and being conscious that the psalmist has suffered similarly). It can also be genuinely therapeutic, as they are taken on a journey – perhaps from despair to hope – ending up in a different place from where they started.

This pattern within the Psalms connects with a major biblical theme – namely death and resurrection. Thus the psalmist may start in a place of 'death', but is 'raised' to a place of vision. Indeed, in quoting the first words of Psalm 22 when dying on the cross ('My God, why have you forsaken me?'), Jesus may have been consciously evoking the underlying pattern of that psalm. For, although it starts with despair, it ends in triumph:

In the congregation I will praise you… for the Lord has not despised the suffering of the afflicted one, but has listened to his cry for help… Future generations will proclaim his righteousness to a people yet unborn.

Jesus may also have been alluding to this prevalent pattern in the Psalms when he taught (in Luke 24) that 'it is written in the Psalms… that the Christ must suffer and rise again'. For the very shape of so

many psalms is one of suffering followed by a kind of resurrection.

Jesus' quoting of this psalm at his crucifixion proves quite eye-opening for several reasons. First, it reveals how deeply the Psalms had penetrated into his own life – the Psalms were Jesus' own 'prayer-book'; if Jesus treasured the Psalms as the place where he learned to pray, his followers would do well to treasure them too. Second, it shows how he saw the Psalms as also containing aspects of *prophecy*. Thus the psalmists were not only describing their own (or Israel's) situation but were often experiencing things which would find a fulfilment in the Messiah when he came.

Praise the Lord.
  Praise God… in his mighty heavens.

Praise him for his acts of power…

Praise him with the sounding of the trumpet…

praise him with timbrel and dancing…

praise him with resounding cymbals.

Let everything that has breath praise the Lord.
  Praise the Lord!

Psalm 150

This explains why the New Testament writers quote the Psalms so frequently, seeing in their pages uncanny prophecies concerning Jesus:

- Jesus was the 'anointed king', the one seated on the royal throne (Psalms 2, 45, 72);

- Jesus was the one who suffered and cried out to God in despair, who was utterly obedient, but who was vindicated in glory (Psalms 16, 22, 40);

- Jesus was the one whom God had invited to 'sit at God's right hand' and was now a special 'high priest' (Psalm 110 – the text most frequently quoted in the New Testament).

This 'messianic' reading of the Psalms gives a whole new layer of meaning to them. For, although we can appreciate them as written in ancient Israel, we can also see them as mysteriously fulfilled in Christ. Readers can thus sense that not only the psalmist, but *Christ himself* has been through similar suffering.

In a remarkable way, the Psalms have continued to inspire people down the centuries. For God's people have repeatedly found that those things which the psalmist proclaims can similarly be celebrated today: God's faithfulness to his purposes, the power of his word, and the strength of his love.

Proverbs

'Pride goes before
 destruction,
a haughty spirit before a fall.'

Proverbs 16:18

*(a proverb very similar to words
found in Herodotus, the fifth-
century BC Greek historian).*

Spring colours in the Judean desert
between Jerusalem and Jericho.

Though written so long ago, the book of Proverbs comes across as remarkably contemporary. Its pithy sayings have a timeless quality, pinpointing many themes of life as lived in any culture and in any age.

'Education, education', emphasize our modern politicians; and the editors of Proverbs would have readily agreed. For we are seeing here how seriously the people of Israel took this issue of passing on wisdom to the next generation. This is wisdom lived, tested, discussed at the city gate, and then, crucially, passed on in the home. There were parallels to this, of course, in other ancient cultures (see pp. 104–105), but Proverbs upholds a distinctive perspective: that true wisdom – the best education – comes from God and from obedience to him. So the repeated motto of Proverbs is unequivocal: 'the fear of the Lord is the beginning of knowledge'.

The wise path, therefore, is not a secular or idolatrous life, but one lived before Yahweh: 'the name of the Lord is a strong tower – the righteous run into it and are safe'. Thus, even though Proverbs does not focus overtly on the 'religious' aspects of life (with only a few references to worship), some chapters are filled with references to 'the Lord'. We

are thus reminded that *all life is God's life* – at home, at work, by day and by night: '*all our paths* are in full view of the Lord'.

Proverbs falls into two main sections. The first nine chapters are an extended invitation to a father's 'son' to choose wisdom. From chapter 10 onwards there is a continuous stream of single-verse proverbs, many of which draw a contrast between the two possible ways to live. This pattern is broken for some slightly longer 'sayings of the wise' (chapters 22–24). In the final two chapters there are the 'sayings of Agur' and of 'King Lemuel', with a (justly famous) epilogue devoted to extolling a 'wife of noble character'.

In the opening overture the young and the 'simple' are encouraged to seek after understanding and discretion. Wisdom will keep them safe; it is more valuable than rubies. Gradually this wisdom becomes personified in a female form, with Wisdom bidding people to come to her. By contrast the woman Folly tries to allure people instead towards her house – deliberately echoing the allurement of the adulteress (warned about just a few chapters earlier). To follow *her*, however, spells disaster: 'there is a way that appears to be right, but in the end it leads to death'. This strong warning will then underlie all the subsequent proverbs. Beneath their often humorous form there will be a note of urgency. Readers will have to choose. The path of evil, however attractive, does not pay; the wicked will eventually receive their due punishment.

The sequence of 515 proverbs begins by setting up numerous contrasts between wisdom and folly. Will we aim for righteousness or wickedness; diligence or laziness; integrity or crookedness; love or hatred? Will we aim for pride or humility; discernment or mockery; kindness or cruelty; generosity or stinginess? Will we be truthful or lie; be patient or quick tempered; care for the poor or ignore them; hate bribes or be greedy? Above all, will we gratefully receive instruction (even rebuke, if necessary), or will we mock our teachers? 'Whoever heeds correction shows prudence.' Not surprisingly, then, there is a strong emphasis on the value of parental discipline: 'Start children off in the way they should go, and even when they are old they will not turn from it.' Proverbs has no naïve view as to the essential goodness of human beings; left to our own devices, we will wander. Wisdom accepts that it needs boundaries, guidance and direction. 'Discipline your children, for in that there is hope.'

In a telling phrase, we learn that 'where there is no revelation, the people cast off restraint; but blessed are those who heed wisdom's instruction'. The people of Israel knew they needed not only good human advice but also divine revelation – as now contained in Israel's Law. And Proverbs knows we will always fall short and need God's mercy: 'Those who conceal their sins do not prosper, but those who confess and renounce them find mercy.'

Towards the end, the proverbs take the form of similes: 'Like apples of gold in settings of silver is a ruling rightly given.' 'As iron sharpens iron, so one person sharpens another.' The similes are drawn from across the spectrum of life: human activity is compared to birds and lions, snow and rain, teeth and vinegar, door-hinges and broken walls, perfume and churning milk – even leg amputation and nose bleeds! The sayings positively sparkle with wit. Here's a graphic example: 'Like one who grabs a stray dog by the ears is someone who rushes into a quarrel not their own.'

The book closes with an extended eulogy of wisdom as found in a 'noble wife' – busy both at home and in her business dealings. 'Beauty is fleeting,' concludes Proverbs, 'but a woman who fears the Lord is to be praised.'

***

Proverbs is packed full of sound advice. No wonder some people aim to read its 31 chapters every month – a chapter each day. Others have its sayings on their business calendars. No wonder too that Jesus' own teaching reflects its influence, with his pithy sayings reflecting this 'wisdom' tradition. In this sense, Jesus was a 'sage'.

Proverbs' contribution is not just that it reveals how God's reality permeates all of life; it also gives a tantalizing portrait of personified Wisdom:

I raise my voice to all humankind… The Lord brought me forth as the first of his works… I was formed long ages ago, at the very beginning, when the world came to be… Blessed are those who listen to me… those who find me find life.

Proverbs 8:4, 22–23, 32, 35

Within Proverbs this presentation of 'Lady Wisdom' is clearly a device to draw the reader towards the wisdom found in God. It is a pictorial way of saying that there is no true wisdom apart from God, and that God makes himself known by his wisdom. Moreover, if wisdom is foundational in creation, then to follow the path of wisdom is to live life *as we were created to do*. Choose wisdom and you will find your created, God-intended destiny. As the saying goes, 'For best results, follow the Maker's instructions.'

The New Testament writers, however, became convinced that Jesus was the *very embodiment* of God's wisdom: Christ 'has become for us wisdom from God', writes Paul, and in him 'are hidden all the treasures of knowledge'. So they naturally returned to Proverbs' imagery and used it to explain Jesus' unique significance – as the agent of creation, and the one through whom human beings can gain a personal knowledge of their creator God. So, not surprisingly, some of Jesus' invitations sound remarkably similar to those offered by Wisdom in Proverbs: 'Whoever finds me finds life... come to me and I will give you rest.'

I was young and now I am old,
  yet I have never seen the righteous forsaken...

They are always generous and lend freely;
  their children will be a blessing.

Turn from evil and do good;
  then you will dwell in the land forever.

For the Lord... will not forsake his faithful ones...
  the offspring of the wicked will perish.

Psalm 37:25–28

Key chapters in Ecclesiastes

'There is a time for everything'
(chapter 3)

The futility of wealth
(chapters 5–6)

'Remember your Creator'
(chapter 12)

'Enjoy life with your wife, whom you love, all the days of this your meaningless life.'
Ecclesiastes 9:9

Solomon is associated with many things, including the building of Israel's only fleet near Eloth (modern Eilat?) on the shores of the Red Sea (1 Kings 9:26). This model shows the likely design of boats in that period.

Ecclesiastes

'Vanity of vanity,' says the Teacher. 'Everything is meaningless!' These famous opening words warn us that Ecclesiastes will be a strange book. For it voices a host of negativities: human life is described twenty-seven times as 'meaningless', seven times as a mere 'chasing after the wind'. 'In this meaningless life of mine I have seen a wicked man living long in wickedness.' This then causes the Teacher to give the cynical advice: 'Do not be over-righteous and do not be over-wicked; avoid all extremes.' And there are a range of other apt one-liners which might appeal to the Eeyores of this world.

Even in ancient times people questioned why the book was in the Old Testament at all. Perhaps, as with Job and some psalms, its role is to give believers a biblical mandate for honesty in expressing their doubts? Or perhaps instead it is designed deliberately to show what life looks like *when we leave God out of the picture*; if so, it becomes an implicit warning against a secular worldview – a kind of back-handed call to faith.

Yet, even if true, matters are not quite that simple. For a start, the Teacher's standpoint is *not* one of total atheism or disbelief – these are the dark shadows that fall across a would-be believer. Then there is the puzzling epilogue, which commends the Teacher's writings as 'true' but which also puts a critical distance between the standpoint of the book's final editor and that of the Teacher.

Thus the writer of the epilogue warns that the Teacher's apparently wise sayings may also serve like 'goads', prodding the sheep on to discover other things; in other words, they may not in themselves have conveyed the complete story but are designed to prompt readers to their own further enquiry.

This critical distance between the final editor and the Teacher then opens up the possibility that Ecclesiastes is a brilliant teaching device in which its readers *are fully intended* to find themselves critical of some of the Teacher's musings. The device is similar to that found in the book of Job. There we learned at the end that much of what Job's friends were saying was wrong. This means we go back to the text and find ourselves saying increasingly, 'Yes, but…!' or 'No!' Ecclesiastes could well then be intended similarly as a *deliberately provocative* text – as a foil by comparison with which we can move towards the truth.

If so, this might explain some of the book's apparent contradictions. For example, we are told that righteous living is important, but in the next verse that righteous people often get what the wicked deserve. Yet this is precisely what we might expect in a book designed to provoke, rather than to teach systematically. The book is precisely a profound wrestling with these apparent contradictions which are so hard to harmonize. So, just as good teachers today are often those who do not simply 'spoon feed' their pupils but rather intrigue them, so Ecclesiastes gradually teases out of its readers their own answers. This is indeed wisdom, but not served up on a plate – a biblical wisdom that taunts and teases us.

There is no obvious structure to Ecclesiastes – except that in the opening half the Teacher observes the worlds of pleasure, study and hard labour, before moving to some tentative conclusions in the second half. And the style combines proverbial one-liners, brief reflections on particular themes, and even short poems. Yet the overall themes are clear. Working with a strong understanding of God's transcendence, it is an extended exploration on the apparent futility of life. Death, in particular, is a problem – because it seems to hit both the good and the bad in an arbitrary way. Within Ecclesiastes, then, there are some recurrent themes:

- Wisdom, though often useful, is sometimes not properly valued and always has its limitations.

- Toil and labour may be pointless, especially when others seemingly reap the benefits.

- History seems to keep repeating itself.

- Hedonism and pleasure-seeking do not deliver.

- The wise and foolish will face the same destiny in death.

- The future is always unknown.

- Human life is filled with envy, evil, scheming, 'frustration, affliction and anger', all of which will look so pointless in future generations.

There are also some insights that are touched upon only once:

- The disadvantages of living and working on one's own.

- The pointless upheavals caused by people seeking advancement.

- The dangers of using too many words or making foolish vows.

Time and purpose

'There is a time for everything, and a season for every activity under the heavens:
a time to be born and a time to die,
a time to plant and a time to uproot…
a time to weep and a time to laugh…
a time to search and a time to give up,
a time to keep and a time to throw away…
a time to be silent and a time to speak,
a time for war and a time for peace
God… has made everything beautiful in its time.
He has also set eternity in the human heart;
yet no one can fathom what God has done from beginning to the end…
No one knows when his end will come.'

The editor's epilogue:
'The Teacher searched to find just the right words… the words of the wise are like goads.'

'Of making many books there is no end, and much study wearies the body.'

'Here is the conclusion of the matter: Fear God and keep his commandments, for this is the duty of every human being. For God will bring every deed into judgment, including every hidden thing, whether it is good or evil.'

- The uselessness of material riches.

- The stupidity of excessive nostalgia and of foolish laughter.

- The wisdom of obeying rulers (even though they are often more foolish than their followers).

- The importance of keeping engaged with tasks (even though some will not succeed) and not waiting for the 'ideal' conditions.

The Teacher is reflecting both on his own experiences and those of others. He has worked very hard to apply his mind – he is what we might call a 'reflective analyst' or a 'monitor evaluator'. Yet now, having apparently achieved a measure of wisdom, he seems to go through a period of not valuing it any more. The reader feels he will use his acquired wisdom in ways that become self-destructive, despising his wisdom or seeing it too as 'meaningless': 'With much wisdom comes much sorrow; the more knowledge, the more grief.'

So it is encouraging in the book's second half when he interrupts his musings with statements about the value of enjoying life to the full and pursuing wisdom – *even though there remain aspects of both these pursuits which he cannot understand.* 'So I commend the enjoyment of life.' The Teacher is reconnecting with life, no longer standing on the touchline as a critical non-participant. He is seeing 'life under the sun' as a gift of God to be enjoyed in the here and now. Yes, the ways of God are mysterious; but *our human inability to understand everything does not suck all the meaning out of life.* The Teacher has found some solid ground and has drawn back from falling into the abyss of despair. His final command (to 'remember your Creator in the days of your youth') thus comes across as the insight of a person who has struggled much, but has now reached a calm assurance.

* * *

Ecclesiastes takes us on a profound journey. We are taken into a dark valley but given clear signals that there is light at the end of the tunnel. Yet, seen in the light of the New Testament, one senses that the real light to lift the Teacher from despair would be the resurrection of Christ. The Teacher, looking at death solely from an Old Testament perspective ('under the sun'), is understandably worried that death seems to treat good and bad alike. Yet what if in due course Israel's God did do something new in human history? If so, the Teacher is giving brilliant expression to the complexities resulting from not having yet received God's *full* revelation.

So Ecclesiastes is a marvellous precursor to the gospel, acting like a dark shadow that serves to reveal by contrast the light of the resurrection. Having read Ecclesiastes we realize why the resurrection was such good news when it hit the first-century world. And we also find that the way its final editor has opened up a measure of critical distance (effectively saying 'this is true as far as it goes') paves the way for later readers to *say the same about the whole book*: 'this is true, but God's ultimate revelation can take us so much further'. Ecclesiastes thus positively invites fresh interpretation in the light of the New Testament.

So, if the Teacher has hit an impasse, the New Testament will assert that Christ's resurrection offers a way through. That's why, when Paul in Romans 8 explicitly reflects on life's 'frustrations' as seen in 'creation', he asserts that believers in the resurrection have a new hope. If the Teacher could have seen this, that which to him seemed dark and empty would have been bathed with light and filled with meaning and purpose.

Song of Songs

The Song of Songs is one of the Old Testament's hidden gems: a series of poems extolling the joys of human relationships and sexual love. Modern readers, presuming the Bible would be a closed book on such an intimate subject, are often surprised by its erotic nature. Yet here we find a lover in close contact with his beloved, as they talk together about their love and their physical desires.

At times the book seems a little disjointed (suggesting an anthology of songs). Yet there is also a sense of a dramatic progression: from first meeting, to sexual encounter, to the desire to maintain this love into the future.

Proverbs had hinted that 'the way of a man with a girl' was one of four things 'too wonderful' to be described – so it remained hidden and under cover. Here in the Song of Songs, the veil is removed – not totally (the poems do not become pornographic) – but enough for us to know that human, sexual love does not lie outside God's purposes.

Song of Songs

The ancient Israelites were not Platonists – seeing matter as evil and our sexual natures as somewhat degrading – but affirmed the physical aspects of life as good gifts to be received from the God who had created them.

The book has only eight chapters and the basic features are clear: there are alternate poems (from the beloved to her lover and vice versa), interrupted on several occasions by comments from a group of female friends attending the woman. This locates the love poems within the context of ancient marriage ceremonies in which the bride would be accompanied to the bridal chamber by her female companions. So, although there are moments of total privacy, this public dimension to the book ensures that the poems do not come across simply as private desires for illicit sex. They publicly celebrate the love of the bridal couple and even implicitly encourage them to consummate their love ('drink your fill, O lovers').

This marital context becomes explicit in several references to marriage and to the woman as a 'bride'. It is also seen in the exclusive nature of the relationship, as seen in the woman's hopes: 'close your heart to every love but mine; hold no one in your arms but me'. Overall there is a sense of responsibility that removes the book from being merely an encouragement to 'free love'. So three times the bride counsels her female companions 'not to awaken love until it so desires'. This is passion that has appropriately kept itself under control until the appointed 'day'. Given the strong social and legal frameworks within Israel's Law, which required virginity in the marriage bed (something replicated to this day in various Middle Eastern cultures), it could hardly be otherwise.

The opening chapter is full of anticipation. By the end of that first chapter, however, there is already a reference to their bed and there are no longer any rude interruptions from the bride's female friends. The bridal couple are thus seemingly on their own, looking back on different episodes from their courtship, and the lover is praising his bride for her beauty. Towards the end of chapter 4, there are then clear hints that they are about to consummate their love: 'My bride… you are a garden, a fountain closed off to all others'; to which she replies, 'Let my lover come into his garden'; and he is soon saying, 'I have come into my garden, my bride.'

So the subsequent chapters have a slightly different feel. There are suggestions of further lovemaking, but also an increased longing from the bride that her husband should not be absent too long. She suggests going out again into the countryside or desert for some time on their own. They come back and have a brief discussion with her female friends about the marriage prospects of the bride's younger sister, but the book closes with the bride boasting of what she can give her husband and with him seeking out her company once more. And she replies yet again: 'Come away, my lover.' Yet again they

The lovers' conversation

The lover's invitation
'Arise, my darling, my beautiful one, come with me. See! The winter is past… the season of singing has come… How beautiful you are!… Like a lily among the thorns is my darling among the young women…'
'You have stolen my heart… my bride… with one glance of your eyes… How delightful is your love… how much more pleasing is your love than wine!… Your eyes are like doves… your teeth like a flock of sheep… your lips are like a scarlet ribbon… your navel like a rounded goblet that never lacks blended wine… May your breasts be like the clusters of the vine, the fragrance of your breath like apples, and your mouth like the best wine.'

The beloved's response
'My lover is to me a sachet of myrrh resting between my breasts… How handsome you are!… Like an apple tree in the forest is my lover… I delight to sit in his shade… He has taken me to the banquet hall and his banner over me is love… His left arm is under my head, and his right arm embraces me… My lover is radiant… his mouth is sweetness itself… his legs are pillars of marble… This is my friend, O daughters of Jerusalem!'
'Place me like a seal over your heart… for love is as strong as death, its jealousy as unyielding as the grave. It burns like a blazing fire… Many waters cannot quench love!'

'Take me away with you – let us hurry! Let the king bring me into his chambers.'
Song of Songs 1:4

disappear over the horizon to enjoy their love and life together.

So the book has a reasonably coherent narrative flow. It also has a number of sexual references (some more veiled than others): there are four extended descriptions of the lovers' physical charms – normally working down from the head to the foot. And some of its phrases have become justly famous, speaking of love in a way that is truly timeless.

* * *

The book proclaims that sex is a good thing; so too are the human longings for intimacy and relationship, for identity and meaning, which our sexual desires represent. And sex is not only good because it is the means of having children; for the Song of Songs never once mentions that important subject! Here marital sex is being enjoyed in its own right.

The Song achieves this by picking up the imagery of the Garden of Eden (Genesis 2). There Adam and Eve enjoyed God's creation of each other and were naked without being ashamed; sex in that garden was implicitly something good within God's creation. So now here the man and woman enjoy sex in their own garden of delights. That original love story is here being replayed and enjoyed. And, although sin has subsequently distorted all human relationships, something of the original is being restored.

This was an important message at the time, but even more so today – when people often presume that faith and sex simply don't mix. At the same time, the Song knows that sex can be highly dangerous: hence its repeated warning to avoid arousing sexual desire and its reminder about the 'jealousy' of sexual love. Given that our modern cultures have gone the other way – idolizing sex – this becomes its key message.

However, despite this focus on physical sex, the Song is not aiming primarily to be a biblical sex manual! Instead it is helping its readers to identify with the couple's friends – that is, rejoicing with them without envy and recognizing in the public sphere that such private sexual intimacies are fully appropriate within the context of marriage. In this way it has the same effect as the injunction later in the New Testament: 'Marriage should be *honoured by all*, and the marriage bed [literally *coitus*] kept pure' (Hebrews 13:4). Marital sex, even though private, must be publicly honoured, respected and promoted.

But does the Song only teach about sex? No. By ensuring that sex was affirmed as a good thing, the Song made it possible for the marriage relationship *as a whole* to be seen as a good part of God's intentional creation. That, in turn, enabled Old Testament prophets and New Testament apostles to use marriage as a key analogy for God's covenantal relationship with his people. This, the best example of human relationships, could now be taken to teach about the most important relationship of all. Indeed marriage came to be seen as reflecting a prior reality – the eternal covenant love which God has for all his people. So elsewhere in the Old Testament God is portrayed as the loving husband who is passionately committed to his people (see especially Hosea). Similarly, in the New Testament, Christ is portrayed as the bridegroom, deeply committed to the church, which is his bride (see Ephesians 5 and Revelation 19).

And what is true corporately proves true at an individual level too. Many individuals down the centuries have been able to experience God's love for them personally as something deeply intimate: 'He has taken me into the banquet hall, and his banner over me is love!'

You are the most excellent of men
and your lips have been anointed with grace.

You love righteousness and hate wickedness;
therefore God, your God, has set you above your
companions by anointing you with the oil of joy.

All glorious is the princess within her chamber;

In embroidered garments she is led to the king;
her virgin companions follow her.

Led in with joy and gladness,
they enter the palace of the king.

Your sons will take the place of your fathers;
you will make them princes throughout the land.

Psalm 45:2, 6–7, 13–16

Prophecy

The Old Testament's final section is devoted to prophecy: both the so-called 'major' prophets (Isaiah, Jeremiah, Ezekiel and Daniel) and the twelve 'minor' prophets (see p. 158).

Prophecy was very important within Israel. This community believed that Yahweh (unlike the gods of the nations) was *a speaking God* – who had revealed himself to people like Moses, and whose words were therefore to be treasured. Yet this God continued to address his people; and for this task he raised up 'prophets' who would 'speak forth' his word. 'The word of the Lord came' to the prophets (we often read), and they spoke it out.

Sometimes this word focused on predicting future events, but often it simply diagnosed present situations or challenged people to make suitable responses (prophecies were thus much more than just predictions). Sometimes this divine word might come in the form of poetry (and oracles), but equally it might sound like a sermon (as especially in Jeremiah). Sometimes the word would be specific, addressing imminent events; sometimes more abstract – painting the big picture of God's dealings with his people. One common theme was the danger of idolatry, another the reality of God's judgment but also his blessing – if only his people would repent.

As seen above (p. 88) Elijah and Elisha were major prophetic figures in the ninth century BC, but they did not leave behind written books. Thereafter prophetic groups became a recognized phenomenon within Israel and Judah, gaining a reputation for calling people to repent (see for example, 1 Kings 22:24; 2 Kings 17:13). Almost certainly Isaiah, for example, would have gathered around him a 'support group', which would have collected together his various prophecies. This may, in turn, have led to the development of a 'school' of prophecy which stood in recognizable continuity with Isaiah's original ministry.

With Jeremiah we know he had a secretary, Baruch, who painstakingly wrote down his messages – despite the fierce opposition from Judah's king (see Jeremiah 36, described below, p. 140). This incident alerts us to the challenges involved in preserving these unpopular messages in a context of civil unrest and impending war. Yet somehow they – and the words of the other major prophets – were indeed preserved. How exactly they were then assembled into the books we now possess is a process that cannot be determined. Even so, when we read these books we need to listen out, not just for the voice of the original prophets, but also for the voice of their final editors, who arranged the prophecies in such a way as to emphasize certain key points.

The prophets' different contexts
Isaiah lived in Judah in the late eighth century (c. 760–680 BC). He advised Kings Ahaz and Hezekiah, but died during the reign of King

Manasseh (according to a later tradition, being sawn in two by this rebellious king). Many of his prophecies relate to key events during that period (described in 2 Kings: see pp. 89–91): Judah being attacked by Syria and Israel (734/3 BC); Israel being destroyed by the Assyrians (722/1 BC); and Sennacherib's menacing approach up to Jerusalem's walls (701 BC). However, chapters 40–55 seemingly speak of a much later situation – of the return from exile in Babylon (in the late sixth century BC); and chapters 56–66 look forward into a yet more distant future. Thus many suggest these final prophecies emanate from a later period, but were bound together in one volume because they so clearly continued the big story of God's dealings with Israel – as first outlined in Isaiah's earlier prophecies.

Jeremiah began his prophetic ministry in the 'thirteenth year' of Josiah's reign (c. 626 BC). His prophecies then span more than forty years, and give us the inside story of those critical years both before and after the two devastating assaults on Jerusalem by the Babylonians (in 597 and 586 BC). Jeremiah thus lived through the most painful episode in Judah's history; he also saw his own predictions of judgment come tragically to fulfilment.

Ezekiel's prophetic ministry overlapped with Jeremiah's final years. Ezekiel, however, was located in Babylon, having been deported in 597 BC. His prophecies begin in the 'fifth year' of the exile and predict Jerusalem's final overthrow (in 587/6 BC); his later prophecies (concluding in 571 BC) look forward to Israel's restoration.

Daniel too was deported but found himself admitted into King Nebuchadnezzar's court. On several occasions throughout his long life he had critical interchanges with different kings – sometimes interpreting their dreams or announcing judgment to come. The book's second half, however, contains a series of colourful visions which, while set in the Babylonian exile, scan history's future horizons in such a way as to bring its focus down to the second century BC. These visions also develop a more 'apocalyptic' style (see p. 156). This makes it hard, not only to date the book's final compilation, but also to classify it: thus, although Daniel is included here as a 'prophecy', in the Hebrew Bible the book is listed instead among the 'writings'.

Looking back over these four major books, one can see the critical importance of the first book, Isaiah. For its three main sections, strategically put together in the canon, provide a comprehensive framework for understanding Israel's past, present and future: the book looks back to the era before the exile, then deals head-on with the trauma of the exile, and finally points forward to further divine actions in the future. All subsequent biblical prophecy then begins to make sense when read within this framework.

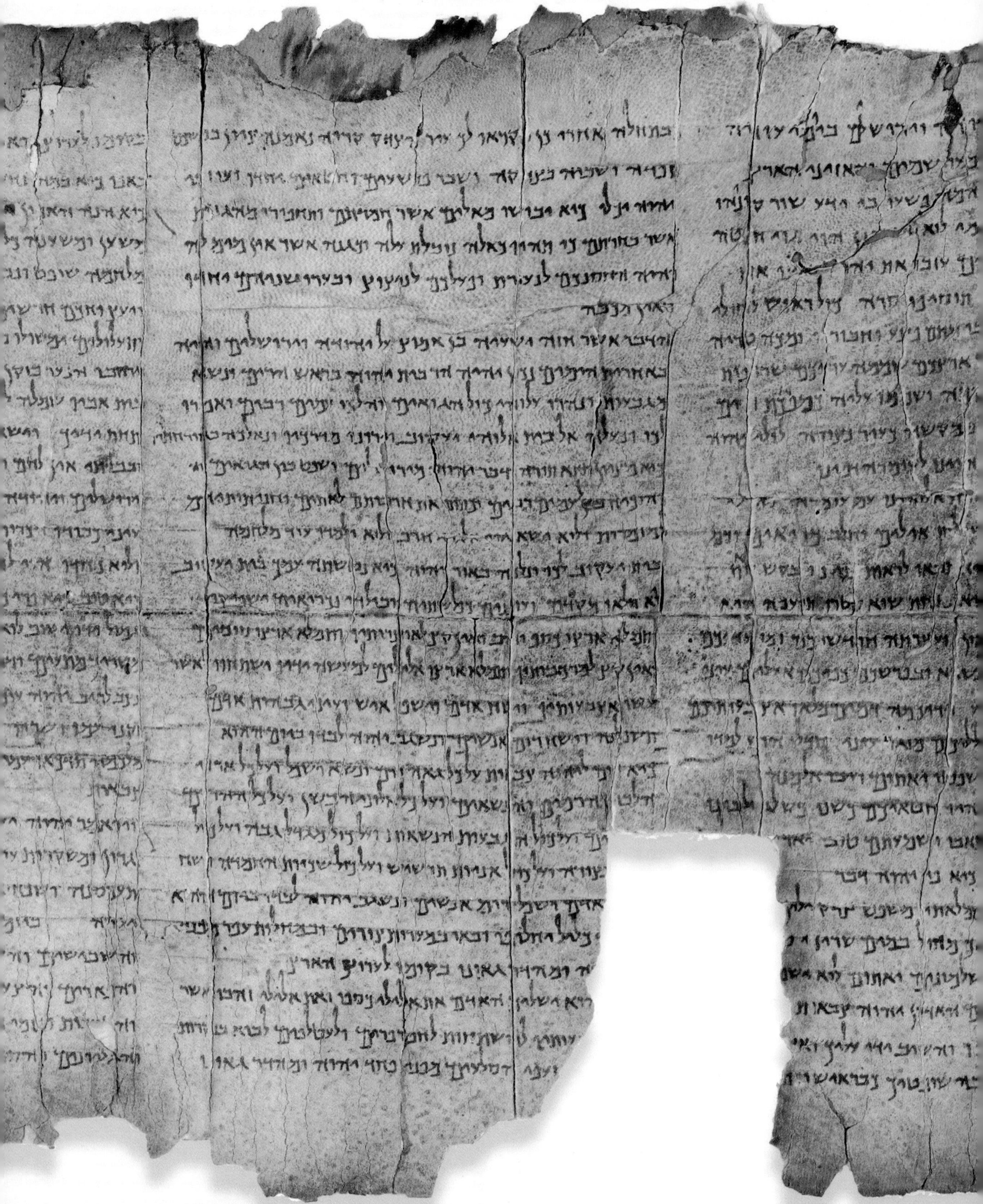

Isaiah

Isaiah is the longest and perhaps the most famous of the prophetic books. Isaiah himself lived in Jerusalem in the late eighth century BC during a tumultuous period in Judah's history; while many of the prophecies located later in the book speak of Israel's return from exile in the sixth century BC (see further p. 134). So this book accompanies God's people throughout a critical period in their history.

Throughout the book God's purposes are presented on a cosmic canvas. Here we see Israel's God portrayed as the Creator who is sovereign over his world, as the Holy One who judges his people, and as the one who acts with compassion as their redeemer, bringing rescue and restoration. On the canvas too, are the nations far away from Israel, who will come to see the great works of Israel's God. Isaiah's vision is international. The book also contains many texts which speak of a mysterious individual (described variously as a 'child', a 'servant' and as 'one who suffers') who will introduce this new, universal phase in salvation history. Who can this be?

Isaiah thus inspires and intrigues in equal measure. No other Old Testament book is quoted as much in the New Testament. And few books have quite its force and power. Isaiah himself had received an awesome vision of God on his throne, being 'high and lifted up'; and that same vision can have a similar effect on those who, centuries later, read this book's remarkable prophecies.

1. Judgment and redemption for Judah (chapters 1–12)

The opening five chapters contain some startling visions of Judah and Jerusalem. Yahweh speaks of his people as rebellious children who have 'turned their back on the Holy One of Israel' and who offer meaningless sacrifices because they practise injustice and bribery. The 'faithful city has become a harlot' and is liable to judgment for its pride and idolatry, its murder and oppression of the poor. Yahweh has looked for justice and found only bloodshed; his people have 'spurned his word' and are trusting in their own human strength.

So Yahweh will summon other nations to roar at his people like a lion; they will be humbled and 'go into exile for lack of understanding'. Yet in this act of judgment Yahweh will redeem Zion, purging it of its evils, and make it instead the 'city of righteousness'. Indeed 'in the last days' the 'mountain of the Lord's temple will be raised above the hills'; 'the word of the Lord will go out from Jerusalem; and the nations will beat their spears into pruning hooks'.

In chapter 6 there is a brief account of Isaiah's own commissioning.

Key chapters in Isaiah
The song of the vineyard (chapter 5)
Isaiah's vision in the temple (chapter 6)
'To us a child is born' (chapter 9)
The joy of the redeemed (chapter 35)
Jerusalem's rescue under King Hezekiah (chapters 36–39)
'Comfort my people, says your God' (chapters 40–45)
The suffering servant (chapter 53)
'Come, all you who are thirsty' (chapter 55)
'The Spirit of the Lord is upon me' (chapter 61)

Left: The complete text of Isaiah has been preserved in this manuscript (dating to c. 100 BC) – the longest of the Dead Sea Scrolls (discovered at Qumran in 1947).

'I saw the Lord seated on a throne, high and exalted… Above him were seraphs, each with six wings… And they were calling to one another: "Holy, holy, holy is the Lord Almighty; the whole earth is full of his glory."'
Isaiah 6:1–3

'The earth will be filled with the knowledge of the Lord as the waters cover the sea.'
Isaiah 11:9

'You will keep in perfect peace those whose minds are steadfast, because they trust in you. Trust in the Lord forever, for the Lord, the Lord is the Rock eternal.'
Isaiah 26:3–4

While worshipping in Jerusalem's temple 'in the year that King Uzziah died' (742 BC), Isaiah has a vision of Yahweh and his holiness. After receiving a sign of God's forgiveness for his own sin, Isaiah responds to God's call: 'Here am I. Send me!' So he is charged to tell this people that their hearts have become calloused; they will be sent far away, with only a tiny remnant being left. In reality Jerusalem's population would not be taken into exile for another 150 years, but Isaiah has been given the big picture: dark clouds are now hanging over the city.

Next, King Ahaz is attacked by the joint forces of Israel and Syria (c. 734 BC). Isaiah tells him not to be worried, since both these kings will soon be overthrown by the king of Assyria, and then he prophesies against both Israel and Assyria. Meanwhile Jerusalem will be spared an Assyrian invasion and so will proclaim: 'The Lord, the lord, is my strength and my defence; he has become my salvation.'

Interspersed through these chapters is a string of prophecies which point to a more distant future. There is the puzzling sign Isaiah gives to Ahaz: 'a young girl [or virgin] will give birth to a son and call him Emmanuel [God with us]'. There is a prophecy that those in Galilee will one day see a great light – because 'a child is born' who will 'reign on David's throne for ever', being called the 'Prince of Peace'. And from David's line there will grow a righteous 'branch', a person filled with the Spirit who will gather in the Gentile nations. Evidently the God who is working in Isaiah's day for his people's rescue has also got some longer-term plans for an even grander rescue operation.

2. God rules over all nations (chapters 13–27)

There then follows a series of extended oracles against other nations. Isaiah foresees Judah's exile in Babylon in the distant future, but also how Babylon, that proud 'morning star', will be thrown down. Next up is the more immediate threat of Assyria: this too will be crushed. As for the other nations – such as Philistia, Moab, Syria (Damascus), Cush (Sudan/ Ethiopia), Egypt, Edom, Arabia and Phoenicia (Tyre) – all these will also see Yahweh's judgment, and some of them will bring tribute to Zion.

There are oracles too against Judah's leaders: they are 'forgetting God their Saviour', not remembering their 'Rock and fortress'. Even so, Jerusalem will not experience destruction at this time. God's people are to learn their lesson: Yahweh truly 'contends with them through warfare and exile'; and these are the means by which their sins are 'atoned for'.

All this is set against the backdrop of a more universal act of judgment, perhaps at some much later date. 'On that day' Yahweh will show his healing power to Israel's historic enemy, Egypt; and indeed (in Isaiah 19) Egypt and Assyria will be ranked ahead of Israel in God's list of his treasured possessions! When will that 'day' come?

3. Hope and judgment when facing Assyrian invasion
(chapters 28–35)

The oracles continue. As the Assyrian invasion looms, judgment is pronounced on the northern kingdom of Israel ('Ephraim'). Yet the spotlight soon reverts to Isaiah's own Jerusalem, where the prophet detects spiritual complacency and a false reliance on other political powers (such as Egypt). The only true course is to rely on Yahweh: 'The Lord will be the sure foundation for your times, a rich store of salvation, wisdom and knowledge.' 'The Lord longs to be gracious to you; he rises to show you compassion... Blessed are all who wait for him!' So Isaiah urges the people to 'return to him whom they have so greatly revolted against'.

This was a tough message, urging Judah to trust in God's defence against Assyria. Would they respond? More importantly, however, was Isaiah correct? It sounded good in theory, but *would* Jerusalem survive?

4. The story of Jerusalem's reprieve under Hezekiah
(chapters 36–39)

That key question explains why the next four chapters are given over to describing what happened when Sennacherib, king of Assyria, marched against tiny Jerusalem – even though these chapters recap almost word for word the account found in 2 Kings (18:17 – 20:19: see p. 91).

Isaiah continues to prophesy through the crisis, and his words prove true: Yahweh indeed rescues his people, and Jerusalem is spared! This powerful episode gave dramatic evidence of Yahweh's commitment to his people. Yet Isaiah had already warned Jerusalem of the real threat *for the longer term* of destruction and exile. Those distant skies, full of storm and menace, would not disappear just because there had been this marvellous break in the clouds under Hezekiah.

This then explains the importance of chapters 38–39, where Hezekiah thanks Yahweh for a reprieve after an illness but then stupidly shows off all his treasures to some envoys from Babylon. Isaiah then prophesies about that more distant future when the storm clouds will indeed envelop Jerusalem: 'All that your fathers have stored up will be carried off to Babylon... and some of your descendants will be taken away to the palace of the king of Babylon.'

5. Return from exile and the work of the 'servant' (chapters 40–55)

This is the sombre background for the famous next words in Isaiah:

Comfort, comfort my people... Speak tenderly to Jerusalem and proclaim to her that her hard service has been completed... [and] that she has received from the Lord's hand double for all her sins.

Isaiah 40:1–2

Return from exile

Isaiah graphically describes why Israel's sin had made the exile an inevitable necessity (e.g. 42:23–25; 47:6; 51:17ff.). Yet the exile's *end* is painted even more dramatically – as a new and greater 'exodus' (43:16–17; 44:7; 48:21; 51:9–11; 52:4). The most famous passage is as follows:

'How beautiful on the mountains are the feet of those who bring good news, who proclaim peace, who bring good tidings, who proclaim salvation, who say to Zion, "Your God reigns." ... *When the Lord returns to Zion, they will see it with their own eyes. Burst into songs of joy together, you ruins of Jerusalem, for the Lord has comforted his people, he has redeemed Jerusalem. The Lord will lay bare his holy arm in the sight of all nations, and all the ends of the earth will see the salvation of our God.'*
Isaiah 52:7–10

The 'suffering servant'
This time of restoration and joy, however, is inextricably tied up in some way with the unexpected suffering of God's 'servant':

'He was despised and rejected, a man of sorrows and acquainted with grief... We esteemed him not... But he was pierced for our transgressions... Each of us has turned to his own way, and the Lord has laid on him the iniquity of us all... He was led like a lamb to the slaughter... After the suffering of his soul, he will see the light of life... by his knowledge my righteous servant will justify many and he will bear their iniquities.'
Isaiah 53:3, 5, 6–7, 11

Suddenly we are taken to a time when some great tragedies concerning Jerusalem are about to be a thing of the past. What 'hard service' are we talking about? What time are we in?

Almost certainly these next chapters in Isaiah refer to a much later period towards the end of the exile (c. 540 BC); hence the several references to Cyrus, the Persian king who allowed Jews to return to Jerusalem (see pp. 128–29). In this section, then, we have Yahweh's promises to restore his people from exile because, by means of that exile, their sins have been paid for.

Ruins of the palace of Cyrus the Great in Pasargadae, built as the first capital of his empire between 546 and 530 BC (near Persepolis and now in Iran).

These are some of the most inspiring chapters in the Bible. Yahweh is the sovereign Lord, the everlasting God, the unique creator; the one who controls nations' destinies; the one who calls Cyrus his 'anointed' and inspires him to set the exiles free (though Cyrus himself does not acknowledge Yahweh). 'I AM the Lord; I will not give my glory to another or my praise to idols;' 'apart from me there is no Saviour'.

So, although Israel may feel insignificant or uncared for, it is not so: Yahweh will be the Mighty One of Jacob, their powerful king and mighty Redeemer. They may say, 'The Lord has forsaken me,' but truly they are 'engraved on the palm of his hands'. 'Can a mother forget her baby?' No, they are the people whom he 'formed in the womb for himself'. 'I will not forget you. I have swept away your offences like a cloud... Return to me, for I have redeemed you.' Israel's God will 'comfort Zion' and 'have compassion on his afflicted ones'. He will 'remember their sins no more'; he will 'pour out his Spirit'. He will judge Babylon for its pride and use Cyrus, his chosen ally, to bring about its destruction. He will pass the 'cup of his wrath' from Israel to her oppressors and will help the exiles return to their land:

"I will carry you, and I will rescue you.' Although Zion has felt like a widow, she will now have numerous children and know Yahweh as her 'husband'.

In response Israel must be Yahweh's 'servant' in the world and bear witness to his great identity; for Yahweh desires that all people recognize his righteousness: 'Turn to me and be saved, all you ends of the earth... Before me every knee will bow.' All this is then summarized in a famous passage (from Isaiah 52, see p. 133). Israel's return from exile will be 'good news' – the moment of rescue, redemption and great comfort – and will be a clear sign of God's saving power; for Yahweh himself will, as it were, return to Jerusalem and be installed as her true king.

Yet there is another key strand in these chapters: on several occasions we are introduced to a mysterious 'servant' figure who will play a key role in God's purposes. As already seen, Israel as a nation is supposed to be Yahweh's servant, so on some occasions the servant may rightly be identified with Israel. Yet Israel is also chastised for being a blind servant, so this *righteous* servant figure gradually emerges as a unique individual who will perfectly fulfil this role for Israel, indeed *as* Israel:

- 'Here is my servant, my chosen one in whom I delight. I will put my Spirit on him and he will bring justice to the nations.'

- 'It is too small a thing for you to be my servant to restore the tribes of Jacob... I will also make you a light for the Gentiles....'

- 'My wise servant will be raised and lifted up and exalted.'

Yet, unexpectedly, we are then given a graphic description of the suffering this 'servant' will have to endure (Isaiah 53, see p. 133). Not surprisingly the New Testament writers quote this passage frequently, seeing here uncanny predictions of Jesus' crucifixion and resurrection (see further p. 201). For now we simply note that, within Isaiah's original prophecy, the suffering of this servant figure is inextricably linked with the restoration of Israel from exile. When the righteous servant suffers, this will be a sure sign that the exile is finished and that the sin (which caused that exile) has been fully forgiven. It will also thereby be the moment when God's 'salvation' will indeed go out to the 'ends of the earth'.

6. Hope and judgment in the future: the new heaven and earth
(chapters 56–66)

The book's final chapters have further oracles, which contain yet more critique of Israel for her continued sinfulness. There is idolatry, sorcery, even child sacrifice; God's people are rebellious and will not remember him; despite their religious fasting, there is continued

'Do not fear, for I have redeemed you;
... you are mine.

When you pass through the waters,
I will be with you...

Since you are precious and honoured in my sight,
and because I love you...

Do not be afraid, for I am with you.'
Isaiah 43:1–2, 4–5

injustice, violence, abuse of the poor and disregard for the sabbath: 'righteousness stands at a distance, truth has stumbled in the streets'. As a result their 'iniquities have separated them from God'.

All too evidently Israel continues to be sinful – which is why it cannot be the 'servant' through whom Yahweh brings his salvation to others; though called to be a 'light to the nations', Israel has itself been plunged into darkness.

In this dire situation the prophet portrays Yahweh deciding to intervene directly *himself*, putting on his armour and bringing about salvation with 'his own arm': in this way, 'the Redeemer will come to Zion, to those in Jacob who repent of their sins'. Once again the New Testament writers will see this fulfilled, remarkably, in Jesus' coming to Jerusalem (hence Paul quotes this verse in Romans 11: see pp. 235–37); thus Jesus, they claimed, was to be identified, not just with Yahweh's righteous 'servant', but even with Yahweh himself!

Moreover, Yahweh still has other purposes to be worked out: there is a vision of Jerusalem's Temple becoming an inclusive 'house of prayer for all nations'; there are visions of the 'wealth of the nations' being brought to a glorified Mount Zion. Above all, in the final two chapters there are repeated promises that Yahweh will create 'a new heaven and a new earth', with Zion being a place of unsullied peace and prosperity. In an echo of the imagery of chapter 2, the 'wolf and the lamb will feed together… they will neither harm nor destroy on all my holy mountain'.

As these final visions develop, it becomes increasingly difficult to see them as fulfilled in that first return from exile in the sixth century BC. So it is intriguing when Jesus refers to two passages from this section of Isaiah. One spoke of a person filled with God's Spirit who would 'proclaim the year of the Lord's favour'; the other of the Temple being 'for all nations'. He was indicating thereby that some of these unfulfilled aspects in Isaiah – even though the ultimate vision of a 'new heaven and a new earth' must wait – were being implemented through him.

* * *

When read as a whole, Isaiah's overall purpose is clear. Human beings, though inclined to rebel against God, are to trust in God. The book therefore presents God's uniqueness – his awesome power, righteousness, judgment and love – so that people might turn from any rival sources of confidence and instead trust in their creator, redeemer and judge.

The book also assumes that God is intimately involved in world affairs. The turbulent geo-political world of the Ancient Near East was all under his control. God's people were not to think their actions went unseen by him or their sufferings unnoticed, but rather to see his

'We have not brought salvation to the earth.'
Isaiah 26:18

'In repentance and rest is your salvation… in quietness and trust is your strength.'
Isaiah 30:15

'All our righteous acts are like filthy rags'.
Isaiah 64:6

hand at work – sometimes in judgment, sometimes in deliverance, but always in righteousness. This understanding of divine providence would prove the single most important lesson that God's people needed to learn at that time. For it was only because the people of Judah learned to affirm that their God *had* been at work – even in the desecration of Jerusalem – that they clung on to their faith. And, if so, the Bible itself might never have been preserved. After all, why continue with this talk about Yahweh if he was so obviously powerless?

> *Not to us, Lord, not to us*
> *but to your name be the glory,*
> *because of your love and faithfulness.*
>
> *Why do the nations say,*
> *'Where is their God?'*
>
> *Our God is in heaven;*
> *he does whatever pleases him.*
>
> **Psalm 115:1–3**

In particular, the importance of Isaiah 40–66 cannot be over-stated. Without this, the message would have been straightforward: that Israel's confidence in Yahweh had been vindicated through his delivering Jerusalem in the days of Hezekiah. Yet that message, on its own, would have been quite incapable of making sense of the city's subsequent destruction. The book's second half is therefore a vital addition, producing a robust framework – strong enough to deal with both good times and bad, with both God's mercy and his judgment.

Isaiah's depiction of the future is also vital. For not only does it lift our gaze to the ultimate goal of human history – in the 'new heaven and new earth'; it also gives us the basic vocabulary to understand what might happen next *within* Israel's history, pointing forward to an even more glorious redemption and a yet deeper 'return from exile'. This is then the place where Christian readers find it legitimate to see some of Isaiah's prophecies being fulfilled in Jesus. He is the 'child', the 'suffering servant', the 'branch', the Davidic 'king', the 'light for the Gentiles' – not least because Jesus evidently applied Isaiah's words to himself on several occasions. In addition, he spoke of himself as the 'stone' (which Isaiah twice saw as being 'laid in Zion' by God); and his proclamation of the kingdom picked up the language of Isaiah 52: he was proclaiming the 'good news': that in him Israel's God was truly reigning over his people once more. In him the longed-for 'end of exile' was thus finally becoming reality.

Jeremiah

Jeremiah is the longest prophetic book in the Bible: fifty-two long chapters packed with urgent warnings from Yahweh. The dark clouds of God's judgment are steadily advancing; and Jerusalem is overrun by the Babylonians (in 597 and 586 BC) – precisely as Jeremiah had foretold. This tragedy is therefore described in several places in the Old Testament (for example, Jeremiah 52 is almost identical to 2 Kings 25). Yet what we have in Jeremiah, uniquely, is the *inside story* of these events – told by someone living in Jerusalem during that horrendous period. And it is also acutely personal – giving us Jeremiah's *own* inside story as he voices some of his personal distress.

Jeremiah's ministry spanned more than forty years. His prophecies cluster around four main seasons within that longer period (followed roughly in our outline below). Yet many prophecies are not specifically dated and in several places, even though there are time indicators, the order of events has been jumbled up. This was probably for thematic reasons, but may also have been due to the sheer difficulty of collating this (sometimes unpopular) material in very adverse conditions. So, like readers of Anne Frank's memoirs (or other material smuggled out from a besieged city), we should read Jeremiah appreciating the courageous determination of those who preserved these prophecies for us.

1. Prophecies from an early or unclear date (chapters 1–19)

Jeremiah is commissioned by Yahweh: he is to be fearless and is given some visions that symbolize Yahweh's imminent judgment. There then follows a string of powerful prophecies that denounce Judah for forsaking Yahweh and for 'backsliding' in their relationship with him. There is social injustice, disregard for the sabbath, the shedding of innocent blood (even including child sacrifices) and rampant idolatry. Its kings and officials, its priests and its people are all equally to blame. 'The prophets prophesy lies, the priests rule by their own authority, and my people love it this way.' Nobody 'deals honestly and seeks the truth'; 'truth has perished; it has vanished from their lips'. 'My people are fools, they do not know me… They are skilled in doing evil; they know not how to do good.' Judah is committing spiritual 'adultery', 'exchanging their glory for worthless idols'.

In response Yahweh announces that he will banish his people, forsaking those he loves. On one occasion, when standing by the Temple gates, Jeremiah states that Yahweh will even destroy his own 'house'. People keep talking about 'the Temple of the Lord', evidently trusting that this sacred place will be protected by Yahweh, but this is

'I appointed you as a prophet to the nations… I have made you a fortified city… They will fight against you, but will not overcome you, for I am with you and will rescue you.'
Jeremiah 1:5, 18–19

a false trust; instead they have made it into a 'safe place' which hides their evil-doing – a 'den of robbers'.

In all these ways Yahweh's covenant is evidently being broken, so its curses are coming into effect. God's people have been given three precious gifts – the Temple (where Yahweh was present), Jerusalem (where his kings exercised his rule) and the Promised Land (their 'inheritance'); all three of these, however, were now in danger of being taken away.

One day, after visiting a potter's house, Jeremiah teaches how the house of Israel is like clay in a potter's hand. Just as a potter may adjust what he is making if it is marred in some way, so Yahweh will adjust his plans according to a nation's response: 'If a nation repents, I will not inflict the disaster I had planned.' So Yahweh is wooing his people ('Return, faithless Israel... for I am your merciful husband') and hoping these warnings will move them towards repentance.

So Jeremiah offers the people some potential liturgies of repentance

'Let not the wise boast of
* their wisdom...*

but let those who boast boast
* about this:*
that they understand and
* know me,*
that I am the Lord, who
* exercises kindness,*
justice and righteousness...
* for in these I delight.'*
Jeremiah 9:23–24

Jeremiah hears a key message when at a potter's house in Jerusalem: ' "Can I not do with you, house of Israel, as this potter does?", declares the Lord... "I am preparing a disaster for you." ' (Jeremiah 18:6, 11).

– some words that express what Judah needs to say to Yahweh. There are powerful calls to trust in God and 'boast' only in him. Yet his message falls on deaf ears, and a sad sense of the inevitable descends. These 'stiff-necked' people will not change; after all, a leopard cannot change its spots, and 'the heart is deceitful above all things'. Judgment is coming, come what may.

2. Jeremiah's ministry around 605 BC (chapters 25–26; 35–36; 45)

Thus far the book has consisted mainly of prophecies and sermons with very few narrative comments. From chapter 20 onwards, however, Jeremiah's prophecies are tied more explicitly to particular historical episodes. Six times events are explicitly dated to the time of King Jehoiakim (609–597 BC), with four of those being tied expressly to the 'fourth year' of his reign. This 'fourth year' is itself identified as the year when Egypt was defeated by Babylon at the battle of Carchemish (605 BC). So Jeremiah prophesies against Egypt, warning of its defeat. More importantly, he foresees a time when the 'cup of God's wrath' will be drunk by each of the surrounding nations – and Judah will not be spared. Instead 'the whole country will be desolated and [you] will serve the king of Babylon for seventy years'. Now at last the threat of Judah's exile is named explicitly (though with the ray of hope that it will only last for *two or three* generations).

A reed pen on parchment: in ancient times the task of producing a repeat copy of a document – as Jeremiah's secretary, Baruch, was forced to do after King Jehoiachim's reaction – was always a painstaking one.

'I know the plans I have for you... plans to prosper you and not to harm you, plans to give you hope and a future... You will seek me and find me when you seek me with all your heart.'
Jeremiah 29:11, 13

Several times we hear of Jeremiah ministering in the Temple. On one occasion he is warning worshippers of the coming disaster, when suddenly he is arrested, with some officials pressing for his death. Others, however, argue that the prophet Micah had predicted similar disasters and had not been put to death. So Jeremiah is released. Yet, unlike Micah and Isaiah, Jeremiah has to minister when that prophesied judgment is actually imminent; and evidently he will now be identified as a political traitor – the death-threats will only intensify.

King Jehoiachim's hostile attitude towards Jeremiah becomes all too clear. He bans Jeremiah from the Temple. When Jeremiah asks his secretary, Baruch, to take his place in the temple precincts, reading out Jeremiah's prophecies on and off for nearly a year, Baruch is eventually hauled off for interrogation by the temple officials. They tell the king, who asks for Baruch's scroll to be read to him. Every five minutes he then uses a knife to cut off that section of the scroll, immediately throwing it in the fire. The whole scroll is destroyed. Jeremiah promptly dictates all his prophecies again to Baruch, but there could hardly be a clearer illustration of the nation's refusal to hear Yahweh's word. Judah's king simply dismisses it line by line.

3. Jeremiah's ministry under King Zedekiah from 597 BC (chapters 20–24, 27–29)

Things are no better ten years later. By this time the Babylonians have already made their first attack on Jerusalem, deporting Jehoiakim's successor (confusingly called Jehoiachin) and appointing Zedekiah in his place. Jeremiah's activity can be summarized as follows:

- He predicts that the Babylonians will be back to plunder yet more of the Temple's furnishings and will take more inhabitants into exile. So an official (called Pashur) puts him in the stocks for a day.

- In response to Zedekiah's questions Jeremiah states that Yahweh is working *against* the city: only those who surrender will live.

- He pronounces that Jehoiachin will never return from exile and that none of his offspring will sit on David's throne.

- In a letter addressed to the exiles he encourages them to 'seek the welfare of the city', promising that Yahweh has good purposes for them: their captivity will end after seventy years. Those in Jerusalem, however, can expect further distress – death, the sword, starvation or exile.

- Jeremiah puts a wooden yoke around his neck as a sign that they will soon be under Babylon's yoke. When Hananiah breaks the yoke (predicting peace within two years), Jeremiah denounces him as a false prophet who will die very soon. And he does.

Within this gloomy scenario, however, a new hope is emerging. In a powerful chapter (23) Yahweh announces that, because his people's leaders have been false shepherds, *he himself* will be his people's true shepherd: 'I will gather the remnant of my flock and will bring them back to their pasture.' Moreover, 'I will raise up to David a righteous Branch, a King who will reign wisely.' So people will speak not so much about the great exodus from Egypt, but of the great return from exile.

4. Jeremiah's ministry around the fall of Jerusalem in 587/6 BC (chapters 30–34; 37–45)

So there is hope: God will act, there will be a new exodus and a new kingship. Despite Jerusalem's imminent judgment, there will be a return from exile. These prophecies of restoration pick up a few earlier hints, but now become more frequent – in the so-called 'Book of Consolation' (chapters 30–33). This may never have been a separate 'book' but is a useful way of describing these four distinctive chapters that focus on this positive message. It contains some of the book's most famous passages (see box, right) and reveals Jeremiah's conviction that he knows God will not reject his people. Indeed, linked with their restoration from exile, Yahweh will also inaugurate a radically new covenant relationship with his people – one marked by deep obedience from the heart, personal knowledge of God and an assurance of total forgiveness. It is a powerful vision, but the question is left hanging: how exactly will God do this and when?

Meanwhile, the Babylonian siege engines are surrounding Jerusalem. Bizarrely, Jeremiah is instructed by God at this point to buy his cousin's plot of land in Anathoth (Jeremiah's home village just outside Jerusalem). God intends this as a dramatic sign that, after the economic downturn and after their return to the land, 'fields

---

The 'book of consolation'

'I will bring back my people from captivity and restore them to the land... They will serve the Lord their God and David their king whom I will raise up for them. So do not fear, O Jacob my servant... I am with you... I will discipline you but only with justice... I will restore the fortunes of Jacob's tents... So you will be my people and I will be your God.'
Jeremiah 30:3, 8–11, 18, 22

'I have loved you with an everlasting love; I have drawn you with loving-kindness... He who scattered Israel will watch over his flock like a shepherd. For the Lord will ransom Jacob and redeem them... They will shout for joy on the heights of Zion... I will refresh the weary and satisfy the faint.'
Jeremiah 31:3, 10–12, 25

'The days are coming... when I will make a new covenant... I will put my law in their minds and write it on their hearts. I will be their God, and they will be my people. No longer will they teach their neighbours, or say to one another, "Know the Lord," because they will all know me... For I will forgive their wickedness and will remember their sins no more.'
Jeremiah 31:31, 33–34

Right: The 'Babylonian Chronicles' are a series of tablets, recording the principal events of each year from 747 to 280 BC. This one describes the years 616–607 BC, including the dramatic destruction of the Assyrian capital, Nineveh, in 612 BC (see p. 166).

Below: 'My people have committed two sins: they have forsaken me, the spring of living water, and have dug their own cisterns, broken cisterns that cannot hold water' (Jeremiah 2:13).

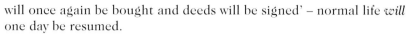

will once again be bought and deeds will be signed' – normal life *will* one day be resumed.

Jeremiah is then arrested and is thrown into a cistern. An Egyptian courtier, however, pulls him out and from now on Jeremiah is kept captive within the palace, occasionally having conversations with anxious King Zedekiah. 'Is there any word from the Lord?' asks the king. 'If you surrender,' replies Jeremiah, 'your life will be spared and the city will not be burned down.'

Zedekiah did not surrender, however, and after an eighteen-month siege, the city fell. Contrary to Jeremiah's advice, the escaping inhabitants flee to Egypt – taking Jeremiah with them. So the last we hear of this long-serving prophet is when he speaks at a large conference in Egypt, warning that the Babylonians will soon be invading Egypt too. So Jeremiah, the prophet who had predicted the exile, himself ends his days in exile – thus sharing in the very fate that he had tried to avert. Rejected by his people, he was also ejected from his own city, sharing in the judgment placed upon his people. Yet in this he was revealed as a true prophet, and these tragic events were simultaneously the moment of his vindication.

5. Prophetic oracles against all nations including Babylon
(chapters 46–51)

Appended at the end are various oracles against the surrounding nations – Egypt, Philistia, Moab, Ammon, Edom, Damascus, Kedar and Hazor, Elam and Babylon itself – indicating that Yahweh's judgment on his own people was part of a more universal judgment. These oracles are relentlessly negative – except for those concerning three nations (Moab, Ammon and Elam), which Yahweh promises to restore. As expected, the prophecies against Babylon are particularly harsh. Yet only now do we discover that these prophecies were sent (courageously) by Jeremiah to the *first* batch of exiles in Babylon – that is, around the same time as his letter which encouraged them to settle down (see p. 141). Jeremiah clearly had discerned both the short- and long-term prospects for God's people.

He also was no less opposed to Babylon than his fellow-Jews; but only now do we see his true colours. Evidently, Jeremiah's prophecies against his own nation had all been born from compassionate commitment to his people. He was not a remote judge, criticizing from a distance; nor was he a traitor. He was someone speaking solemn truth in love. For in days of deception, the kindest person resolutely speaks the truth – even though people do not want to listen.

***

The book of Jeremiah proved a vital resource for the people of Judah after the trauma of 587/6 BC. Without it, they might have been driven either to despair or to atheism. Instead Jeremiah's message gave them the tools with which to rebuild: the awareness that Jerusalem's fall was not a sign of Yahweh's weakness but rather of his power and judgment, and the bright hope that he would restore his people within seventy years. Thus its two great themes – of judgment followed by salvation – contained the vital seeds of the nation's renewal. And, after their return, it will have acted as a powerful incentive not to make the same mistakes again, but to be a people marked by loyalty to Yahweh alone, walking in obedience to his covenant.

Modern readers can find themselves similarly being given some powerful tools of spiritual renewal as they consider these two great themes of God's judgment and his salvation. They can also learn much from the example of Jeremiah himself – learning from his struggles in prayer (see box, right) or from his brave stance in a nation's public life. Thus in his almost solitary opposition to prevailing opinion there

There are more autobiographical sections in Jeremiah than perhaps in any other Old Testament book. Not only does he describe his own calling to be a prophet as a young man (in chapter 1), we are also given some of his personal prayers which he prayed to God in response to that calling – especially when suffering persecution for fulfilling this unpopular task:

Oh, my anguish! The agony of my heart! My heart pounds within me. I cannot keep silent... They keep saying to me, 'where is the word of the Lord?' I have not run away from being your shepherd; you know I have not desired the day of despair. What passes my lips is open before you. Do not be a terror to me; you are my refuge in the day of disaster... Hear what my accusers are saying... They have dug a pit for me.'
Jeremiah 4:19; 17:15–17; 18:19–20

This comes to a head when Jeremiah complains:

You deceived me, Lord, and I was deceived... I am ridiculed all day long... The word of the Lord has brought me reproach... But if I say, 'I will not speak any more in his name', his word is in my heart like a fire... I am weary of holding it in... Cursed be the day I was born!... Why did I ever come out of the womb to end my days in shame?'
Jeremiah 20:7–9, 14, 18

Jeremiah's honesty here, as he wrestles before God, has been an encouragement to many – especially to those facing unenviable tasks on God's behalf.

O God, the nations have invaded your inheritance;
  they have defiled your holy temple,
    they have reduced Jerusalem to rubble...

They have poured out blood like water...
  and there is no one to bury the dead.

How long, Lord? Will you be angry forever?

Pour out your wrath on the nations
  that do not acknowledge you...

for they have devoured Jacob
  and devastated his homeland.

May your mercy come quickly to meet us,
  for we are in desperate need.

God our Saviour...
  deliver us and forgive our sins
    for your name's sake.

Psalm 79:1, 3–9

is something reminiscent of a Nelson Mandela or a Martin Luther King. Why stand up for your convictions when you are going totally against the tide?

Jeremiah's example has also reminded Christian readers of Jesus. Jesus was explicitly compared to Jeremiah (Matthew 16:14) because he spoke out so strongly against his nation and warned of Jerusalem's destruction. He even used Jeremiah's own words when describing the Temple as a 'den of robbers'. Eventually we see Jesus being rejected, like Jeremiah, as a false prophet and sharing undeservedly in that very judgment he himself had predicted.

This clear link with Jesus provides the key for interpreting Jeremiah appropriately in our own day. For when we ask how this clear biblical teaching about God's judgment relates to our contemporary world, the cross of Jesus resolves the issue. Jesus clearly affirmed God's capacity to judge; and he would have seen the troubles of Jerusalem – both past and future (both in 587/6 BC and AD 70) – as revealing this judgment. Yet Jesus also saw his own death as the means whereby that judgment could be averted; he deliberately took upon himself the judgment he had predicted. In this way, as the New Testament writers later explain it, Jesus' cross becomes the place where God's judgment is *both fully revealed and then fully removed*. So Jeremiah's two great themes – of judgment and salvation – come together at the cross. And those who face the cross squarely, heeding its warnings but hearing its promises, are taken (like the readers of Jeremiah) on a cleansing journey through repentance to restoration.

Lamentations

After Jeremiah comes Lamentations, a short book which expresses despair after Jerusalem's fall. Although not explicitly written by Jeremiah, it has always been associated with him, for we know that he composed 'laments' even before the city's fall (see Jeremiah 11:18–20).

Four of its five chapters are acrostics – the first word of each verse beginning with the next letter in the Hebrew alphabet (see also Psalms 25, 34 and 119). This gives a sense of thoroughness as every aspect of grief is rehearsed: bewilderment and loss, hot anger and attempted blame-shifting, demanding questions and resigned despair. This stylistic discipline makes this an 'ordered grief', enabling the writer to express real anger and doubt, yet within the fixed framework of ultimate faith in God.

The writer acknowledges this tragedy comes from the curses established within Yahweh's covenant against Israel's sin. Yet he protests that it is excessive, with no real 'comfort' in sight. Instead he waits for God – as expressed in the famous verse in the very centre of the book:

Because of the Lord's great love we are not consumed, for his compassions never fail.
They are new every morning; great is your faithfulness!

Lamentations 3:33–34

'How deserted lies the city...
All the splendour has departed
from Daughter Zion...
All her people groan as they search for bread...
'Is it nothing to you, all you who pass by?...
Is any suffering like my suffering...
that the Lord brought on me?'
Lamentations 1:1, 6, 11–12

Ezekiel

The book of Ezekiel was composed entirely in exile. Ezekiel himself came from a priestly family and must have been one of the first deportees, taken to Babylon after Nebuchadnezzar's attack in 597 BC. His prophetic ministry thus overlaps with Jeremiah's ministry; and, despite being so far apart geographically, they are fully agreed – Yahweh's judgment will be followed by his active involvement to restore them.

Even so, Ezekiel's prophecies have a slightly different feel. Being so many miles away from his home, many of his prophecies are 'ecstatic' visions – as he is transported in 'visions of God' to Jerusalem. And all his prophecies are deeply coloured by his profound vision, described at the outset, of God's glory and presence.

Prophecies of judgment from 593 to 587/6 BC (chapters 1–24)

The book of Ezekiel begins with this awe-inspiring vision of God's glory.

Ezekiel and the exiles would have been living close to the River Euphrates, and he sees his powerful opening vision 'by the Chebar canal'.

In the fifth year since the start of the exile (c. 592 BC), Ezekiel sees 'what looks like four living creatures', with an array of faces, wings and wheels; above them is a throne on which is seated a 'figure like that of a man', blazing with light and rainbow colours: 'this was the appearance', writes Ezekiel in deferential terms, 'of the likeness of the glory of the Lord'. Ezekiel falls face down but is called to his feet, is touched by God's Spirit, and is commissioned to prophesy fearlessly to the 'rebellious house' of Israel. For seven days he sits among the exiles, completely overwhelmed.

Then, having had a repeat vision of God's glory, he is given some bizarre instructions: he is to lie on his side for over a year (430 days) in order to symbolize God's judgment (for 430 years) on the kingdoms of Israel and Judah. These (and other) symbolic actions, some quite shocking, are all a dramatic way of portraying the 'sword, famine and plague' which will be experienced by Jerusalem because of its rebellion. Only a small remnant will survive and eventually return. Even Yahweh's 'treasured place' (the Temple) will be 'desecrated by evil foreigners'. 'Then they will know that I am the Lord.' This last phrase will be repeated often in Ezekiel's later prophecies, indicating Yahweh's chief purpose in these momentous events.

One year later Ezekiel has another vision. That same 'figure like that of a man' takes him in the Spirit to the Temple in Jerusalem and shows him what is going on: priests revelling in their idols, others worshipping the sun-god, and some women mourning for the goddess Tammuz; moreover, 'the city is full of injustice and the land full of bloodshed'. Yahweh issues a decree of death upon all in the city – apart from those who are grieved by these 'detestable things' and who are therefore marked on the forehead by a 'man clothed in linen'. Meanwhile Ezekiel sees the four 'living creatures' (whom he now recognizes to be the 'cherubim'). They leave the Temple and come to the 'mountain east of the city' (the Mount of Olives) – God's glory has made a dramatic exit. The city, thus abandoned by Yahweh, is now ripe for judgment: the glory of God's presence (known in Hebrew as *shekinah*) has departed, but will it ever return?

There then follow some more symbolic actions and a string of prophecies (perhaps received during the next nine months or so), which confirm that judgment on Jerusalem is imminent. Jerusalem is like a useless piece of vine-wood, now consigned to the flames and, as in the days of Noah, only a few 'righteous' people will be spared in the coming conflagration. And these 'righteous' can be clearly defined as those who have 'turned from their wickedness' in repentance. No amount of godly ancestry, Ezekiel solemnly warns, nor indeed prior acts

Medieval manuscript from the opening of the book of Ezekiel in the Lambeth Bible (c. AD 1145); it depicts Ezekiel eating a scroll (Ezekiel 3:1–3).

Ezekiel would have been in a refugee camp – perhaps in mud-brick houses as here – and sharing the plight of his fellow exiles.

of righteousness, will help on that day: 'the soul that sins will die', but 'those who turn from their wicked ways will live'.

In two extended allegories, designed to shock, Ezekiel portrays Jerusalem as a young woman, whom Yahweh had adopted at birth, but who has now adopted the role of a prostitute. Like her older sister, she has given herself to idolatry and sought out foreign lovers (such as Egypt, Assyria and Babylonia); and the last of these 'lovers' will now expose her. There have been child sacrifices and the desecration of Yahweh's sabbath – above all, she has been forgetful of Yahweh's covenant love, and so will drink the 'cup of ruin'.

On one occasion (expressly dated to the summer of 591 BC), Ezekiel is approached by the Jewish elders in exile. They sit down, asking for a prophecy. Yet the 'word of the Lord' comes that even the exiles are 'rebellious'. Ezekiel retells Israel's history, showing how God's people have been consistently idolatrous – in the desert and in the Promised Land, the 'most beautiful of all lands'; they have thus rendered the land unclean. Yet, each time, Israel has been spared Yahweh's full wrath because that would only serve publicly to 'profane the name' of Yahweh.

God's concern for his name then opens up a window of hope, that this judgment on Israel will not be final: Yahweh will 'gather them' and establish a renewed people in the land. For now, however, Jerusalem's days are numbered. There is no one, from Yahweh's perspective, who can 'stand in the breach' and prevent the calamity.

Then, on 15 January 588 BC, Ezekiel is told by Yahweh that the Babylonian armies are starting their siege of Jerusalem. He is also warned that the next day his wife, who is the 'delight of his eyes', will die. When this happens, Ezekiel is not to mourn, but to warn his countryfolk that Yahweh is about to desecrate his own sanctuary – that which had been the 'delight of *their* eyes', their 'heart's desire', and the 'object of their affection'. The axe is ready to fall.

Oracles against the nations from 587 to 571 BC (chapters 25–32)
At this critical moment the book has an extended 'pause'. The tension has been building up, with the tragic fall of Jerusalem likely to occur any moment. Now, however, Ezekiel's attention is diverted towards

Israel's neighbours. In nine prophecies (six of them being dated to particular days in the years 587 to 585 BC), he denounces any neighbours who are gloating over Jerusalem's predicament and warns that *they too* will soon experience Yahweh's judgment.

Unlike those in Isaiah and Jeremiah, however, these 'oracles against the nations' do not include Babylon – perhaps because Ezekiel himself is now located there in exile. Instead his oracles focus on Egypt and the trading city of Tyre, both of which would be attacked by the Babylonian armies in the coming years. Ezekiel denounces the arrogance of their rulers and raises a 'lament' for their overthrow, using images of trees being toppled and powerful lions being tamed.

Prophecies of restoration after Jerusalem's fall: 587/6 BC
(chapters 33–39)

Then the news reaches the exiles of Jerusalem's fall. At this point Ezekiel's mouth is opened once more to speak about Israel; and what comes out is a remarkable series of prophecies which foretell Israel's eventual restoration. Perhaps the most memorable prophecy portrays the people of Israel as a valley filled with dry bones: when Ezekiel prophesies to the bones, Yahweh's Spirit reassembles the bones, puts flesh on them, and the corpses come to life. This dramatic picture of resurrection signifies Yahweh's restoration of his people: though they are as good as dead, he will 'put his Spirit in them' and then 'settle them back in their own land'. Similarly, in an extended prophecy concerning the people as being like lost sheep, we hear great promises about how Yahweh will *himself* be their shepherd (see box, right).

Yet Israel should not be under any illusion: 'I am not doing this for your sake, but for the sake of my holy name, which you have profaned.' Thus it will be a totally undeserved act of covenant love. Moreover, God's desire to produce a holy nation has not changed; even if they have been cleansed and forgiven, they are still called to serve him without compromise – or else a similar judgment may come upon them again.

A vision of God's restored presence: the new Temple 573 BC
(chapters 40–48)

The book closes (appropriately for a priest like Ezekiel) with an extended vision of a new Temple set in the midst of a rebuilt Jerusalem in a restored land. Back near the beginning, Ezekiel had seen Yahweh's glorious presence departing from the city. Now, after lengthy descriptions of the new Temple complex, 'the glory of the Lord' returns and 'fills the temple'.

A detailed picture of this new Temple's worship and regulations is developed. Ezekiel then describes a deep river flowing down eastwards

The divine shepherd gathers his people

I myself will search for my sheep... I will rescue them from where they were scattered... I will bring them into their own land... I will tend my sheep and... shepherd the flock with justice... I will place over them one shepherd, my servant David, and he will tend them... they will know that I... am with them and that they... are my people.
Ezekiel 34:11–16, 23, 30

I will sprinkle clean water on you... I will remove your heart of stone and give you a heart of flesh. And I will put my Spirit in you... Then you will live in the land I gave your ancestors... This land that was laid waste has become like the garden of Eden.
Ezekiel 36:25–27, 35

You... will know that I am the Lord, when I will open your graves and bring you up from them... David my servant will be their prince for ever. I will make an everlasting covenant of peace with them... I will put my sanctuary among them forever. My dwelling place will be with them; I will be their God and they will be my people.
Ezekiel 37:13; 25–27

Like Jeremiah, Ezekiel foresees for Israel an amazing restoration from exile: it will be like a new creation – introducing a new Eden, based on God's resurrection power. These great pictures – of a divine shepherd, an eternal Davidic prince, of resurrection and God's Spirit – would inevitably be picked up by the New Testament writers as pointing to the realities revealed in Jesus.

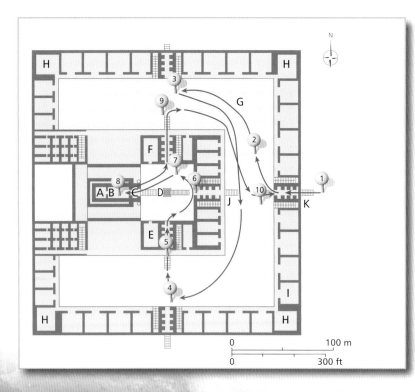

Ezekiel's tour of the visionary temple (chapters 40–43)

Beginning at the main gate, Ezekiel is taken up some steps to a passageway (1), which then leads to the outer courtyard and the plaza (2). He is shown the north gate (3) and the south gate (4) and is then taken through into the inner courtyard (5). Once inside he is taken to the east gate (6), then to the north gate, which includes rooms for preparing the sacrificial animals (7), and finally through a porch and 'main room' into the Most Holy Place (8). He then leaves the inner courtyard through the north gate, where he sees the priests' quarters (9), and exits the Temple by the east gate. From here, Ezekiel sees the return of 'the glory of Israel's God' (Ezekiel 43:1–12).

A: Most Holy Place. B: Main room. C: Outer courtyard. D: Altar. E: Chamber for altar priests. F: Chamber for priests who serve in the Temple. G: Outer court, with 30 rooms. H: Outer kitchens. I: 30 outer rooms. J: Sabbath gate for the ruler. K: Main east gate.

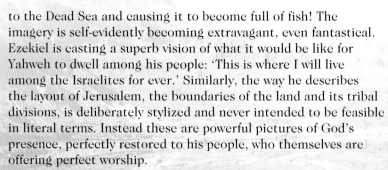

to the Dead Sea and causing it to become full of fish! The imagery is self-evidently becoming extravagant, even fantastical. Ezekiel is casting a superb vision of what it would be like for Yahweh to dwell among his people: 'This is where I will live among the Israelites for ever.' Similarly, the way he describes the layout of Jerusalem, the boundaries of the land and its tribal divisions, is deliberately stylized and never intended to be feasible in literal terms. Instead these are powerful pictures of God's presence, perfectly restored to his people, who themselves are offering perfect worship.

It is a mouth-watering ideal, designed to captivate the exiles' hearts. For in prophesying a literal restoration of Israel to the land, Ezekiel senses that this is a foretaste of a deeper work, when God will be among his people – that ultimate reality which the New Testament will refer to as 'heaven' or the 'New Jerusalem'. So the final words of the book (which deliberately sound similar to 'Jerusalem' in Hebrew) give a new name to this, the ultimate city: 'The Lord is there.'

* * *

Although Ezekiel's message (of judgment and restoration) is similar to Isaiah's and Jeremiah's, his perspective is slightly different. For Ezekiel is one of the few Old Testament books written *entirely* in Babylon, so we are hearing the voice of Israel in the depths of her exile. Secondly, Ezekiel combines themes that might otherwise be kept separate: for example, the absolute sovereignty of God with human responsibility. Above all, as a prophet who was also a priest, Ezekiel gives a forthright call for spiritual and moral regeneration under godly leadership, but combines this with a desire for the Temple's renewal as an institution offering true worship. Here, then, are the building blocks for Israel's post-exilic life. Like a new Moses, Ezekiel is rebuilding Israel's foundations – for its political leadership, for its Temple worship, for its obedient life in the Promised Land. In this sense this book is truly restorative.

This expansive vision of God's desire to restore his people would prove highly influential in the New Testament era. Jesus himself picks up this language in Ezekiel's final vision, claiming that 'streams of living water' will flow out from *him*. In this way he subtly claims to be the longed-for new Temple – and indeed to be bringing to us the very presence of God (see p. 211). This explains why the New Testament writers then saw in Jesus' coming the deeper fulfilment of the restoration prophesied by Ezekiel. In Ezekiel 34 God had said that *he himself* would come and shepherd his people: now in Jesus here was the true shepherd, the new David and indeed the new Temple – all in one! Then, when they gained a new experience of the Holy Spirit (see p. 221), they would readily have noted Ezekiel's clear statements about God 'placing his Spirit' within the hearts of his restored people. And, at the very end, when seeking to cast a vision of God's ultimate dwelling among his people, the author of Revelation could hardly avoid adapting the powerful imagery of Ezekiel's final vision.

*By the rivers of Babylon we sat and wept
  when we remembered Zion.*

*There on the poplars
  we hung our harps,*

*for there our captors asked us for songs...
  they said, 'Sing us one of the songs of Zion!'*

*How can we sing the songs of the Lord
  while in a foreign land?*

*If I forget you, Jerusalem,
  may my right hand forget its skill.*

*May my tongue cling to the roof of my mouth...
  if I do not consider Jerusalem
    my highest joy.*

*Remember, Lord, what the Edomites said
  on the day Jerusalem fell...
    'Tear it down to its foundations!'*

Psalm 137:1–7

Daniel

The story of Daniel begins in 605 BC when Daniel (perhaps no more than ten years old) is deported from Jerusalem to Babylon (see p. 91). Then he is selected, along with three other young Israelites, to enrol in a 'fast-track' educational programme designed for up-and-coming courtiers.

Once in the king's court, however, Daniel takes a brave stand for his Jewish heritage, refusing the king's food and asking for vegetables only. This conflict between Yahweh and the secular pagan court will then be played out over the coming years in other, more serious ways:

- **Interpretation of the king's dream.** When King Nebuchadnezzar has a dream but refuses to divulge its contents to his magicians, Daniel successfully interprets it. The dream had been of a large statue, composed of four different metals, which was eventually smashed by a rock. Daniel explains that Nebuchadnezzar's kingdom is the first of four that will rise and fall, eventually being replaced by an indestructible kingdom established by the 'God of heaven'.

Key chapters in Daniel

Daniel and his friends thrown into a furnace (chapter 3)

Belshazzar sees some writing on the wall (chapter 5)

Daniel in a den of lions (chapter 6)

Four beasts and the 'Son of man' (chapter 7)

Nebuchadnezzar confesses that Daniel's god is the 'God of gods'.

- **A fiery furnace.** When the king then expects all Babylon's citizens to worship a vast golden image, Daniel's three friends are thrown into a 'fiery furnace' for refusing to do so. Miraculously, however, they emerge unscathed after Nebuchadnezzar has spotted a fourth person walking around with them in the fire – someone who 'looks like a son of the gods'. Again the king honours the God of Israel and confesses that he alone can 'save in this way'.

- **Interpretation of a second dream.** When the king has another dream (about a large tree cut down), Daniel predicts the king will be banished from his court until he 'acknowledges that heaven rules'. Twelve months later, after a moment of arrogant self-congratulation, the king indeed goes into some isolation, where he shows symptoms of madness. But when he 'praises the Most High', his sanity is restored.

- **Words on the palace wall.** Many years later, one of Nebuchadnezzar's successors, King Belshazzar, holds a feast using goblets snatched from Jerusalem's Temple. A mysterious hand starts writing four Aramaic words on the wall: 'Mene, Mene, Tekel, Parsin'. Daniel interprets that the king has not 'honoured the God who holds your life in his hand',

'If the God we serve is able to save us, then he will deliver us from the blazing furnace and from Your Majesty's hand. But even if he does not, we want you to know... that we will not serve your gods or worship the image of gold you have set up.'
Daniel 3:17–18

King Darius, who assumes the throne in the generation after Daniel (ruling from 522–486 BC), gives an audience to his Crown Prince Xerxes: as depicted in the stone reliefs in Persepolis (c. 5th century BC).

and explains the four cryptic words: 'God has numbered the days of your reign... you have been weighed in the scales and found wanting... your kingdom is to be divided between the Medes and Persians.' That very night Belshazzar is killed and replaced by Darius the Mede.

- **The lions' den.** Finally, some officials, deliberately trying to frame Daniel, persuade this new king to issue an irrevocable decree requiring that only he, Darius, be worshipped for thirty days. By now Daniel is an old man, but he continues his life-long practice of praying three times a day by an upstairs window facing Jerusalem. So he is arrested and thrown into a den of lions. The next morning, however, much to the king's relief, he is found safe and well. So Darius (like Nebuchadnezzar before him) issues a decree proclaiming the importance of reverencing the 'God of Daniel'.

Belshazzar's Feast, by Rembrandt van Rijn (1606–69).

At this point the narrative sequence stops and we are given instead the contents of some visions that Daniel received over a lengthy period. The first is perhaps the most famous. Daniel sees 'four beasts' coming up out of the sea, the last of which has ten horns on it. He is told that these beasts represent four kingdoms, the last of which will 'devour the earth', and the ten horns are its kings. However, another king (represented by another horn) will arise, who will deliberately oppress 'the saints of the Most High', but this king will in turn be replaced by an 'everlasting kingdom' administered by the 'saints'.

Daniel in the Lions' Den (1872), by Briton Rivière (1840–1920).

Before receiving this explanation, however, Daniel has seen God sitting in his heavenly courtroom as the 'Ancient of Days' and being approached by 'one like a son of man, coming with the clouds of heaven,' who is immediately given by God an 'everlasting dominion' and 'authority' over 'all peoples'. This mysterious figure is an exalted one, human in form but divine in function; and part of his role is evidently to represent the 'saints' – when he rules, they rule.

Two years later, Daniel has a vision of a ram being attacked by a goat which soon grows four horns, one of which becomes enormous. An angel, Gabriel, explains that this relates to the distant future and speaks of the kings of Media and Persia being replaced by the 'king of Greece', himself being succeeded by four smaller kingdoms; from these will arise a 'stern-faced' king who will seek to destroy 'the holy people' but will himself be destroyed – though 'not by human power'.

Some time yet later Daniel takes to heart Jeremiah's prediction that the 'desolation of Jerusalem would last seventy years'. Confessing that his people have not kept God's 'covenant of love', he pleads that Yahweh might 'turn away his wrath' and bring honour to Jerusalem and those that 'bear his name'. At this point Gabriel appears again to explain that the 'seventy years' really represent a much longer period of time: 'seventy "sevens" are decreed for your people and your holy city to finish transgression, to atone for wickedness, to bring in everlasting righteousness, and to anoint the most holy.'

More details are given relating to an 'Anointed One' who will be 'cut off' and another figure who will set up an 'abomination of desolation' in the Temple. Despite much speculation as to these figures' identity, the main point is clear: although there will be an imminent return, the exile will only come to an end in the distant future – when the

INTERPRETING DANIEL

Daniel is one of the most difficult books in the Old Testament to interpret. There are major debates about the date of its composition. It purports to describe events between c. 605 BC and 536 BC, but there are features which might suggest it was written much later.

- There are apparent confusions about the monarchs of the period, and there is no evidence for a king called Darius reigning before Cyrus.

- Other biblical books make no reference to a first group of exiles being deported in 606 or 605 BC (only in 597 BC).

- Chapters 2 to 7 are not written in Hebrew, but in Aramaic – the language common in Palestine in the post-exilic period.

- Several times a 'history lesson' is given which traces the passing of four mighty kingdoms (normally identified with Babylon, Media, Persia and Greece), with reasonably clear allusions to Alexander the Great (336–323 BC) and the hated Seleucid ruler, Antiochus Epiphanes IV (175–164 BC). These could be descriptions written *after* the event, perhaps just after Antiochus' desecration of the Temple (167 BC).

Good responses to these concerns have been made, and much of the book has features which *prima facie* appear historical. A further possibility is that only the later chapters (8, 10–12), which identify the 'fourth beast' with the Greek empire, date from the second century. If Jesus then implies that Rome, not Greece, was really the 'fourth beast', then perhaps the 'Greek' interpretation is effectively updated and superseded by the New Testament writers in the light of Jesus' teaching. After all, the revelations given (in chapters 2, 7, 8–9) would have actively encouraged each succeeding generation to wonder if theirs was the time of fulfilment. Jesus then announces that *his* is the generation when the exile is truly going to come to an end.

Interpreting Daniel in this way emphasizes the possibility of real prophetic prediction (it is not all fabricated after the event), while also allowing that some of the later chapters show signs of later re-application of those original prophecies.

***

The visions (in chapters 7–12) are in the genre of 'apocalypse' – a distinctive form of Jewish literature that became increasingly common in the centuries between the Old and New Testaments (see further pp. 177 and 288).

'Apocalypse' is from the Greek word for an 'unveiling' or 'revelation'. Ancient apocalypses normally took the form of a narrative of events in heaven (often including a cosmic battle between good and evil), now revealed by an angel to a human recipient. Readers thought these heavenly events were metaphorical ways of describing a real situation being faced by the readers in the present: they helped readers to see their own circumstances from God's perspective – a view of the present from the vantage point of heaven.

'transgression' (which first caused the exile) will be atoned for fully.

The fourth and final vision occupies the book's last three chapters. Daniel sees a 'man dressed in linen' with a 'face like lightning', who reveals what is written in the 'Book of Truth'. Daniel learns of the endless tension between the 'kings of the north and south'. One particular 'king of the north' will 'vent his fury against the holy covenant', abolishing the Temple's daily sacrifice and setting up the 'abomination of desolation'. Yet eventually he 'will come to his end', and Daniel's people will be delivered: 'Multitudes who sleep will awake, some to everlasting life, others to shame and everlasting contempt.' Daniel then asks the 'man clothed in linen' about the timing of all this. He is given a cryptic answer (concerning '1,335 days') and told that goodness and evil will continue alongside each other throughout this lengthy period. The last words addressed to him are personal, encouraging Daniel that at the end he will rise to receive his allotted inheritance.

*Why do the nations conspire
and the peoples plot in vain?*

*The kings of the earth rise up
against the Lord and against his anointed.*

*The One enthroned in heaven laughs;
and terrifies them in his wrath, saying,*

*'I have installed my king
on Zion, my holy mountain.'*

*Therefore, serve the Lord with fear
and celebrate his rule with trembling.*

Psalm 2:1–2, 4–6, 10–11

* * *

Despite many uncertainties in interpreting this book (see opposite), its main theme is clearly the sovereignty of God, who is seated on his throne and controls all history; behind the human conflicts there is a heavenly war overseen by God. So, even amidst persecution, God is in control, and the 'Son of Man' is defending God's 'saints'.

The book is, therefore, one of hope. Its opening stories would have encouraged the faithful that, even in the days of exile, this Yahweh had been powerful in giving Daniel his wisdom. And its closing visions would have assured them that tiny Judah, though buffeted by the super-powers of its day, would in God's time give rise to an everlasting and worldwide kingdom. At that time the exile would *truly* be over: complete atonement would be available, and the nations would see the inauguration under Israel's 'Son of Man' of an eternal kingdom. Not surprisingly, the New Testament writers – inspired by Jesus describing himself as the 'Son of Man' – would conclude that this was truly fulfilled in Christ.

Minor Prophets

Relief of the Assyrian army,
c. 688–630 BC.

After the lengthy prophetic books (Isaiah, Jeremiah, Ezekiel and Daniel), we come to the so-called 'minor' prophets – a collection of shorter prophecies made over a wide period of Israel's history (c. 780–499 BC). This subsection within the Bible has also been known as the 'book of the twelve'. The works of the twelve different prophets have probably been gathered together as a unit since at least 100 BC. This happened in order to ensure that the smallest books among them did not get lost. It also helps us today to value the contributions of those smaller books, knowing that, if they necessarily only give a partial picture, they are complemented by themes in other books. So, for example, Nahum's exclusive focus on the forthcoming destruction of Nineveh is nicely balanced by the story of Jonah, which reveals Yahweh's capacity to have mercy on that same city. Meanwhile, Obadiah's focus on Edom finds parallels in Joel and Amos. The books can also usefully be compared with the major prophets (with whom several of them were contemporary).

Key chapters in the Minor Prophets

God's love for his people (Hosea 11)

'I will pour out my spirit' (Joel 2)

'Let justice roll on like a river!' (Amos 5)

'Nation will not take up sword against nation' (Micah 4)

'Not by might, but by my Spirit!' (Zechariah 4)

'Who can endure the day of his coming?' (Malachi 3–4)

The order of the twelve books can appear slightly haphazard – though it has clearly been motivated in part by some desire for a historical order. Thus Hosea and Amos evidently concern the northern kingdom of Israel in the eighth century; while the last three (Haggai, Zechariah, Malachi) evidently relate to Judah after the first return from exile in 539 BC. So when Joel consistently comes in the top half of the list, this may mean that the compilers of the twelve believed it to be an early work, not a late one. Whether they had independent evidence for this, we cannot now know.

The books are summarized here in a likely historical order. This makes it easier to understand their particular messages against the backdrop of the biblical storyline (see pp. 12–13). Yet, please note, there remain major questions about the historical dating of both Joel and Jonah – with both perhaps being much later (for quite different reasons) than suggested here.

Finally, there are of course scholarly debates about the original form of these books. In particular, are Zechariah 9–14 and Amos 9:11–15 later additions to their respective books? Parts of Micah, too, may show signs of being edited during the post-exilic period. However, there are some good arguments for taking the opposite view – that the books were first 'published' in roughly their present form. For our purposes here these debates are largely immaterial; and, hopefully, the summaries offered will commend the idea that the books, as we now have them, do make unified sense.

Amos

The oldest prophecy collected into the book of the twelve minor prophets is that of Amos (c. 760 BC). This shepherd from Tekoa (in the southern kingdom of Judah) was called to speak out fiercely against the northern kingdom of Israel. His opening picture is of Yahweh 'roaring from Zion' and much of what follows is focused on judgment. After oracles against the surrounding nations, the spotlight is turned briefly towards Amos's own Judah and thereafter, squarely and inexorably, on Israel. Their status as God's people does not exonerate them but makes them even more liable to his judgment: ' "I will not turn back my wrath," declares the Lord.'

The reasons have to do with social justice: 'they sell the righteous for silver and the needy for a pair of sandals'; 'you have turned justice into poison'. So Yahweh declares that he hates their religious feasts: 'Even though you bring choice fellowship offerings, I will have no regard for them. Away with the noise of your songs! But let justice roll down like a river, righteousness like a never-failing stream!'

Despite Yahweh's previous judgments, such as famine and drought,

'I was neither a prophet nor the disciple of a prophet, but I was a shepherd, and I also took care of sycamore-fig trees. But the Lord took me from tending the flock and said to me, "Go, prophesy to my people Israel." '
Amos 7:14–15

Prophets ministering in the eighth century

159

his people have not returned to him. 'Prepare to meet your God, seek the Lord and live; then the Almighty will be with you, just as you say he is. Perhaps the Lord will have mercy.' Yet, despite this possibility of repentance, the overall sense is that this is now too late. This is conveyed to Amos through a series of visions: of locusts, then of fire, of a plumb-line and then of a basket of ripe fruit. When he sees the first two, Amos cries out for mercy and Yahweh relents. But when he sees the plumb-line (presumably a benchmark of upright living) he is told: 'I am setting a plumb-line among my people; I will spare them no longer.' And the final vision only confirms that Israel is now 'ripe' for judgment: 'I will turn their religious feasts into mourning; I will make that time like mourning for an only son... I will fix my eyes on them for evil.' And (in a way that is bitterly ironic for those who have been disregarding Yahweh) Yahweh will now give them what they want: 'I will send a famine – a famine of hearing the words of the Lord; people will stagger, searching for the word of the Lord, but they will not find it.'

Thus a devastating prophecy came true. In 722 BC (within a generation of Amos's first preaching) the northern kingdom was indeed taken into exile by the Assyrians (see p. 90). Subsequent readers would have sensed the incredible truth of Amos's prophecy and noted its clear warning: God's people were liable to judgment if they abandoned his ways. For Amos dramatically reveals God's passionate commitment to social justice and practical righteousness. Yet God does not totally abandon his people. In a surprising twist at the very end, Amos foresees Israel's restoration after exile. Like other prophetic books, Amos thus sees a pattern of exile and restoration, of death followed by resurrection, of judgment as the prelude to salvation and rescue.

'The sovereign Lord does nothing
without revealing his plan
to his servants the
prophets.'
Amos 3:7

Amos was a shepherd from Tekoa, a small village (top left) surrounded by the terraced hillsides common in Judea.

Hosea

Around twenty years later Hosea is given a similarly urgent message for Israel – though its tone is slightly different. We hear the same strong warnings but also far more of God's passionate love. This comes about through Hosea's own context. He is a resident in the northern kingdom – not a visiting critic from the south – so his words of judgment are spoken with tenderness to his own people. More poignantly still, Hosea's own marriage reflects the pain of rejected love. His wife, Gomer, may have been a prostitute and certainly proves unfaithful – with Hosea even being instructed by Yahweh to 'buy her back' from her adultery. And Gomer's third child may not have been Hosea's; even so, he is called to raise the child as if his own.

This painful family situation is used to teach the prophet – from the inside – what God himself is going through in relation to his people: his overtures of 'steadfast love' are being spurned, and his faithfulness answered by an unfaithful people committed to spiritual adultery. Yahweh is a grieving husband, a divine cuckold.

After three opening chapters (with each speaking clearly about both the forthcoming judgment and also Yahweh's intention to restore his people), Hosea lays out the charges against Israel: 'There is no faithfulness, no love, no acknowledgment of God in the land. There is only cursing, lying and murder, stealing and adultery.' 'Lawsuits spring up like poisonous weeds.' Their worship of Yahweh is insincere, causing Yahweh to state clearly that he 'desires mercy' (hesed), not sacrifice. Instead genuine prophets are dismissed as fools. Indeed there is a calf-idol in Samaria and worship of Baal; worse still, cult prostitution is being practised on numerous hills. The priests are no better; and the royal family regularly misbehaves. Israel is 'arrogant', 'like a stubborn heifer', and 'has forgotten his Maker'.

So 'the days of reckoning are at hand'. 'A whirlwind will sweep them away.' They call out to Egypt and Assyria for help, but in vain. 'They will not remain in the Lord's land;' 'Samaria will float away like a twig on the surface of the waters.'

Yet Yahweh's heart is evidently being churned up: 'How can I give you up, O Israel? My heart is changed within me; all my compassion is aroused.' We hear the anguish of a loving husband looking back to the days of first love ('when I found Israel, it was like finding grapes in the desert'); we hear a father nostalgically reflecting on his children's early years ('when Israel was a child, I loved him'). And at the end, even though judgment is about to fall, there are passionate hints at the possible restoration of God's people – if only they will return to Yahweh bringing words of heartfelt repentance. To this Yahweh gladly responds: 'I will heal their

'I will betroth you to me…
in righteousness and justice,
in love and compassion.'
Hosea 2:19

'Sow for yourselves
*   righteousness,*
reap the fruit of unfailing
*   love,*
and break up your
*   unploughed ground;*
for it is time to seek the Lord,
*   until he comes*
and showers righteousness
*   on you.'*
Hosea 10:12

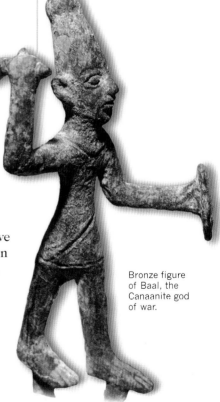

Bronze figure of Baal, the Canaanite god of war.

waywardness and love them freely. I will be like dew to Israel; he will blossom like a lily.'

As with Amos, the awful events of 722 BC, when the threatened judgment indeed came to pass, are never described (perhaps because both prophets died beforehand). Hosea's prophecy, however, is distinctive, because it is one of the most emotive – indeed emotional – books of the Old Testament. He sees into the very heart of God: the compassionate one who, though he will not tolerate entrenched disobedience, longs to bring his people back into a relationship of love and faithfulness. This portrait of God is the closest within the Old Testament to that used by Jesus in his parable of the prodigal son – as the father runs out, losing all his dignity, to meet his wayward but now returning child.

'Come, let us return to the Lord... on the third day he will restore us, that we may live in his presence... let us press on to acknowledge him.'

Hosea 6:1–3

Jonah

Jonah is named in 2 Kings (14:25) as a prophet from Galilee who lived during the reign of King Jeroboam II (781–753 BC); so, conceivably, he might have known either Amos or Hosea. Yet dating the *book* of Jonah is quite a different matter – with the story's final composition perhaps being much later.

Jonah's story is justly famous. When called to preach against Nineveh, Jonah heads off in the opposite (westerly) direction, boarding a ship bound for Tarshish (possibly Spain). But when a great storm develops, Jonah confesses to the non-Israelite crew that he is fleeing from Yahweh; he is to blame for their predicament and so he urges them to cast him overboard. This they eventually do, but Jonah is caught by a big fish, which three days later returns Jonah to dry land. So Jonah goes to Nineveh and preaches its imminent destruction, only to get an amazing response – with the king himself calling for repentance and fasting.

This greatly displeases Jonah. We now learn that this had been Jonah's complaint at the very outset – namely that Yahweh, being a 'compassionate and gracious' God, might 'relent of sending calamity' and thus leave Jonah looking very stupid. Jonah's worst-case scenario has just occurred: Yahweh's enemies have been forgiven! So he sits on a nearby hill in a grumpy mood, perhaps still hoping to see the city's destruction. Yahweh, however, challenges his right to feel angry and uses the blighting of a shady vine (which Jonah had been enjoying) to show that he cares for Nineveh far more than Jonah cared for the vine: 'Nineveh has more than 120,000 people. Should I not be concerned about that great city?'

The book is seen by the New Testament as demonstrating God's pattern of salvation, as Jonah goes down into 'death' but is brought

back in resurrection life. Yet, in its own context, it teaches two further important lessons.

First, even if Israel is God's chosen people, Yahweh's heart goes out to *all*. So, just as Israel can experience his judgment (as seen in Amos and Hosea), Israel's enemies, conversely, can experience his mercy. Secondly, Jonah's truculence reveals that a prophet can preach a message of judgment from a spirit of anger. True prophets, however, if called to preach judgment, will be moved by Yahweh's compassion. Moreover they are glad when they are proved wrong! When people repent and the threatened disaster is averted, they should be the first ones to rejoice. This then shows that Old Testament prophecy is not all a matter of *literal prediction* (of events that will definitely occur, come what may). Instead, much of it is *spiritual warning* (of events that *might* occur, if there is no repentance).

'Then they took Jonah and threw him overboard' (Jonah 1:15): as depicted in a medieval Armenian manuscript (dated 1266).

Joel

There are few indications in the short prophecy of Joel as to its date. It may belong to this early period, but it could come from much later. Its focus is on an imminent (or recent?) devastation caused by a swarm of locusts, which Joel sees as a warning of a severe devastation soon to be brought about by a military invasion:

Put on sackcloth and mourn. Let all who live in the land tremble, for the day of the Lord is coming, a day of darkness and gloom. The Lord thunders at the head of his army... Rend your heart and not your garments; return to the Lord your God.

Joel 1:13; 2:1–2, 13

Yahweh then responds mercifully to his people's repentance: 'I will drive the northern army from you; I will repay you for the years the locusts have eaten.' This then triggers a vision of what will happen in the more distant future – 'in those days' God will 'pour out his Spirit on *all* people', 'for on Mount Zion there will be deliverance... among the survivors'.

Moreover, at that time Yahweh will gather all the nations together for judgment. In a dramatic reversal God's people will 'beat their ploughshares into swords' and execute judgment on Yahweh's enemies – on *this* 'day of the Lord' he will 'roar' from Zion, not against them (as in Amos and Hosea) but on their behalf. The prophecy ends with an idyllic picture of hills dripping new wine and of Jerusalem as a peace-filled city, enjoying Yahweh's dwelling in its midst: 'The Lord dwells in Zion!'

This focus on Zion/Jerusalem indicates that Joel (unlike Hosea, Amos and Jonah) was preaching in the southern kingdom of Judah. It may also suggest a quite early date, since this more optimistic 'Zion theology' became less frequent in the period leading up to Jerusalem's fall (in 587/6 BC). If so, Joel is predicting not a military invasion by the Babylonians, but rather some coastal raids by the inhabitants of Philistia, Tyre and Sidon (the three enemies Joel explicitly names). The over-riding message is clear, however: Yahweh's judgment is real, but repentance brings great blessings; judgment gives way to salvation, 'scattering' to 'regathering'. And those blessings are also projected forward into a more distant future when Yahweh will bring blessing to *all* people. Thus in the New Testament Peter will see the gift of the Holy Spirit on the day of Pentecost as a fulfilment of Joel's prophecy: the time of restoration has arrived!

Micah

Micah too lived in Judah. Unlike Joel, however, his ministry can be dated with confidence to the last third of the eighth century (c. 735–700 BC), for Micah expressly predicts the fall of Samaria (in 722 BC). He also predicts that the Assyrians will cause trouble in his own home area (the low foothills to the south-west of Jerusalem) and twice warns that the enemy will reach 'even to the gates of Jerusalem' – as indeed happened in 701 BC (see p. 91).

Micah sees this as Yahweh's response to Judah's sins. The nation's rulers are condemned for 'hating good and loving evil'; and false prophets are castigated for adjusting their messages according to the payment received. When people argue that Jerusalem is safe because 'the Lord is among us', Micah bravely warns that Zion will instead be 'ploughed like a field' and Jerusalem will become a 'heap of rubble'. This is the first attack on Jerusalem in the minor prophets and was a key prophecy remembered a century later in the days of Jeremiah (see p. 140).

At this point Micah's prophecy suddenly takes the opposite tack, speaking of how 'in the last days' the mountain of the Lord's Temple will be established as chief among the mountains (words also found in his contemporary, Isaiah). Here is the great alternative scenario – with the Temple becoming a source of worldwide peace. Which of these two very different visions for Jerusalem will come to pass? Or will *both* come true – with judgment in the short term being followed later by international renown?

Micah's prophecies thereafter oscillate between these two extremes:

- There will be exile and the loss of Judah's king, but Yahweh himself will rule over Mount Zion and restore dominion to Jerusalem.

- Israel will be abandoned, but eventually a child will be born in tiny Bethlehem who will shepherd God's people and bring peace 'to the ends of the earth'.

- Yahweh accuses Israel of ill-gotten gain and dishonesty, and warns of judgment to come, yet, when Israel acknowledges its wrong-doing, Yahweh promises to 'extend its borders'.

This is the classic prophetic mixture of judgment and blessing, warning and promise. So, although there is an imminent threat, the big picture is one of long-term survival: there will be restoration, forgiveness and covenant faithfulness; the nations will acknowledge Yahweh; God's people will be 'gathered in' and God himself will rule over his people.

'He has shown all you people
    what is good.
And what does the Lord
    require of you?
To act justly and to love
    mercy,
and to walk humbly with
    your God.'
Micah 6:8

'Who is a God like you,
    who pardons sin…?
You will again have
    compassion on us;
you will tread our sins
    underfoot
and hurl all our iniquities
    into the depths of the sea.'
Micah 7:18–19

Prophets ministering in the seventh century

Nahum

Nahum refers to Assyria's defeat of Thebes (the capital of Egypt), which took place c. 662 BC, and predicts the fall of Assyria's own capital, Nineveh (which occurred in 612 BC). So he is prophesying between these dates – two generations after Micah and roughly a hundred years after Assyrian forces had taken northern Israel into exile. During that time Assyria has pestered southern Judah, but the time is nigh, predicts Nahum, when Nineveh's days of abusive power will end.

In contrast to the book of Jonah, which held out hope for Nineveh, in Nahum its overthrow is certain. Yes, 'the Lord is slow to anger', but he 'will not leave the guilty unpunished'. Nahum's prophecy gives graphic detail as to the storm hanging over Nineveh's head: 'Woe to the city of blood... many casualties, piles of dead, people stumbling over the corpses...' At the end, Nahum addresses the king of Assyria directly: 'Nothing can heal you; your wound is fatal. All who hear the news about you clap their hands at your fall, for who has not felt your endless cruelty?' Meanwhile Judah will have its 'splendour restored', being set free from Nineveh's 'shackles'. So Nahum's brief prophecy presents us with two key aspects of Yahweh's character: 'the Lord is good, a refuge in times of trouble' but 'with an overwhelming flood he pursues his enemies into darkness'.

'The Lord is a jealous and avenging God...
His way is in the whirlwind and the storm.'
Nahum 1:2–3

Zephaniah

Zephaniah (a great-great grandson of good King Hezekiah) was also prophesying around this time (c. 630 BC), but his message contains a darker story for Jerusalem. Three times Zephaniah talks about the coming 'day of the Lord', but each time this means judgment on all peoples, including Jerusalem. This is because Jerusalem's inhabitants are practising idolatry (worshipping Baal and Molech) and complacently presuming that Yahweh never does anything 'either good or bad'. If they want God's protection, they must 'seek righteousness and seek humility'.

In a central section there is a series of oracles against those nations that have mocked God's people, but then Zephaniah reverts to warning Jerusalem: 'the city of oppressors' is rebellious, accepting no correction, and 'does not draw near to her God'. So the day of judgment comes – on Jerusalem and the wider world.

Yet beyond it, on the other side, there is a whole new world: a humbled Jerusalem, filled with international worshippers, and an obedient 'remnant' restored to the land and enjoying God's presence. In a final picture of great tenderness, Zephaniah promises God's people:

'The Lord will take great delight in you, he will quiet you with his love and rejoice over you with singing.'

Habakkuk

Habakkuk's prophecy comes a generation later. The positive reforms of King Josiah (c. 621 BC; see p. 91) may have been triggered in part by warnings such as Zephaniah's. By now, however, any good has been negated through the recent policies of King Jehoiachim (c. 605 BC; see p. 91). So, when Habakkuk complains to God about the violence prevalent in society, the perversion of justice and the paralysis of the law courts, he receives a chilling response: 'I am raising up the Babylonians, that ruthless and impetuous people, whose own strength is their god.'

At this Habakkuk makes a second complaint: 'Your eyes, O Lord, are too pure to look on evil; why then are you silent while the wicked swallow up those more righteous than themselves?' And he waits for a reply. This comes in the form of an extended oracle against the Babylonians in which Yahweh admits that this nation is proud, greedy and full of bloodshed and idolatry; so, even though it will be delayed until the 'appointed time', Babylon will surely drink the cup of God's judgment.

The Barren Fig Tree, by James Tissot (1836–1902).

Habakkuk then responds with a long prayer in which he recasts this oracle into a dramatic portrait of Yahweh acting in power to avenge his enemies and to 'deliver his people'.

Habakkuk is reeling slightly from the sheer power of this revelation but he closes by adopting a patient stance, 'waiting for the day of calamity to come on the nation invading us'. He concedes that before the Babylonians experience these judgments, Jerusalem will experience them first. Yet he comes to a position of settled faith in the midst of difficult days: 'Though the fig-tree does not bud... yet I will rejoice in the Lord... the sovereign Lord is my strength.'

'For the earth will be filled with the knowledge of the glory of the Lord as the waters cover the sea.'
Habakkuk 2:14

Obadiah

Obadiah is probably the only minor prophet to have been ministering during the period of the exile (587/6–539 BC). His book, the shortest in the Old Testament, is an oracle against Edom (Judah's neighbour to the south-east). There had been some long-standing tension between the two nations; but now the Edomites have gone so far as to 'rejoice over the people of Judah in the day of their destruction' and indeed to 'march through the gates in the days of their disaster'.

Sela (later named Petra, both meaning 'rock') was the chief city of the Israelites' long-term enemies, the Edomites. Two hundred years earlier Judah's King Amaziah (798–769 BC) had routed their army, throwing many to their deaths from the 'top of a rock' (2 Chronicles 25:12); now Obadiah denounces them for rejoicing over the fall of Jerusalem (587/6 BC).

Almost certainly this refers to Jerusalem's fall at the hands of the Babylonians in 587/6 BC. Edom evidently joined in the plunder, settling old scores. This act of treachery was then remembered by the exiles in Babylon (see Psalm 137) and probably underlies the other oracles against Edom found in Jeremiah, Lamentations and Ezekiel. Obadiah adds his voice to the sense of outrage at this act of unbrotherly revenge: 'your deeds will return upon your own head'. In due course Mount Zion will be a place for 'holy deliverance', but 'the house of Esau will be set on fire'; and Israelite 'exiles' will return and re-occupy part of the Promised Land. At which point, Obadiah concludes, the 'kingdom will be the Lord's'.

Visible beyond Edom's old high place of sacrifice is 'Aaron's tomb' on one cliff-top, and the city's stronghold on the other.

Haggai

The date for Haggai's short prophecy can be placed remarkably precisely: the 'second year of King Darius' is 520 BC. The first exiles had returned in 539 BC, but work on the rebuilding of the Temple had ground to a halt because of opposition (Ezra 1–6, pp. 97–98). Haggai's encouraging prophecies serve to stir up a renewed determination to do this important work and the Temple is duly completed some four years later (516 BC).

Haggai chides the people for building their own houses while questioning whether it is right to build Yahweh's 'house'. 'Give careful thought to your ways,' Yahweh declares; the recent bad harvests have come about 'because my house remains a ruin'. This message stirs up Joshua (the high priest) and Zerubbabel (the Jewish 'governor of Judah'). Three weeks later work is begun to clear the Temple foundations.

Haggai's next prophecy is succinct ('"I am with you," declares the Lord') but, one month later, he is given a slightly longer message! Aware that some may be discouraged, through comparing their current paltry efforts with the Temple's 'former glory', Yahweh commands them to 'be strong... my Spirit remains among you'. Yahweh will 'shake the nations', and 'the glory of this present house will be greater than the glory of the former house'.

Eventually, two months later, the foundation stone is ready to be laid. Haggai promises that from this very day God's people will experience a new measure of God's blessing and that Zerubbabel will be like a 'signet ring' to Yahweh – 'chosen' by the Lord.

Zechariah

Zechariah then picks up the same themes. His first prophecy comes one month before Haggai's last, being the familiar call: '"Return to me and I will return to you," declares the Lord.' Three months later, however, Zechariah receives a series of colourful visions:

- He sees an angel asking the Lord Almighty when the 'seventy years' of his anger against Jerusalem will cease, and the reply comes: 'I will return to Jerusalem with mercy and there my house will be rebuilt… The Lord will again comfort Zion.'

- 'Four horns' are thrown down, and Zechariah is told these represent those nations which proudly scattered Judah into exile.

- A man with a measuring-line rebuilds Jerusalem: Yahweh himself will be a 'wall of fire' around the city and 'its glory within'.

- Joshua, the high priest, is then tempted by Satan; but Yahweh clothes Joshua with rich garments and promises that, if he proves faithful, he will lead the Temple worship. He and his fellow priests are told they are 'symbolic of things to come' and that in due course Yahweh is going to 'bring my servant, the Branch', who mysteriously will somehow provide atonement for all people 'in a single day'.

- Zerubbabel, having laid the Temple's foundation stone, is told he will also instal the capstone to shouts of praise.

- He sees a flying scroll going out to curse those who swear falsely and a woman in a basket being transported to Babylonia (a symbol of wickedness being removed from Jerusalem).

- Finally he sees four chariots taking out God's peace to the four compass points of the earth.

Zechariah is then told to place a crown on Joshua's head. If many expected Zerubbabel to be crowned king in light of the many promises that the Davidic kingship would continue, Zechariah daringly favours Joshua, signalling that any such 'kingship' will be merged with the priesthood: 'he will be a *priest* on his *throne*'. Yet his words are clearly speaking prophetically, not so much of Joshua himself but of the 'Branch', who will both 'build the Temple' and be 'clothed with majesty'

'Who dares despise the day of small things?'
Zechariah 4:10

'Not by might nor by power but by my Spirit.'
Zechariah 4:6

– words that inevitably would fuel expectations for the arrival of this newly styled priest/king.

There follows a discussion about fasting and then an extended prophecy concerning Jerusalem's future glory: the 'City of Truth', the 'Holy Mountain', will be repopulated by returning exiles and will enjoy God's blessing from the time of the Temple's re-foundation.

The final six chapters of Zechariah (chapters 9–14) come across slightly differently. Chapters 9–11 are introduced as a single oracle but have at least four different sections:

- an oracle against the nations;

- a prophecy about the arrival on a donkey of Jerusalem's king (*not* Zerubbabel) who will bring peace to the ends of the earth;

- a prophecy about Yahweh saving his people as their shepherd;

- a strange episode in which the prophet is called himself to take the role first of a good shepherd and then of an evil one, but he is paid a pittance for his troubles as a good shepherd (only thirty pieces of silver) and throws the money 'to the potter'.

Chapters 12–14 are similarly introduced as a single oracle. Again there are several different sections, though here they are all connected with an eschatological vision of what Yahweh will do 'on that day', including prophecies about:

- Jerusalem as an 'immovable rock';

- Jerusalem and the 'house of David' being given a 'spirit of grace and supplication'; they will weep, 'looking on the one they have pierced' as though 'grieving for a first-born son';

- a fountain in Jerusalem which will cleanse people of sin and mark the end of idolatry and false prophets;

- Yahweh's chosen shepherd being struck by the sword, causing his sheep to be scattered;

- a final prophecy with various ingredients: standing on the Mount of Olives, enabling people to flee the city; Jerusalem being elevated, with water flowing from the city to the east and west; and

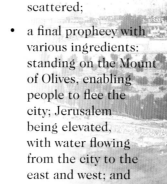

Yahweh ruling over the whole earth, blessing people from all nations who celebrate the feast of Tabernacles in Jerusalem.

These final chapters have more of a 'scatter-gun' approach, looking into the distant future in ways that are quite mysterious. Even so, there are some fairly consistent themes: Yahweh's continued commitment to his people, and his desire to use Jerusalem to vindicate his purposes in the future; also his promise to shepherd and rule his people, while also sending a mysterious other figure to be that shepherd and ruler on his behalf.

These six chapters are then quoted by the Gospel writers with remarkable frequency (see p. 175). For in these bizarre prophecies they saw predictions of an equally bizarre and unexpected weekend in Jerusalem – focused on a figure who was a humble king riding a donkey over the Mount of Olives, a good shepherd who was rejected and sold for a pittance, indeed an 'only son' whose death would lead to much weeping and yet deal with sin. So, just when we might think that Zechariah has lost the plot, we discover instead that he may have been given particular insight into God's ultimate plot and purposes.

Malachi

There is only one prophet in this final category – namely Malachi, whose prophecy is dated to c. 480 BC, or even much later to the fourth century. Malachi announces that Yahweh is coming in judgment in response to various malaises in contemporary Judah:

- People are questioning Yahweh's power and have not appreciated his love for them; they are effectively robbing God through not contributing the full amount of their pledged tithing.

- The priests have not followed the model of reverence seen in their ancestor Levi; people are showing contempt for Yahweh's name by offering diseased animals in their sacrifices.

- People are wearying God by claiming that he is not bothered by evil behaviour; there are cases of intermarriage with foreign women and, worse still, instances of divorce.

Yahweh responds to some of these issues directly: the priests will experience a particular form of humiliation; although Yahweh 'loves' the Temple, the abuses in its worship will not matter because 'pure offerings' will eventually be brought from all over the world; meanwhile, married couples are to 'guard themselves in their spirit' and not to 'break faith'; and those who 'fear the Lord' should know that their

Prophets ministering after 500 BC

God looks down from heaven
*   to see if there are any who seek God.*

Everyone has turned away,
*   all have become corrupt...*

Oh, that salvation for Israel would come out of Zion!
*   When God restores his people,*
*   let Jacob rejoice and Israel be glad!*

Psalm 53:2–3, 6

names are written in Yahweh's 'scroll of remembrance'. The main message, however, is that Yahweh will judge his people:

See, I will send my messenger to prepare the way before me. The Lord you are seeking will come to his temple... But who can endure the day of his coming?... For he will be like a refiner's fire... See, I will send you the prophet Elijah before that dreadful day.

Malachi 3:1–2; 4:5

These words strongly suggest that even if Yahweh will come in some acts of judgment in the short term, he will also come *in person*. In prophetic writing the idea of Yahweh's 'coming in judgment' was commonplace, but it did not signify that *Yahweh was himself going to arrive in person*. Here in Malachi, however, the metaphors are sounding remarkably literal: the people will be sent an advanced messenger (comparable to Elijah) and then 'the Lord' *himself* will 'come to his temple'.

No wonder Mark's Gospel would start with these very prophecies when advancing the claim that Jesus was none other than Yahweh visiting his people in person (and that John the Baptist was the Elijah-figure sent to 'prepare the way for *the Lord*'). Malachi thus becomes the brilliant last voice from the Old Testament, signalling that the next important event in this all-encompassing biblical story would be the arrival of that story's *author* – none other than Yahweh himself in person.

THE MINOR PROPHETS QUOTED IN
THE NEW TESTAMENT

The minor prophets, looking through the imminent clouds, glimpsed the bright new future that lay beyond – that time when there would be a proper restoration from exile (and yet more besides).

The New Testament writers then see this as fulfilled in the coming of Jesus. This was the time, they claimed, when the exile truly came to an end, because Jesus had achieved the forgiveness of sins; moreover Yahweh had come to dwell with his people; and the nations had come into the kingdom of God. So they often quote texts from the minor prophets, pointing out their fulfilment in Christ:

Old Testament prophecy	New Testament fulfilment
Amos 9:11–12 ('I will restore David's fallen shelter...').	Key text quoted by James, Jesus' brother, in affirming that Gentiles may now enter the people of God because Israel's 'restoration' has been accomplished through Jesus (Acts 15:16–17).
Hosea 1:10 ('In the place where it was said to them, "You are not my people," they will be called "children of the living God"').	Quoted by Paul and alluded to by Peter in their arguments for Gentile inclusion in the people of God (Romans 9:25; 1 Peter 2:10).
Hosea 6:6 ('I desire mercy, not sacrifice').	Quoted twice by Jesus in his debates with the Pharisees (Matthew 9:13; 12:7).
Hosea 11:1 ('Out of Egypt I called my son').	Quoted by Matthew as a prophecy fulfilled by Jesus returning after his flight to Egypt as a child (Matthew 2:15).
Jonah 2:2–9 ('You... brought my life up from the pit'; 'salvation comes from the Lord').	Jonah's three days in the fish are seen by Jesus as a sign of his own death and resurrection (Matthew 12:39–40).
Joel 2:28–32 ('I will pour out my Spirit on all people').	Quoted by Peter as being now fulfilled in the gift of the Holy Spirit on the day of Pentecost (Acts 2:17–21); its apocalyptic language may also have influenced Mark 13:24 or Revelation 6:12.
Micah 5:2–4 ('Out of you [Bethlehem] will come one who will be ruler').	Quoted by King Herod's advisers when asked the expected birthplace of the Messiah (Matthew 2:6).
Habakkuk 2:4 ('But the righteous will live by their faithfulness').	Quoted by Paul as the key text for understanding 'justification by faith' (Romans 1:17).
Haggai 2:6 ('I will once more shake the heavens and the earth').	Quoted by the author of Hebrews in his vision of God establishing his 'unshakeable' kingdom (Hebrews 12:26–27).
Zechariah 9:9 ('See, your king comes to you, riding on a donkey').	Explicitly quoted by two of the evangelists as a prophecy fulfilled by Jesus when he entered Jerusalem (Matthew 21:5; John 12:15).
Zechariah 11:12–13 ('So they paid me thirty pieces of silver').	Alluded to by Matthew as a prophecy (along with others in Jeremiah) fulfilled by Judas Iscariot in selling Jesus the good shepherd for this paltry sum (Matthew 27:3–10).
Zechariah 13:7 ('Strike the shepherd and the sheep will be scattered').	Quoted by Jesus when predicting Peter's denial on the night of his arrest (Mark 14:27).

THE STORY SO FAR:
BETWEEN THE TESTAMENTS

So the Old Testament comes to an end. As we look back on this body of literature, how do we make sense of the story thus far? Or, to put the same question more historically, what were the truths with which every reader of the Old Testament had been thoroughly imbued by the time Jesus was born?

Three great truths had been established within Judaism by that time: monotheism, election and eschatology. These three concepts, which initially may sound rather forbidding, can be unpacked as follows. First, *monotheism* describes the belief, seen throughout the Old Testament, that there is but *one* God. Jewish people in Jesus' day would have regularly recited from Deuteronomy (6:4): 'Hear, O Israel: The Lord our God, the Lord is one.' They were not '*poly*theists' (believing in *many* gods), nor even *heno*theists (that is, believing their god was *one* of many), but monotheists. All other so-called 'gods' were non-existent figments of other nations' imaginations. Moreover, this one, true God was the God who had created the universe, who now sustained his world, and who would one day be its judge: he was the one '*from* whom, *through* whom, and *to* (or *for*) whom all things existed'. Israel's God was therefore the creator, sustainer and judge.

Moreover, the Old Testament story – filled as it was with so many smaller stories about God's involvement with his people – made it abundantly clear that this God was no absentee 'landlord'. On the contrary, he is dynamic and active. In particular, he had acted in the time of Moses to redeem his people from slavery in Egypt; he was thus a God who delighted to rescue and who was deeply committed to those he called his people.

This leads us to the second great conviction within Old Testament faith – namely election. Election refers to God's active choice of his people. Most pages of the Old Testament asserted that the people of Israel, despite their many failings, were God's 'chosen' ones, the 'elect' with whom the Lord had entered into a binding covenantal relationship. This relationship was described in the much-repeated biblical phrase: 'I will be their God, and they will be my people.' And it was based on divine promises, which came with a matching expectation of obedience. Much of the Old Testament was thus the story of how this divine promise (first made to Abraham) had been worked out in actual history, and how God's people had come to experience both the blessings and curses intrinsic within this unique relationship. Of course, this exclusive focus on Israel then left a major unanswered question: what was God's will and purpose towards those *outside* Israel, the so-called 'Gentiles'?

176

The third great conviction, established especially in the later Old Testament writings, was that this God was going to do something dramatic for his people in the future – precisely as an outworking of his earlier promises. To describe this strand of biblical hope, we here give the name *eschatology*. Commonly, this word (based on the Greek word for 'last things') is used to refer to the ultimate end of our space-time universe – the 'last days' before the *end of the cosmos.* Within Old Testament thought, however, the 'last days' described that time when *God would do for Israel that which he had promised them*: he would usher in the 'age to come', when Israel's kingdom would be established, and in this new age the Gentiles would somehow be brought under the reign of Israel's God.

First-century Jews were not therefore waiting for the 'end of the world' (as we might use that term today) but rather for this prophesied era of fulfilment within the ordinary course of human history. Throughout most of the Old Testament's prophetic writings there was this insistence that God had better plans in store for his people. But when and how would these come to pass? The divergent responses to the urgent questions of eschatology then explain the various parties within Judaism, which we will shortly encounter in the New Testament era (see pp. 182–83).

So these were the three great pillars of Old Testament faith: there was only *one God,* who had *called a people* into a binding covenant, and who one day would *act in fulfilment* of those covenant promises. The generations after the last prophet (traditionally understood to be Malachi) were therefore marked by a keen sense of anticipation and waiting. If there seemed to be no more direct prophecy, then at least the 'apocalyptic' writers could give their version of how events would soon unfold. Some of these works (for example, 3 and 4 Esdras, 1 and 2 Baruch) would be collected into the Old Testament's apocrypha (also known as the 'inter-testamental' writings). In these and in other more historical books (such as 1 and 2 Maccabees), God's people kept alive their sense of identity and destiny, tracing their past and staring forwards into the future. Yet the true 'voice of the Lord' was strangely silent; and the Romans had overpowered the land.

It was in these dark days, when biblical hope seemed dashed by harsh reality, that there suddenly appeared in Israel the long-awaited voice of a prophet – the voice of one calling in the desert, 'prepare the way for the Lord!' And so, at long last, the great Old Testament story was kicking into gear once more. The age of fulfilment – the big second instalment in God's single master plan – was about to begin!

Possible dates for the writing of the books of the New Testament

	GOSPELS	HISTORY	LETTERS	APOCALYPSE
40 AD				
45			James?	
48			Galatians	
50				
51			1 Thessalonians	
52			2 Thessalonians	
53				
54			1 Corinthians	
55			2 Corinthians 1–9	
56			2 Corinthians 10–13 1 Timothy?	
57			Romans	
60			2 Timothy?; Hebrews*; 1 Peter*; Jude*	
61			Colossians Philemon Ephesians	
62	Mark* Luke*	Acts*	Philippians	
63				
64			Hebrews**; 1 Peter**; 2 Peter?*	
65	Matthew* Mark**			Revelation*
68				
70				
72			Jude?** 2 Peter?**	
75	John*		1, 2, 3 John*	
80	Matthew** Luke**	Acts**		
85			1, 2, 3 John**	
90	John**			
95				Revelation**

* Earliest possible date   ** Latest possible date
For further detail on historical events in the New Testament, see p. 219.

THE
NEW TESTAMENT

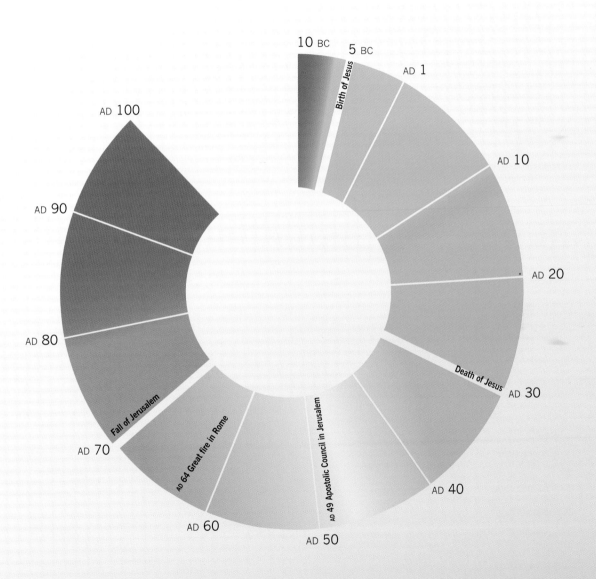

10 BC
5 BC
Birth of Jesus
AD 1
AD 100
AD 10
AD 90
AD 20
AD 80
Death of Jesus
AD 30
Fall of Jerusalem
AD 70
AD 64 Great fire in Rome
AD 49 Apostolic Council in Jerusalem
AD 40
AD 60
AD 50

INTRODUCING THE NEW TESTAMENT

The New Testament consists of twenty-seven books, composed over a fifty-year period (c. AD 45–95) by those who were convinced that Jesus of Nazareth was Israel's long-awaited Messiah. Each writer therefore sees his work as a continuation of that one biblical story which we have been tracing through the pages of the Old Testament. That story had focused on a 'covenant' (or 'testament'), that God had promised to Israel through people such as Moses and Abraham. These writers, however, were now convinced that God had fulfilled this covenant promise by sending Jesus; yet he had done so in some new and surprising ways – hence the apt title, the 'New Testament' (or 'New Covenant').

Four different writing styles
Within the twenty-seven books (as we saw above, p. 178), there are four main genres:

- the **Gospels** (accounts of Jesus' life);
- the **Acts of the Apostles** (a short history of the early church);
- the **letters** or **epistles** (written by Paul and others to the first Christian congregations);
- and, finally, the book of **Revelation**, also known as the Apocalypse (which contains prophetic and apocalyptic material similar to that found in Daniel: see p. 156).

So the New Testament, despite being quite short, has a rich variety. Accordingly, we should not read it in a monochrome way, but value these different styles. When reading the epistles, for example, we can expect to find apostolic teaching and to receive some fairly direct instructions about Christian living. With the book of Acts, however, we should not expect to find such doctrinal statements or ethical commands but rather a real-life story – full of ups and downs; it is written to encourage us, but our own quite different circumstances may mean we cannot live out this story in exactly the same way. (On the special issues when reading Revelation, see p. 289.)

Dating the books
Further detail on the likely dates of composition for the various New Testament books can be found below (on pp. 184–85, 232 and 271). When we put these dates together (as on p. 178), one striking feature is that many of Paul's letters (some dating to the AD 50s) were probably written *before* the first edition of a written Gospel (c. AD 60–65). This means that Paul's teaching provides vitally important material for understanding the story of Jesus – for this is what was being publicly taught about Jesus around the Mediterranean within just twenty years of the crucifixion. If then, as many think, Galatians is Paul's earliest letter, its opening phrases are very significant, because Paul is evidently already convinced that Jesus is in some way *divine*.

Another point to note is that, for many scholars, the vast majority of the New Testament was written down before AD 70 – the year when Jerusalem's Temple was destroyed by the Romans in accordance with Jesus' predictions. Those tumultuous events, which effectively brought to an end the world known to Jesus and his disciples, may well have acted as an incentive for the apostles to commit things to paper before it was too late. The exceptions, I suggest, were the Gospels of Matthew and John; the short epistles written by John in Ephesus; and the book of Revelation. Yet even these may have all been completed by AD 85 or earlier. The New Testament (unlike the Old Testament) was therefore written down within a quite narrow band of time and within at most two generations of the original events.

Putting the books together
Admittedly, it took a much longer time for the books to be carefully vetted and checked for their authenticity. The final definitive list (or 'canon') of

Page from Codex Sinaiticus, a virtually complete version of the Bible in Greek, transcribed between AD 325 and 360.

New Testament books as we know it, dates to AD 367 (in a letter of Athanasius from Alexandria). Yet this slow process should not be taken as a sign of incompetence by the early Christians. On the contrary, it is a sign of the great care they took to double-check with as many people as possible before making a rash decision. After all, its rapid expansion meant that by the AD 250s the church was an organization stretching from Britain to Mesopotamia. So, in the days before telecommunication, such double-checking would be a painfully slow process. This meant, inevitably, that some of the smallest letters were particularly hard to verify and confirm (see p. 270).

In reality, however, the major contours of the New Testament were already established and agreed by the middle of the second century. During that century, there was a spate of Gnostic writings which tried to supplement or contradict the apostolic writings, offering alternative (and often bizarre) accounts of Jesus' teaching, and

which often claimed special 'insider' sources of spiritual revelation. The Christian church, however, was well able to detect the authentic from the spurious, making wise judgments about what genuinely went back to the apostolic era. And, despite many modern speculations, there is strong evidence that they got it right.

So we should come to the New Testament not only with some confidence but also with some expectation that in its pages we will be given an authentic portrait of Jesus. It may be a very small book, quite vulnerable to criticism; but, through the centuries, it has proved to be like dynamite.

The background to the New Testament

To better understand the New Testament, we need to appreciate its complex context. At one level, it is a predominantly Jewish book, deeply indebted to the Old Testament and strongly coloured by events within Judaism during the previous few centuries. At another level, however – precisely because it was proclaiming the news about Jesus to the whole world – it is also coloured by the ancient classical world.

The Jewish background

The majority of first-century Jews would have embraced the beliefs set out above (p. 176): they believed their God was the one, true God; that they were his people and that he had given them unique promises. Yet, more politically, their major concern was the occupation of their homeland by Rome. The Roman armies, led by Pompey, had entered Jerusalem in 67 BC and the whole country was part of a Roman province ('Syria-Palestina'). Herod the Great and his successors might have been their immediate rulers, but they were puppet-kings under the authority of Rome.

So, throughout Jesus' ministry, Palestine is a place of seething unrest. Jesus' contemporaries longed for independence from this pagan domination, which seemed so contrary to prophecies that their God would usher in his kingdom. Yes, they had experienced 100 years of comparative independence after the Maccabean revolt under the Hasmonean rulers (from 167 BC); but Pompey's arrival had crushed all that. The result was bitter resentment and increasing protest. Thus there were several uprisings (for example, when Herod died in 4 BC); and in due course there would be the major Jewish revolt (AD 66), culminating in the Roman siege of Jerusalem and the Temple's destruction (AD 70). Jesus lived in a context in which it would take only a small spark to send the whole thing up in flames. The longing for a rescuer-figure (a Messiah) was only increasing; so Jesus would need incredible care when he spoke about his messiahship or the arrival of the kingdom of God.

Jesus thus had to plot a course for his ministry that was visibly distinctive from the agenda of the four main groupings that had emerged within Judaism in response to this crisis situation:

- The **Sadducees**, made up largely of the ruling classes in Jerusalem, were the most content with the Roman occupation; being focused on the Pentateuch, not the prophetic books, they did not entertain strong prophetic hopes that paganism would be removed.

- The **Pharisees**, by contrast, who were more popular among ordinary people, strongly desired God to rescue his people; yet they insisted God would only act when his people were 'holy' and not compromising with Gentiles (for example, in observing sabbath and dietary regulations).

- The **Essenes** took this concern for holiness even further, establishing a close community at Qumran (near the Dead Sea), where their corporate life was supposed to replicate the holiness of the Temple.

• The **Zealots** became increasingly impatient in the period after Jesus and began actively to pursue a military solution.

The pagan background

Yet Jewish people had to interact with the wider culture – not only in Galilee but especially in the so-called 'Dispersion' (or 'Diaspora'). Many Greek cities thus hosted large Jewish communities (established several hundred years before); and it was in such communities that the Christian message would first take root once it left the shores of Palestine.

In the eastern half of the Mediterranean people spoke Greek. Effectively Greek culture had spread through the exploits of Alexander the Great (336–323 BC). His successors (the Ptolemaic dynasty in Egypt and the Seleucids in Antioch) strongly asserted this Greek (or Hellenistic) influence, which in turn triggered a fierce backlash from the Jews (the Maccabean revolt of 167 BC). When the eastern Mediterranean came under Roman rule, Rome allowed the local Greek culture to continue. So the predominant civilization was either Hellenistic Greek or Greco-Roman.

This culture was hugely indebted to the values of classical Athens. In religious terms the gods of the Greek pantheon (Zeus, Athena and so on) were still in vogue, but this polytheism could easily absorb other deities. Different philosophies were also influential: there was Platonism (with its strong contrast between the body and the soul, and between the material world and the world of ideas) and, later, Epicureanism, which took a quite hedonistic and nihilistic view of life: 'Eat, drink and be merry, for tomorrow we die!' This introduced a negative approach to the possibility of life after death, but perhaps the majority believed (following Plato) in the immortality of the soul. No one, however, believed in the resurrection of the body – that human bodies would be raised to new life after death.

This is the world in which the message of Jesus' resurrection was first proclaimed. Paul's speech in Athens (see p. 225) illustrates well this clash of cultures as he proclaimed how the God of Israel had recently revealed himself through the death and resurrection of Christ.

The so-called 'Mona Lisa of the Galilee': this beautiful floor mosaic (for a dining-room in Sepphoris, near Nazareth, from the early 200s AD) reveals the influence of Greek pagan ideas on Jesus' native land.

The Athenian 'acro-polis' (or 'high city'), topped by the Parthenon temple (built 448–432 BC), encapsulated the spirit of classical Athens.

Gospels

The four Gospels introduce us to the person at the centre of the whole Bible: Jesus Christ. The English word 'gospel' (derived from an Anglo-Saxon phrase referring to 'God's news') is used to translate a Greek word (*ev-angellion*) that means 'good news'. This word is used by Mark at the start of his account: 'The beginning of the good news about Jesus the Messiah.' He was almost certainly using it as a shorthand title for his work, and ever since it has been used as a way of describing the four books that were written about Jesus. They are all 'good news' and the four Gospel writers are known as the four 'evangelists'.

This new word 'Gospel', coined especially for these documents, points to their unique and distinctive character. In one sense the Gospels appear to be rather like ancient biographies (which tended to focus, by the way, not on every detail of a person's life but just on their key actions and teachings); yet, in another, they are quite different. This is not because the evangelists were not interested in matters of historical record, but rather because they had an extra purpose: they believed the story of Jesus inevitably contained a life-changing message of good news, which their readers needed to heed.

This means that their accounts were never intended simply to highlight the exploits of a recent hero – exploits which, even if true, would now be merely matters of historical interest. On the contrary, the evangelists understood the person about whom they were writing to have been an authoritative teacher with a message that came from God himself. So this was not just a story to be noted, but rather a message to be heeded. More than that, their accounts all concluded with the story of how this Jesus had been raised by God from the dead. So, even if their readers disputed the truth of this story, the evangelists themselves were clearly convinced that this Jesus was not just a figure from the past but someone who was a living reality in the present. Their goal as evangelists, then, was not simply to record history but to persuade people through that history of the good news found in this now risen Jesus.

In sum, they were both biographers and evangelists, both historians and theologians, convinced that history had been invaded by God, and that only by looking fully at that history could people be introduced to the truth of God. The four Gospels are thus written as an invitation to people in any generation to examine the story of Jesus – in the hope that, through doing this, those people may encounter the reality of God.

The four Gospels: setting and date

Almost every detail of the table opposite has been – and continues to be – a matter of intense debate (for the position adopted here, see my fuller arguments published elsewhere: *Jesus and the Holy City, Jesus and His World*, etc.).

There is a widespread consensus that Mark is written by the John Mark known to us from Acts and at some point in the early 60s, almost certainly

Gospel	Author	Location	Date
Mark	John Mark: native of Jerusalem; companion of Paul and then of Peter (Acts 12:12, 25; 13:13; 15:37; Colossians 4:10; 1 Peter 5:13).	Rome	AD 60–65
Luke	Luke, whom Paul describes as his 'beloved physician' (Colossians 4:14); native of Philippi who travelled to Jerusalem and Rome with Paul (Acts 20:28).	Drafted in Palestine; completed in Rome.	AD 57–59 AD 60–65
Matthew	Jewish Christian, possibly identified with Matthew the tax-collector (Matthew 10:3; Mark 2:14); he may have fled north to Pella in Galilee with other Christians from Jerusalem in AD 67 (see Eusebius, *Church History* 3.5.3).	Syria/Palestine (possibly Galilee region or Antioch: see Matthew 4:24).	AD 75
John	Jesus' 'beloved disciple' (John 21:20), writing in old age; according to Irenaeus (later recorded in Eusebius, *Church History* 3.23.3) John 'lived into the reign of Trajan' (emperor from AD 98).	Ephesus	AD 80–90

in Rome. Papias (a bishop writing c. AD 135) suggests Mark was writing down the 'memoirs of Peter', and there are several places in his text where Peter's influence can be detected.

Far more controversial is the idea that Luke also completed his Gospel in Rome around the same time. Many scholars think Luke dates from after the fall of Jerusalem (in AD 70). Yet it is quite feasible that he researched his Gospel during his two-year stay in Palestine (while Paul was in prison in Caesarea, AD 57–59), finishing it once he reached Rome with Paul in AD 60. Luke and Mark are both mentioned by Paul as being in Rome (see Colossians 4:10, 14), so they may well have known each other's work in draft form, but agreed to write up their separate accounts without trying to conflate them (Luke probably already had an outline structure which, even if slightly different from Mark's, he was not willing to abandon).

Matthew seems to have been writing just after the fall of Jerusalem – a tragic event (though predicted by Jesus) which would cause his fellow Jewish Christians much pause for thought. He seems to have known Mark's text, 90 per cent of which he incorporated into his own work. Unlike Luke, however, he does not appear to have had a prior structure of his own but inserted a large amount of Jesus' teaching into Mark's narrative framework.

John's Gospel remains an enigma. Its author seemingly knew the traditions in the other Gospels but deliberately aimed to give an alternative, complementary account. It reveals an intimate knowledge of Palestinian Judaism and contains many touches that have an eyewitness feel to them. At the same time, it engages creatively with a more Greek way of thinking and has an air of mature reflection. These factors suggest that the apostle John was himself its primary author (even if assisted by colleagues in his community). For towards the end of his life he would be uniquely placed to offer his own original memories of Jesus while setting them within a context of a lifetime's considered reflection.

Note to reader:
Those less familiar with the story of Jesus' life may find it easiest to look first at the outline summaries of his teaching ministry and then the events surrounding his death (pp. 186–87 and 196–97) and then to read the chapter on Mark's Gospel (pp. 198–202). This is because Matthew's Gospel (though it appears first in our Bibles and is therefore treated first in this *Guide*) is effectively an expanded version of Mark which contains the most straightforward description of Jesus' life. Even better, you might like to find a modern version of Mark's Gospel and read this short but powerful text for yourself...

JESUS' EARLY MINISTRY

Jesus' public ministry lasted three years and can be dated with reasonable confidence to the years AD 28–30. He had grown up in Nazareth but moved to make his base of operations at Capernaum (located on the north-western side of Lake Galilee and on the major highway from the Mediterranean to Damascus).

He had been born, however, in Bethlehem, just south of Jerusalem, some time before the death of Herod the Great (in March 5 BC). The details surrounding his birth are only given in the Gospels of Matthew and Luke. Matthew's account focuses on the events in Bethlehem and makes much of the visit from the east of some magi to the young child; he mentions Jesus' family fleeing to Egypt (to escape Herod's campaign of slaughter) and only then mentions Nazareth (as the place to which the family returns). Luke, however, perhaps influenced by interviewing Mary and other women in Galilee, gives an account told far more from Mary's perspective: we hear of Mary being told about the birth by the angel Gabriel, of her visit to her cousin Elizabeth (the mother of John the Baptist), and of her taking Jesus to the Temple – both as an infant and, later, as a twelve-year-old.

Mark, however, starts his account with John the Baptist's preaching just before the adult Jesus starts his ministry. The table overleaf summarizes

The Flight to Egypt, by Gentile da Fabriano (c. 1370–1427).

the rest of Jesus' ministry (before his arrival in Jerusalem) as told by the three so-called 'synoptic' writers ('synoptic' because they looked together at Jesus' life from a recognizably similar perspective or vantage point, especially when compared with John's Gospel). From the table it can be seen how much the synoptic writers have in common (though this table disguises the places where they have episodes appearing in a different order). One can also detect some of the interesting overlaps. Matthew has absorbed most of Mark's material but supplemented it with a good amount of teaching. Luke has some quite different teaching material, especially in parable form. John's account of Jesus' ministry is intentionally quite distinctive. He makes it clear that Jesus went up to Jerusalem each year and only has a limited number of episodes located in Galilee (for example, a wedding feast at Cana, and the healing of a centurion's son). The feeding of the 5,000 is the only Galilean episode to be recounted in all four Gospels.

	Matthew	Mark	Luke
1. The River Jordan and the Judean desert	John the Baptist's preaching (and later imprisonment) Jesus' baptism by John Jesus' temptation in the desert		
2. Galilee (opening ministry)			Jesus' preaching in Nazareth
	Calling of the first disciples		
	Teaching and healing in Capernaum		
			Miraculous catch of fish
	Healing of leper and paralytic		
	Call of Levi/Matthew		
			Jesus anointed by unnamed woman
			List of names of the women in Jesus' party
	Questions about fasting and use of sabbath		
	Jesus accused of working for Beelzebub		
	Healing of man with withered hand		
	Jesus teaching the crowds by lakeside		
	Choosing of the 'Twelve'		
	Sermon on the Mount		Sermon 'on the plain'
	Healing of centurion's servant		Healing of the widow's son at Nain
	Stilling of the storm		
	Healing of the demoniac (on east side of lake)		
	Healing of Jairus' daughter and woman with haemorrhage		
	Healing of blind men and dumb demoniac		
	Commissioning of the Twelve for mission		
	Teaching for disciples on mission		Teaching for disciples on mission
	John the Baptist's questions and Jesus' response		John the Baptist's questions and Jesus' repsonse
	Woes on Galilean cities		Woes on Galilean cities
	Warning against seeking signs		
	Parable of the sower (with subsequent explanation) and of mustard seed		
	Further parables: hidden treasure; wheat and weeds; net, etc.		
3. Sepphoris (Herod Antipas's court)	Death of John the Baptist		
4. Galilee (further ministry)	Feeding of the 5,000 (also in John 6) Walking on water and healing on the plain of Gennesaret		
	Debate about what 'defiles' a person		
	Jesus with Syro-phoenician woman		
	Healing of deaf mute and feeding of 4,000		

	Matthew	Mark	Luke
	Warning against 'yeast' of Pharisees and their seeking 'signs'		
		Healing of blind man at Bethsaida	
			Healing of crippled woman on sabbath
5. On the road from Caesarea Philippi towards Jerusalem	Peter's confession of Jesus as 'Messiah'		
	First Passion prediction		
	Transfiguration		
	Healing of epileptic		
	Second Passion prediction		
	Payment of Temple tax		
	Teaching on true greatness		
			Jesus rejected by Samaritans
	Parable of lost sheep		
	Further teaching on the church and forgiveness		
			Parables of good Samaritan and rich fool
			Mary and Martha
			Warnings against Herod Antipas
	Parable of great banquet		Parable of great banquet
			Parables of lost sheep/ coins and prodigal son; unjust steward and rich man with Lazarus; widow and unjust judge; Pharisee and publican. Cleansing of ten lepers.
6. Approaching Jericho	Teaching on divorce and celibacy		
	Blessing of young children		
	Debate with rich young ruler		
	Teaching on the rewards of discipleship		
	Parable of the labourers in the vineyard		
	Third Passion prediction		
	James and John ask a favour		James and John ask a favour
	Healing of Bartimaeus		
			Jesus visits Zacchaeus in Jericho
	Parable of the pounds		Parable of the pounds

Matthew

Matthew has always been listed as the first Gospel. It provides the most comprehensive account of Jesus' teaching, as well as emphasizing Jesus' fulfilment of the Old Testament. Thus it works well as the opening book of the New Testament, linking its story with what has gone before.

However, this gives to it some qualities that not everyone appreciates initially. Matthew's desire to fit in so much material means his account is quite dense, making it seem matter of fact. Then again, his emphasis on Jesus' Jewish context can seem alien. For example, many readers have been put off by his opening genealogy. For Matthew, this was vital, because Jesus was the divine fulfilment of the promises to Abraham; to us, however, it can seem slightly bizarre.

The Church of the Beatitudes built in 1938 on the traditional site of the Sermon on the Mount (Matthew 5–7), overlooking the Sea of Galilee.

Matthew (chapters)	Setting	Topic
5–7	Calling people to follow his new teaching	The blessings of discipleship in Jesus' kingdom
10	Instructing his apostles	Mission into his world
13	Teaching the crowds in parables	The nature of the kingdom
18	Instructing those joining the Messiah's new community	Living in the Messiah's community (the church)
23–25	Challenging Israel and its leaders	Judgment and division at the 'end of the age'

Many people therefore turn first to Mark's Gospel, which is almost half the length and which immediately arrests the reader with the dynamic ministry of the adult Jesus. That may be a good idea too for readers of this *Guide* (see pp. 198–202; see also pp. 188–89 for a summary of Jesus' adult ministry). For if we read Mark first, this will help us appreciate Matthew all the more. Almost certainly what Matthew did was to use Mark's account as the 'template' for his own writing (see p. 187); so when we note what Matthew has added to Mark's account, we can detect his own particular emphases.

Jesus the authoritative teacher

The most striking contrast between Matthew and Mark is the difference in the amount of Jesus' teaching. Strangely, Mark includes very little of Jesus' teaching, giving only two of his sixteen chapters to it. By contrast, Matthew devotes nine of his twenty-eight chapters to recording Jesus' words without interruption. These are compiled into five 'discourses' (see table above), which punctuate the narrative at regular intervals.

Immediately we see Matthew's concerns. The central point (placed appropriately in the *middle* discourse) is that Jesus has come to introduce God's kingdom. This requires a response – especially from Jesus' own people, Israel; they need to learn how to be his disciples, living as a new community focused on Jesus, and going out to others with this important message. Matthew is anxious that we do not lose Jesus' teaching on all these vital matters – hence his neat and tidy scheme, easily accessible for Jesus' future followers.

What is remarkable in all this teaching is Jesus' authority – seen both in its style and its content. Apart from chapters 13 and 25, most of these chapters are *not* in the form of extended parables (common in Luke); rather, they more often have the form of direct commands. Jesus is assuming a commander's authority and expects to be obeyed (see box, right).

The Sermon on the Mount

'Blessed are the poor in spirit, for theirs is the kingdom of heaven.'
Matthew 5:3

Despite taking less than twenty minutes to read out aloud, this is the most famous sermon of all time. Clearly Matthew has given a condensed summary of Jesus' teaching – delivered at much greater length and perhaps on numerous occasions. Yet in it we see what made Jesus' teaching so distinctive: his vivid images from everyday life and his challenges to conventional teaching.

In the opening 'blessings' (or 'Beatitudes') Jesus outlines the upside-down nature of his kingdom, which stands in marked contrast to the world's ways. The rest of the sermon then elaborates on what it means to live in this new kingdom: a deep obedience to the spirit, not just the letter, of the Law; a sincerity in one's religious practice; a single-minded trust in God's provision; a refusal to judge others but a commitment to love one's enemies.

Throughout, Jesus assumes an incredible authority, giving many direct commands ('do not judge', 'do not store up') and quoting from the Ten Commandments first delivered on Mount Sinai: 'You have heard that it was said, "You shall not commit adultery." *But I tell you…*' Here Jesus invites comparison between himself and Moses – and indeed with God himself. Jesus also expects that, just as at Sinai, so his own words should be obeyed. For he will welcome not those who merely call him Lord, but those who '*do* the will of my Father'. Failure here will be as disastrous as building one's house on sand!

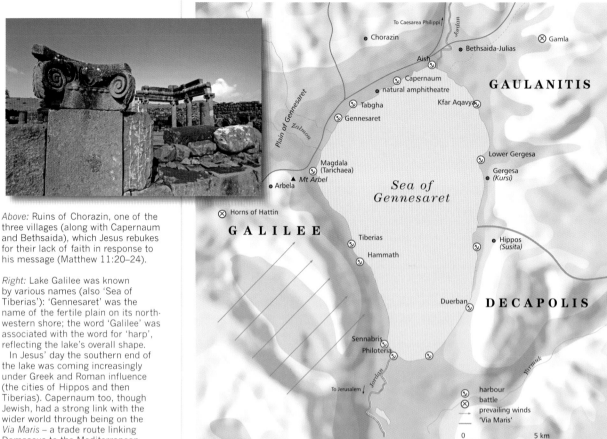

Above: Ruins of Chorazin, one of the three villages (along with Capernaum and Bethsaida), which Jesus rebukes for their lack of faith in response to his message (Matthew 11:20–24).

Right: Lake Galilee was known by various names (also 'Sea of Tiberias'): 'Gennesaret' was the name of the fertile plain on its north-western shore; the word 'Galilee' was associated with the word for 'harp', reflecting the lake's overall shape.

In Jesus' day the southern end of the lake was coming increasingly under Greek and Roman influence (the cities of Hippos and then Tiberias). Capernaum too, though Jewish, had a strong link with the wider world through being on the *Via Maris* – a trade route linking Damascus to the Mediterranean.

Jesus' first disciples, being fishermen, would have spoken Aramaic but also some Greek (for their business transactions). The lake was protected on most sides by high mountains, but when the prevailing winds changed and came down one of the valleys, storms could develop rapidly.

Map labels:
To Caesarea Philippi · Chorazin · Gamla · Bethsaida-Julias · Aish · Capernaum · natural amphitheatre · GAULANITIS · Tabgha · Kfar Aqavya · Gennesaret · Plain of Gennesaret · Zalmon · Lower Gergesa · Gergesa (Kursi) · Magdala (Tarichaea) · Mt Arbel · Sea of Gennesaret · Arbela · Horns of Hattin · GALILEE · Tiberias · Hippos (Susita) · Hammath · Duerban · DECAPOLIS · Sennabris · Philoteria · Yarmuk · To Jerusalem · Jordan · harbour · battle · prevailing winds · 'Via Maris'

Lake Galilee in the 1st century

0 — 5 km
0 — 5 miles

'If anyone will not welcome you or listen to your words… it will be more bearable for Sodom and Gomorrah on the day of judgment than for that town.'
Matthew 10:14–15

Often there is also a solemn note of judgment. Jesus will say to those who disobey him: 'I never knew you. Away from me, you evildoers!' 'As the weeds are pulled up and burned in the fire, so it will be at the end of the age.' 'When the Son of Man comes, [the king] will reply, "Truly I tell you, whatever you did not do for one of the least of these, you did not do for me. Then they will go away to eternal punishment, but the righteous to eternal life."'

Those are the last words of the final discourse. This note of judgment has been steadily increasing and perhaps is seen most pointedly in chapter 23, when Jesus pronounces seven woes against the religious leaders. Matthew's portrait is stark, presenting us with an awesome figure. Yet this is the same Jesus who equally speaks words of comfort: 'Come to me, all you who are weary and burdened, and I will give you rest… for I am gentle and humble in heart.' So, if the final discourse begins with seven woes, we should not forget that the first discourse begins with eight blessings (see p. 191).

Jesus' identity: Moses, Israel, Son of God…

So Jesus' teaching is powerful in itself. Yet Matthew also uses it to build up his presentation of Jesus' unique character. His tidy structure, focused on five discourses, was presumably intended to remind his readers of the five books of Moses (Genesis to Deuteronomy). So a comparison is being invited between Moses and Jesus. If Moses was revered as a major prophet, as the great Law-giver, and as the one who gathered Israel together as a people, this is now true of Jesus – only more so.

Intriguingly Matthew sees this parallel with Moses even in the pattern of their lives. Jesus, like Moses, is born under a repressive regime that tries to kill him (the 'massacre of the innocents' in Bethlehem); and Jesus goes down to Egypt. Then, later, his ministry follows a geographical pattern (being baptized in a river, fasting in a desert for forty days, and going up a mountain to reveal God's laws) that bears an uncanny resemblance to the story of Moses and the Israelites (see p. 62). Matthew is hinting to his Jewish readers that their foundation story is being repeated. Jesus is the new Moses – even a new Israel.

This last suggestion – that Jesus is a new Israel – may seem strange. Yet there is a clear sense in Matthew that, where Israel had failed God (for example in the desert), Jesus instead obeyed God: he was the one faithful Israelite. Moreover, Israel's kings (like David) were assumed somehow to embody the corporate identity of the whole nation; thus, when the Messiah came, he too would carry the destiny of *all Israel* upon his shoulders. This, then, may well be what Matthew is conveying when he presents Jesus as Israel's true king: the magi (or 'wise men') come looking for the 'newborn *king* of the Jews'; much later Jesus is hailed repeatedly as the 'Son of David'; and Jesus' parables often refer to a 'king' – probably a reference to Jesus himself. Jesus is the true king, says Matthew, in whom Israel finds her true destiny.

Yet even these great titles are not sufficient. In the Old Testament Israel's king was sometimes referred to as a 'son of God' (in a metaphorical sense). For Matthew, however, Jesus is the 'Son of God' in a much deeper sense. Indeed for Matthew Jesus is 'God with us' – the active presence of God on earth. That was a phrase (in Hebrew, 'Emmanuel') coined by Isaiah in a prophecy predicting a child's birth. Matthew now sees this fulfilled – not metaphorically, but literally – in the birth of Jesus.

So Matthew presents us with a story of *God himself* coming to visit his people in the person of his Son. And Jesus himself will use this language of divine presence: 'For where two or three come together in my name, there *I am with them*' (my italics). And it is there in his final words: '*I am with you* always.'

All this means, quite remarkably, that Jesus can legitimately be worshipped. Old Testament faith had been built on the solid rock of monotheism: 'Worship the Lord your God and serve him only' (words which Jesus himself quotes during his temptation in the desert). Yet now Matthew shows us how the magi were quite correct to 'worship' the infant Jesus; so too were the disciples when Jesus walked to them on the water; so too were those gathered on the mountain in Galilee as they approached the risen Christ. Despite his Jewish background Matthew teaches that Jesus is to be worshipped. He is not just an authoritative teacher, nor just a new Moses figure; he is also the divine Son of God. Israel's God, the Lord of Sinai, has truly come among his people – 'God with us'.

'You are in error because you do not know the Scriptures or the power of God.'
Matthew 22:29

The moment of fulfilment

If so, then the coming of Jesus was inevitably the most important moment in Israel's history. Other Gospel writers would consider the implications of Jesus for Gentiles and indeed for all human history; but Matthew's prime concern – especially if writing in the aftermath of Jerusalem's tragic destruction (see p. 185) – is with his own people. Matthew thus passionately desires his fellow Jews to see Jesus *as the fulfilment of their own story*: that's why he repeatedly describes things as happening 'to fulfil the prophets'. It is also why his Gospel contains so many warnings. For Jesus had been warning that this was Israel's most critical hour: 'even now', John the Baptist had warned, 'the axe of God's judgment is poised'. This was, as it were, the nation's eleventh hour.

So, once in Jerusalem, Jesus warns the city's leaders of the judgment that is coming and of the forthcoming destruction of the Temple (see box below). He also portrays Israel's God (in his parable of the vineyard) as sending numerous prophets to his people, but they continuously reject them. Last of all the vineyard owner sent his son, but he too is murdered. Although this parable is found in Mark too, Matthew

Jesus' teaching in the Temple

Matthew's final block of teaching summarizes what Jesus said a few days before his death: not only his 'apocalyptic discourse' (see p. 200), but also his sharp words against Jerusalem's religious leaders (the scribes and the Pharisees).

In seven 'woes' he refers to them as 'hypocrites', 'blind guides', 'whitewashed tombs' and a 'brood of vipers'. He castigates them for performing for show: they 'do not practise what they preach'; they 'put heavy loads on people and will not lift a finger to move them'; they 'neglect the more important matters of the law – justice, mercy and faithfulness'. So he predicts, not only that they will persecute his own followers in the future, but also that God's wrath will fall upon 'this generation': Jerusalem's Temple (her 'house') will be 'left desolate'.

These chilling words, showing Jesus' severe opposition to empty religion, also reveal Jesus as a prophet (like Jeremiah), called to warn his own nation of Jerusalem's imminent demise.

If Matthew himself had been persecuted and had witnessed the Temple's destruction in AD 70 (see p. 185), he would have been painfully aware of the truth of Jesus' predictions. He may also have sensed that Jesus, in then walking away from the Temple, was dramatically symbolizing the departure of God's true presence from the sanctuary. So, fittingly, the next two chapters will describe Jesus' further predictions of the Temple's forthcoming destruction, warning people to prepare not so much for that day, but rather for the judgment day of the 'Son of Man'.

recounts Jesus' chilling conclusion, outlining how the vineyard would be given to other tenants: 'the kingdom of God will be… given to a people who will produce its fruit'. Matthew would have seen this as Jesus' solemn prediction that the historic people of Israel would no longer be uniquely 'God's own'; instead God was allowing the Gentiles to join his people.

Matthew's Gospel, despite its strongly Jewish tone, thus turns out to be a Gospel that opens the door far and wide to those outside Israel. If Jesus came for the 'lost sheep of Israel', this was not the end of the story. Instead the pagan magi were a foretaste of people from every nation coming to worship Jesus. And, at the very end, after Jesus' death and resurrection, Jesus explicitly tells his disciples to go out to '*all* nations' with the news of his authoritative rule.

This, then, is a Gospel that is ultimately inclusive. Initially its focus on Israel may seem off-putting; but, if one perseveres, one reaches the deeper truth that *Jesus' mission was through Israel to the whole world*. From now on anyone responding to

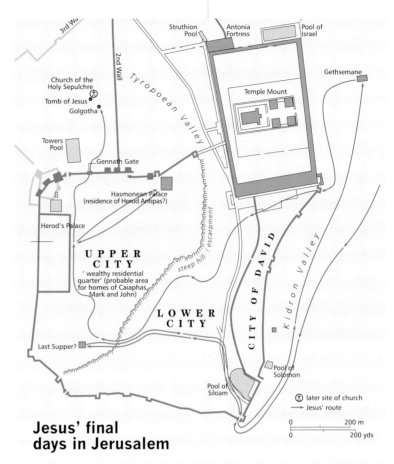

Jesus' final days in Jerusalem

Jesus' teaching could know that they were truly included in God's new people – the community focused on Jesus the Messiah. Yet Matthew's note of warning remains. This is a privilege not to be abused. If God through Jesus warned his people Israel so strongly, the same warning now applies to those claiming to be Jesus' followers.

Thus Matthew's strong teaching has proved to be vital for Jesus' followers ever since. Though a 'tough medicine', it has provided a solid rock on which to build. After all, as Jesus warned, it's no use building on sand.

JESUS' LAST DAYS IN JERUSALEM

Few episodes have been studied in such great detail as Jesus' last week in Jerusalem. All of the Gospel writers slow down their narratives, giving us an unrushed opportunity to sense the significance of those critical days.

The table opposite gives an overview of the various events, as presented in the three synoptic Gospels (see also p. 195 for some detailed maps; see also my book *The Weekend that Changed the World* for a detailed reconstruction).

John's Gospel has a slightly different focus (see further p. 209). In sum, John omits items 2 and 3 and instead gives an extended focus to item 5 (with *five* whole chapters, John 13–17, being devoted to Jesus' Last Supper and his walking to Gethsemane). Thereafter, his account of the events from Gethsemane to the empty tomb (items 6–11; the so-called 'passion narrative') follows the same sequence as the synoptics; yet, once again, John adds a fresh and distinctive perspective:

- we see the soldiers falling back to the ground when they try to arrest Jesus;

- Jesus is interrogated not just by the high priest (Caiaphas) but also by Annas (Caiaphas's father-in-law);

- Pilate and Jesus discuss the nature of Jesus' kingdom;

- on the cross Jesus attends to the distress of his mother, Mary, and then, just before his death, cries out triumphantly, 'It is finished!';

- events at the tomb are told at greater length, with the activity of certain individuals (such as Nicodemus, Mary Magdalene, Peter and John himself) being described in particular detail.

John's account is very vivid and may include his own personal eyewitness memories of that fateful weekend. If John is to be identified with the 'disciple whom Jesus loved' (see pp. 185 and 216), then this disciple was himself present both in the high priest's courtyard (during Jesus' trial) and at the crucifixion (taking care of Jesus' mother, Mary).

The fact that we have four parallel accounts has given rise to lots of questions: how can we receive them as historical if their versions are slightly different, or perhaps retold in a different order? Yet we may at this point be imposing our own modern categories in a way that is unfair. After all, modern eyewitnesses at road accidents can often recall things in slightly different ways; but we do not deduce that because of this the accident never occurred! In fact, slight variances can assure us there has been no collusion. So too with the Gospels. Their slight variances should not be taken as a sign of historical inaccuracy but rather as the legitimate (and indeed desirable) variation to be expected from people describing authentic historical events but from slightly different standpoints.

	Matthew	Mark	Luke
1. From the Mount of Olives	'Triumphal entry' into Jerusalem (Palm Sunday)		Jesus weeps over the city
2. In the Temple	Overturning of the money changers' tables		
	Cursing of the fig tree		
	Teaching in the Temple: i. Questions about Jesus' authority		
	ii. The wedding banquet		
	iii. Further questions: about taxes, resurrection, the Messiah, the greatest commandment		
	iv. The widow's offering		
	v. Seven 'woes' against the scribes and Pharisees		
3. Overlooking the Temple	The apocalyptic discourse		
	Further parables about the 'end of the age'		
4. Bethany (on eastern slopes of Mount of Olives)	Anointing of Jesus 'for burial' by an unnamed woman (Mary Magdalene?)		
5. Within the city	Jesus' Last Supper with his disciples		
	Predictions of Peter's denial		
6. Gethsemane (on lower slopes of Mount of Olives, above Kidron Valley)	Jesus' hour of agony (wrestling in prayer)		
	Jesus' arrest by soldiers, guided by Judas Iscariot		
7. Back within the city	Interrogation before various religious authorities		
	Peter's denial of Jesus		
8. Outside the city	Judas hangs himself		
9. Governor's palace	Interrogation before Pontius Pilate		
	Mockery of soldiers		
			Jesus before Herod Antipas
10. 'Golgotha', outside the walls (the 'place of the skull')	Jesus' crucifixion between two bandits		
	Death and burial in nearby tomb		
	Guards at the tomb		
11. The empty tomb	Jesus' resurrection		
	Women's early morning visit to the tomb		
	Report of the guards		
	Further appearances of the risen Christ		

Mark

Mark's Gospel was probably the first Gospel to be completed. It is by far the shortest and is resolutely focused on the task in hand: to present the claims of Jesus as Messiah and to urge people to respond by becoming his followers (or disciples). The text starts at a lightning pace, with events happening immediately after one another; and yet, once this dynamic tempo has been established, Mark can pause on individual episodes in Jesus' life, as he takes us close up to see Jesus conducting his healing ministry and relating to his disciples.

Mark has thus been deliberately selective, giving us just the bare essentials. And, in drawing us close to Jesus, Mark may be reflecting the influence of Peter (Jesus' leading disciple). For the detail in some stories (for example, Jesus' turning around to face *all* the disciples at the moment when he is rebuking *Peter*) reflects the keen memory of someone very close to the action. Meanwhile John Mark (the author: see p. 184) may also himself have been an eyewitness at one point; for the reference to a 'young man' (or teenager) who ran away naked when Jesus was arrested in Gethsemane may well be John Mark's own signature – as if to say, 'I too was there, though I had little idea at the time what was going on!'

This, then, is a text that is very personal, highly coloured, deeply moving, passionate and urgent. This urgency stems from the author's conviction about the sheer importance of Jesus. Yet it may also stem from his own context – probably writing amid persecution in Nero's Rome. Thus the Gospel's second half emphasizes Jesus' own sufferings and encourages his followers to be ready to 'take up their cross'. At one point Jesus expressly warns that they can expect 'persecutions'. And many wonder whether the Gospel's abrupt ending (it stops in mid-sentence) might be because Mark was prevented from finishing it – perhaps being arrested on Nero's orders. So we should read this text with deep respect – as perhaps the last words of someone passing on the message of Jesus, a message for which he may have been about to pay the ultimate price.

Who is this Jesus? (1:1 – 8:30)

The first half of the Gospel concentrates on the identity and *person* of Jesus. Jesus is on 'stage' throughout the narrative (except in two passages about John the Baptist). So we see him involved in numerous encounters, all of which raise the pressing question: who exactly *is* this Jesus? Even before he comes on stage we have been led to expect the arrival, as prophesied in the Old Testament, of the 'Lord'. Then, at his baptism, God's voice declares: 'You are my Son, whom I love'. Once back in Capernaum there is a forty-eight-hour period in which people see his authoritative teaching, his power over evil spirits and his capacity to heal. Later he heals a paralytic, but provocatively states that this shows how the man's sins have been forgiven. This causes the religious leaders to accuse him of blasphemy – after all, 'who can forgive sins but *God*?' It is a fair question, which Mark's readers are intended to start asking too.

Jesus proceeds to present himself as a friend of sinners and yet also as the 'Lord over the sabbath'. Next he interrupts a terrifying storm on Lake Galilee, causing a sudden, eerie calm. Then he encounters a deranged man (living among the tombs) and restores him to a sound mind. Finally he returns to Capernaum to find that the synagogue ruler's daughter has died: he enters her room and restores her to life. It is as though Mark sees humanity being attacked by four great enemies (disease, demons, disaster and death), but Jesus has defeated each one in turn: he is the victor, the champion!

All this presses towards a climax in chapter 8. After a sensational feeding of large crowds on meagre rations (first among 5,000 Jewish people, repeated later among 4,000 people in Gentile territory), Jesus takes his twelve chosen disciples to the regions of Caesarea Philippi. There he asks them: 'Who do *you* say I am?' Peter finds himself blurting out: 'You are the Messiah!' He senses that Jesus is the long-awaited king. Jesus has been announcing the arrival of the kingdom of God, precisely because he himself is the king!

Mark wants his readers to think the same. In the categories Jesus lays out in his parable of the soils, Mark wants us to be like the good soil, responding to God's word with faith. So, having followed Jesus thus far, we too are invited to answer Jesus' question: 'Who do *you* say I am?'

The so-called 'Jesus Boat' gives a good idea of fishing vessels in the first century; it was discovered in low water near the north-western shore in 1986.

'Prepare the way for the Lord…!'
Mark 1:3, quoting Isaiah 40:3

'Jesus went into Galilee, proclaiming the good news of God: "The time has come… The kingdom of God has come near. Repent and believe the good news!"'
Mark 1:14–15

'I have not come to call the righteous, but sinners.'
Mark 2:17

Opposite: Vineyard above Capernaum, looking across the lake towards what Mark calls 'the other side' (the hills of Gaulanitis).

The 'apocalyptic discourse'

As Jesus walks from the Temple, his disciples comment admiringly on its 'massive stones', but Jesus warns them: 'not one stone will be left upon another'. Later, seated on the Mount of Olives, Jesus then reveals more of this dramatic future. This is often called the 'apocalyptic discourse' because it is indeed a 'revelation' or 'unveiling' of God's future purposes (see pp. 156 and 288).

Yet what is being revealed? Jesus predicts various events (such as the emergence of false messiahs, the setting up in the Temple of the so-called 'abomination of desolation'). These events are advance warnings of the Temple's imminent destruction – hence Jesus' advice, 'When you see [these things], flee to the mountains.' Yet the focus then shifts from the Temple's destruction to the 'day of the Son of Man' when he 'comes with power and glory' – words which seemingly refer to Christ's 'return': see p. 262).

Possibly these are two ways of saying the same thing: the Temple's destruction would confirm Jesus as a true prophet, and he would thus come into God's presence publicly vindicated (see Daniel chapter 7 for this sense of 'coming': p. 156). However, Jesus may have deliberately glided from one key event to the other, seeing God's judgment on the Temple (which marked the end of the disciples' known world) as a foretaste of that day when God would judge all people (marking the *ultimate* end of the whole world). One would occur in 'this generation', the other at a time unknown – even to Jesus. Either way, the key response was to 'be alert and keep watch!'

What did he come to do? (8:31 – 16:9)

Yet there is also the question of this Messiah's destiny and *purpose*. Here we are in for a few surprises. Peter is still thinking in nationalistic terms: he wants a Messiah to liberate Israel from the Romans. Jesus, however, begins immediately to redefine messiahship, predicting his own imminent suffering in Jerusalem. At this, Peter takes Jesus aside and rebukes him. But Jesus turns round and instead publicly rebukes Peter: 'Get behind me, Satan!'

Jesus wants his disciples to be clear: *this* Messiah 'must suffer, be killed and after three days rise again'. Three times over the coming weeks he makes this prediction of his cross and resurrection, but the disciples do not understand. Surely, if Jesus is the Messiah (or the 'Son of Man', as he prefers to describe himself), then both these expected persons are going to be *glorious* figures – not suffering a humiliating death? Yet Jesus insists that these titles must be merged with the prophesied figure of the 'suffering servant' found in Isaiah (see p. 133): 'the Son of Man came to *serve*, and to give his life as a ransom for many.'

Mark's readers therefore find themselves travelling with Jesus' disciples on the road up to Jerusalem and puzzling over this strange teaching. We see James and John still hoping for a political kingdom,

After arriving in Jerusalem Jesus curses a fig tree for not having any fruit on it (despite its not being the season for fruit) and then enters the Temple (Mark 11:1–19); almost certainly this was meant as a dramatic symbol of his judgment upon the Temple – which he saw as similarly 'fruitless'.

proudly wanting special seats when Jesus is crowned king, and hear Jesus' chilling correction. We enter Jerusalem and hear the excited crowds proclaiming that the 'kingdom of our father David is coming!', but sense that they too are in for something of a shock. The next day Jesus dramatically removes the traders from the Temple courts and then uses the Temple for some further teaching; yet the religious leaders are irked by his seeming authority. And in his own parables he hints that they are going to turn against him and kill him. Soon, then, we see Jesus being anointed by a woman in Bethany in an act of intuitive devotion and hear Jesus thanking her for 'preparing his body for burial'. Jesus knows his Jerusalem ministry will end in his death – so too does the unnamed woman – and a sense of the inevitable begins to descend on the drama.

So begins the passion narrative (see p. 196). Mark's version is told slowly and at length. It particularly highlights the story of Peter denying Jesus (perhaps recorded for posterity at Peter's express request); he also emphasizes the darkness that Jesus went through as he hung on the cross ('My God, why have you forsaken me?').

It is also told with great irony. Those mocking Jesus as he dies chide him with having spoken of 'destroying the Temple' and rebuilding it 'in three days'. Jesus had indeed predicted the Temple's destruction, but the 'three days' recalls instead his predictions about his resurrection. If Jesus' prophecies were correct, then *he* was the true Temple, the true presence of God; and his death was the sacrifice through which people might find forgiveness. Not coincidentally, then, the curtain, which screened off the Temple's Most Holy Place, is torn in two at the moment of Jesus' death: the way into God's presence has now been opened, says Mark, by the one dying outside the city wall.

Those gathered around the cross also mock him as the supposed 'Messiah, the king of Israel, who cannot even save himself'. Mark's readers sense that, however, Jesus might well be Israel's Messiah. Yes, he may only have been crowned with a crown of thorns and called the 'king of the Jews' by Pilate in a mocking tone; yet he is actually 'saving' other people in the very act in which he refuses to save himself! So we are grateful that a Roman centurion, unlike the religious leaders, voices the strange idea that is forming in our own minds: 'Surely this man was the Son of God!'

In some ways this confession of Jesus' true identity by a Gentile (even if truer than he himself knew) is the Gospel's climax. (It would certainly have resonated deeply if Mark's first audience were themselves suffering persecution at the hands of such Roman soldiers in Nero's Rome.) Yet for Mark the ultimate climax is Jesus' resurrection: this Messiah, as predicted, was indeed raised by God 'on the third day'. The resurrection means Jesus may well have been more than just a Messiah (after all, the Gospel's opening verses had portrayed him as God's 'Son' and as the 'Lord' himself). It also means that the powerful champion,

Disciples in Mark

Mark's Gospel particularly concentrates on Jesus' interactions with his disciples. We do not hear much of Jesus' teaching to the crowds, but rather his private discussions with his immediate followers.

In this the disciples are portrayed with great honesty. We see them responding to Jesus' initial call, but then being full of doubts and fears. We see them not knowing how to answer Jesus' various questions. On the road up to Jerusalem they argue among themselves and vie for positions of honour; and, once in Jerusalem, their leader, Peter, blatantly denies knowing Jesus, and the rest of them flee from Gethsemane – deserting Jesus to his fate. Moreover, because Mark's Gospel ends so abruptly, we never see them (as in the other Gospels) coming to faith in the resurrection or being 'restored' by Jesus to preach in his name.

This honest account may reflect Peter's first-hand memory – with Peter giving Mark permission to recount the story warts and all. Yet it also helps Mark's readers to feel part of the story: they often identify with the disciples, sharing their doubts and questions, and then find themselves being moved forward on a journey.

This gives particular power to Jesus' words in chapter 8 when he calls those who have confessed him as Messiah now to travel with him up to Jerusalem and 'take up their cross'. Mark's readers find themselves being challenged – like Jesus' first disciples 'on the road' – to ask what it might cost them to follow this Jesus.

'Trembling and bewildered, the women... fled from the tomb. They said nothing to anyone, because they were afraid' (Mark 16:8). Mark's Gospel, itself written amid fear of persecution, ends on a sudden, slightly fearful, note – but one bathed with hope in Jesus' victory over the grave.

'Whoever wants to be my disciple must deny themselves and take up their cross and follow me. For whoever wants to save their life will lose it, but whoever loses their life for me and for the gospel will save it. What good is it for you to gain the whole world, yet forfeit your soul?'
Mark 8:34–36

seen earlier in the Gospel, has conquered death and trampled on humanity's greatest enemy – a massive encouragement to those who now 'take up their cross', perhaps even 'losing their lives for his sake'.

So, although Mark's account is rudely interrupted at this point, his message is plain. This Jesus, Mark affirms, is the Messiah, the Suffering Servant who died for his people. And Mark's readers are invited to heed this truth and, if convinced, to join his disciples, learning 'on the road', and following him through death to their own ultimate resurrection.

Luke

Luke's Gospel has its own distinctive feel. Luke's Jesus is attractively human, the one who welcomes ordinary people to be his friends; and his whole purpose is 'to seek and to save that which is lost'.

There are several possible reasons for this. Luke himself was a Gentile who had probably been a 'God-fearer' (attending synagogue worship as a 'fringe member'); hence his interest in Jesus' welcome to those on the margins: for he himself had been brought inside by this Jesus.

Luke may also have had distinctive sources. Only Luke names women who travelled with the male disciples throughout Jesus' Galilean ministry. If Luke researched his Gospel while in Palestine in the late AD 50s (see p. 185), he may well have met some of these (now elderly) women and so heard *their* unique perspectives. Certainly his account of Jesus' birth seems to be told from the perspective of Mary (whereas Matthew's adopts the perspective of Joseph).

Moreover, Luke has included a whole collection of Jesus' teaching which he inserts once Jesus has set out on the road to Jerusalem (the so-called 'travel narrative': chapters 9–19). This section contains

(see p. 185)

Key chapters in Luke

Jesus' birth and childhood
(chapters 1–2)

Jesus' preaching in Nazareth
(chapter 4)

Parable of the 'prodigal son'
(chapter 15)

Jesus weeps over Jerusalem
(chapter 19)

The risen Jesus on the road to Emmaus
(chapter 24)

View north-westwards towards the hills behind Tabgha (centre) and Capernaum (off to the right), with the Church of the Beatitudes visible amidst the trees.

nearly twenty parables, some told at considerable length (for example, the parables of the good Samaritan and the prodigal son). In these Jesus describes characters in remarkable detail, hinting at their fears and emotions. This then gives Luke's Gospel a very human feel and contributes to a portrait of Jesus himself which is deeply human and personally engaging.

Finally, Luke himself was a doctor (Colossians 4:14), so his medical background will have brought him into contact with human beings at their most vulnerable. As a result his account comes across as deeply empathetic. He is very aware of human needs, both physical and emotional – perhaps being, in modern terms, both a physician and a psychologist.

Luke's Jesus: the forgiving Saviour

> *I bring you good news of great joy that will be for all the people. Today in the town of David a Saviour has been born to you: he is the Messiah, the Lord.*

The angel's word to the Bethlehem shepherds, Luke 2:10–11

Luke emphasizes that his message is 'good news': Christ has come to bring salvation to all. In the rest of his narrative the words 'saviour' and 'salvation' will be used frequently; and in the final chapter they are clearly defined as referring expressly to the 'forgiveness of sins'. So Luke's Gospel is all about forgiveness – God's pardon given to those who repent of their sins:

- John the Baptist calls people to repent; and Jesus warns that people will perish 'unless [they] repent'.

- Simon Peter, when first meeting Jesus, is conscious that he is a

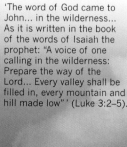

'The word of God came to John... in the wilderness... As it is written in the book of the words of Isaiah the prophet: "A voice of one calling in the wilderness: Prepare the way of the Lord... Every valley shall be filled in, every mountain and hill made low" ' (Luke 3:2–5).

'sinful man'; a woman (probably Mary Magdalene), who anoints Jesus' feet with oil, is told that 'her many sins have been forgiven'.

- Jesus declares that 'there will be more rejoicing in heaven over one sinner who repents'; and, in a parable which contrasts a self-congratulatory Pharisee with a repentant tax-collector, he teaches that the latter went home 'justified before God'.

- And, on his cross, Jesus prays: 'Father, forgive them…'

Luke wants his readers to find in Jesus forgiveness from God. Like the prodigal son, they may be in a 'far country', but if they will return to their father, they can be assured of a warm homecoming. God, says Luke, is a welcoming God who, in Jesus, is seeking those who are lost.

Yet they must return. There is an urgency about this offer. Hence on several occasions Jesus uses the word 'today': *Today* salvation has come to this house'; '*Today* you will be with me in paradise.' These last words, addressed by Jesus to a thief being crucified beside him, epitomize Luke's portrait of Jesus: a helpless, dying thief is offered the gift of forgiveness and eternal life.

God's heart for all people

That episode also makes clear that this forgiveness is available for *all* people – even to an undeserving outcast about to die. Luke's Gospel is remarkable, in this sense, for its universality. In this kingdom of Jesus there are none of the normal divisions created by human beings to exclude others – whether those of wealth, gender or race.

As for wealth, Jesus' parables show how useless it is in God's sight: a rich fool 'stores up things' but dies suddenly because he is 'not rich towards God'; a rich man, experiencing the torment of hell after his death, begs in vain for help from a poor man called Lazarus (whom in life he had dismissed from his care). Jesus expressly pronounces a woe on the rich but a blessing on the poor. His own ministry ensures that the 'poor have the good news preached to them'; and he challenges his hosts to invite the poor to share in their feasts. So the rich may miss out on God's forgiveness. Yet this need not be the case: Zacchaeus, a tax-collector who had become wealthy through dishonest means, gives away half his possessions to the poor and so experiences salvation through welcoming Jesus.

As for gender, Luke's Gospel is remarkably even-handed in its portrayal of men and women, and contains an intriguing series of 'doublets' (combining both a man and a woman):

- Before Jesus' birth there are two songs of praise: the 'Magnificat' (sung by Mary) and the 'Benedictus' (sung by Zechariah).

Jesus' many parables

One of the distinctive features of Jesus' teaching was his use of parables – pictures and stories taken from everyday life that were designed to illustrate the nature of God's kingdom. Mark's Gospel gives one sample occasion when Jesus spoke to the crowd from a boat a few yards from the shoreline, 'teaching them many things in parables'. We then hear a series of parables (a man sowing seed, a mustard seed growing rapidly, a lamp being placed on a stand) and are told: 'the kingdom of God is like this…'

Luke's Gospel then takes this much further, revealing some of Jesus' most famous stories: the good Samaritan, the rich fool, the great banquet, the lost sheep and coin, the prodigal son, the shrewd manager, the rich man and Lazarus, and the Pharisee and the tax-collector, etc. All these are found in Luke's central 'travel narrative' (Luke 9–19) as Jesus sets out from Galilee towards Jerusalem.

Jesus was not just establishing a good rapport with his audience, using images they would easily recognize. He was teasing them to think for themselves about God's way of working in the world. Moreover, many of the stories hooked in his audience in such a way that they would then be shocked by something unexpected – the appearance of a *Samaritan* who was *kind*! In this way Jesus revealed their false assumptions and forced them to engage seriously with the upside-down nature of his kingdom.

- When presented in the Temple, the infant Jesus is welcomed by two aged prophets, Simeon and Anna.

- Jesus warns people in Nazareth, using two biblical examples of godly Gentiles – the unnamed widow in Zarephath (visited by Elijah) and Naaman, the Syrian general (healed by Elisha).

- In Capernaum Jesus heals a servant in the household of a Roman centurion and also heals the son of a widow in nearby Nain. Two of his most controversial miracles include the healing of a paralysed man and a 'daughter of Abraham', previously crippled for eighteen years.

- Before the parable of the prodigal son, Jesus tells two other stories – about a shepherd losing his sheep, and about a woman losing a coin.

Jesus' kingdom is clearly open to men and women alike without distinction. If Luke indeed had interviewed some of the women involved in Jesus' ministry, he had discovered from them a remarkably inclusive Jesus. This Jesus evidently welcomed *everyone* – as seen so clearly when he rebuked his disciples for preventing children from coming to him: 'the kingdom of God belongs to such as these'.

As for race, Jesus was, of course, Jewish; yet his coming was also intended to bring blessing upon the Gentiles. Thus the prophet Simeon

Capernaum, where Jesus ministered for three years. The ancient synagogue dates from between the 2nd and 4th centuries AD. The octagonal building is on the foundations of a Byzantine church built over the house of Peter.

recognized that the infant Jesus was
bringing a 'salvation in the sight of
all people' which would be *both* for
'the glory of God's people, Israel'
and 'a light for revelation to the
Gentiles'. And Jesus himself, though
living within a predominantly Jewish
world, clearly welcomed those beyond
its borders – as seen in his positive
remarks about the Samaritans (the
Jews' historic enemies). So when
Jesus cast a Samaritan as the hero of
his parable, he was being deliberately
provocative. Luke knew Jesus'
audience would have gasped: for them
the idea of a *good* Samaritan was a
contradiction in terms! Jesus was
proving to be dramatically inclusive.

The Jewish story for the whole world

Undergirding Jesus' racial
inclusiveness there was for Luke a
deeper point: namely that Jesus'
coming was when Israel's God had
fulfilled his long-standing plan *to
bless the whole world*. Both Mary
and Zechariah (in their songs before
Jesus' birth) refer to the promises
which Israel's God made to Abraham
– the one whose very name meant
'father of *many* nations'. Luke,
himself a Gentile, seems to have
understood well the Old Testament
teaching that, when Israel's God
fulfilled his promises to Abraham, that
would be the time when 'all peoples on earth will be blessed' (Genesis
12:3). Simeon's prophecy had made just that point.

   In his opening chapters Luke therefore deliberately takes his Gentile
readers back into the *Jewish* world – the place where hopes were
nourished of the Messiah who would 'sit on David's throne' and 'redeem
his people'. He knew that in these distinctively Jewish hopes – and only
there – lay the hope for the blessing of the world. So, if Jesus really was
this Messiah, then all Luke's readers – regardless of racial background –
could be blessed through him. And, when any Gentiles came to believe

*The Return of the Prodigal
Son,* by Rembrandt van Rijn
(1606–69).

Jerusalem's destruction by the Romans, predicted by Jesus at least four times in Luke, is graphically portrayed on the Arch of Titus in Rome: the seven-branched candlestick (the 'Menorah') is being carried into Rome for Titus' 'triumphal entry' into the imperial capital after his sacking of the Temple (AD 70).

'*Jerusalem, Jerusalem, you who kill the prophets and stone those sent to you, how often I have longed to gather your children together, as a hen gathers her chicks under her wings, and you were not willing. Look, your house is left to you desolate. I tell you, you will not see me again until you say, "Blessed is he who comes in the name of the Lord."*'

Luke 13:33–35

in this Jesus, they could be assured that their inclusion within God's kingdom was all 'according to God's plan'.

Luke sees Jesus' universal appeal: thus in the final chapter the risen Jesus sends out his disciples into 'all nations'. Yet there have been hints of this throughout the Gospel – not least when Luke traces Jesus' genealogy back to *Adam* (the head of the whole human race). Jesus, for Luke, is truly the new Adam, the truly human one, the 'Man for others', the one who includes every person within his reach.

Yet finally, Luke is also acutely aware that this universal message has come at a great cost to Israel as a nation. Simeon had predicted that Jesus' coming would be for the 'rising and falling of many within Israel'. Many within Israel would indeed reject their Messiah, and his coming would coincide with the destruction of their cherished Temple and national capital. So Luke highlights four of Jesus' prophecies against Jerusalem, and he makes Jesus' journey up to Jerusalem the defining moment in the city's history – the moment when it missed its true king. Matters thus come to a climax when Jesus looks across from the Mount of Olives at the time of his 'triumphal entry': Jesus weeps for Jerusalem because it 'does not know the things that belong to its peace', and does not recognize in *his* coming 'the hour of its visitation' by God.

Luke, then, cannot tell the good news about Jesus without noting the tragic story of Jerusalem. God has indeed visited his people, but it has beem a moment of both salvation and judgment. As the two people travelling to Emmaus (in Luke's final chapter) discover, God has indeed 'redeemed Israel', not in the expected political sense, but through the death and resurrection of her Messiah. So this final chapter focuses on the importance of Jesus' resurrection. *This* is the moment when God's great plan, for Israel and for the whole world, is put into effect. And all people are invited, in responding to the risen Christ, to find through him the pathway to God's long-intended salvation – the forgiveness of sins.

John

Jesus performed many other signs… which are not recorded in this book. But these are written that you may believe that Jesus is the Messiah, the Son of God, and that by believing you may have life in his name.

John 20:30–31

These words of John take us straight to the heart of John's purpose. John is not giving a comprehensive account (Jesus' complete biography), but a conscious selection – much of the material is not found in the synoptic Gospels, and might otherwise have been lost to posterity. And it has been selected with a purpose: that readers may come to believe (either for the first time, or now more deeply) in the unique identity of Jesus. This belief in Jesus, John is convinced, will then have a spiritual effect – bringing the reader to 'life'!

John's Gospel thus focuses on the person and identity of Jesus. It deliberately contains only a limited number of episodes, because John wants us to delve more deeply into the essential *inner reality* of who Jesus is. For example, in John we do not merely see Jesus feeding 5,000 people; we also hear him teaching that he *himself* is the 'bread of life'. This gives John's Gospel a profound depth. On the one hand, it is a remarkably vivid memory of Jesus' historic ministry; yet it is simultaneously also a profound meditation on all John *now* reckoned Jesus to be.

John's style is therefore marked by multiple layers of meaning. For example, when Jesus speaks of being 'lifted up', this refers primarily to his being 'lifted up' onto the cross; yet it also picks up the language of Isaiah, who had seen God's glory when God was 'high and lifted up'. The cross for John is thus the place of both shame and glory. Then again, John's consistent reference to Jesus' miracles as 'signs' encourages us to see beyond each miracle to that which it *sign*-ifies about Jesus' eternal identity. Thus in his first 'sign' Jesus may turn water into wine, but the deeper *significance* is that Jesus gives abundant, overflowing life.

As an original eyewitness, but now blessed with the gift of hindsight, John has developed some utterly unique lenses – which can see Jesus in at least three, if not four, dimensions. John wants us to put these lenses on and thus be enabled to see that which people, even during the ministry of Jesus, could easily have missed: Jesus' innermost identity as God's incarnate Son. He wants us to see the 'signs of his glory' – the episodes which, when pondered, reveal his true nature, eternal and divine.

Key chapters in John

Jesus turns water into wine
(chapter 2)

Jesus speaks to Nicodemus and a
Samaritan woman (chapters 4–5)

Kind words for a woman caught in
adultery (chapter 8)

Jesus raises Lazarus from the dead
(chapter 11)

Teaching in the 'upper room'
(chapters 13–17)

The risen Jesus by Lake Galilee
(chapter 21)

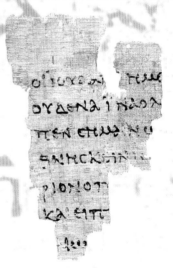

This tiny fragment, containing only 112 Greek letters (though on both sides), would have been part of a much larger book (or 'codex'). This is the earliest surviving New Testament manuscript (C. AD 125) and the text is from John 18:31–38 – thus confirming a first-century dating for the Fourth Gospel. It was discovered in Egypt in 1920.

The 'I AM sayings'

I AM the...
bread of life (chapter 6)

light of the world (chapter 8)

gate for the sheep (chapter 10)

good shepherd (chapter 10)

resurrection and the life (chapter 11)

way, truth, life (chapter 14)

true vine (chapter 15)

'Before Abraham was, I AM!'
(chapter 8)

Jesus' unique identity: the 'Son of God'

John thus wastes no time in revealing Jesus' true identity. In chapter 1 he immediately bombards us with a series of titles for Jesus (see the table below). This is no gradual voyage of discovery, but an immediate trumpet blast announcing the dramatic unveiling of Jesus' all-encompassing identity.

This is a mind-blowing package! Closely examining the titles in this table, we begin to sense that this Gospel will be making vast claims for Jesus. And, sure enough, most of these titles are then developed in more detail in the rest of the Gospel:

- We will see a man called Nicodemus recognizing Jesus as a 'teacher who has come from God'.

- We will see the crowds (after the feeding of the 5,000) proclaiming him as the expected 'Prophet', wanting to make him 'king', and then (when entering Jerusalem) hailing him as the 'king of Israel'. Later, Pontius Pilate will quiz Jesus about his kingdom and be told that it is 'not of this world'.

- We will hear Jesus referring to himself as the Son of Man – an exalted title for someone who reveals God's character and yet who will most truly be 'glorified' when he is 'lifted up' onto a Roman cross.

- We will see Jesus being crucified at the same time as the Passover lambs are being slaughtered in the Temple and hear Jesus speaking of his death in various ways: as a 'good shepherd' 'laying down his life' for his sheep (so they can find safety); or as a seed being planted (so that new life will eventually emerge).

The titles of Jesus referred to in John's opening chapter.

By the author in his prologue	By John the Baptist	By his disciples (on first meeting him)	By Jesus himself
The Word, identified with God			
An eternal being, involved in the creation of the world	The Lord (predicted by Isaiah)		
The source of all human life	The 'Lamb of God who takes away the sins of the world'	Rabbi/Teacher	
The true light that gives light to everyone	The one who comes to his own people and must be 'revealed to Israel'	Messiah	
The one able to make people God's 'children'		The one whom Moses and the prophets wrote about	The Son of Man
The one who became 'incarnate', as a human being	The one on whom the Spirit remains and who baptizes with the Holy Spirit	Jesus of Nazareth	
The only 'Son of the Father', full of 'glory'	The Son of God	The king of Israel	
The source of grace and truth			
The one who makes the invisible God known			

- We will see Jesus as the one who gives the Holy Spirit to his disciples and describes the Spirit in various ways: the Spirit is like 'living water' or a 'stream flowing from one's inmost being', or like a powerful but invisible wind; he is the 'Spirit of truth' who convicts the world of its sin, but dwells within believers and can lead them into 'all the truth'; he is a 'counsellor' who will be their guide and helper.

'In the beginning was the Word, and the Word was with God, and the Word was God… Through him all things were made… in him was life.'
John 1:1, 3–4

Yet there is one title for John that stands supreme: Jesus is the 'Son of God'. The other titles do not take us quite far enough. In particular, 'Messiah' could be quite confusing. Not only did it make little sense to non-Jews, but even for Jewish people Jesus was a Messiah in a surprisingly non-political sense. (Thus in John's Gospel Jesus only once explicitly claims to be the Messiah, when speaking privately to a woman in Samaria – not in Judea, where false messianic expectations were rife.) Moreover, 'Messiah' had never been a title for a *divine* figure (only for a *human* king, sent by God); but this was precisely how John wanted his readers to see Jesus – hence his more than a hundred references to Jesus as the 'Son of God' (or simply the 'Son').

To be sure, even *this* title had occasionally been used of ordinary human beings in the past (as a term of respect, for example, for the kings of Israel); but John had a clever way of making sure his readers knew he was using it of Jesus in a unique 'divine' sense. For, before using the term 'Son of God', he describes Jesus as the '*Word* of God' and makes it clear that this 'Word' is eternal and divine. He is neatly defining his terms, so that his readers will get the message: *this* 'Son of God' was divine; he had been eternally with God 'at the Father's side'; he had shared in the glory of Israel's God and, when he was on earth, this was the creator God, visiting the world *in person*.

Again, this is then explored more fully in the remainder of the Gospel:

- We hear Jesus speaking of having been sent by God from heaven to act with his authority.

- We hear Jesus consistently calling God his own Father and being given the authority to judge human beings, able to raise them to new life; he has 'seen the Father' and been 'in his presence'.

- We hear Jesus placing himself under the Father's authority ('I do nothing on my own but speak only what the Father has taught me') and yet also claiming equality with God

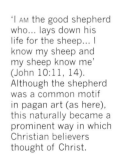

'I AM the good shepherd who… lays down his life for the sheep… I know my sheep and my sheep know me' (John 10:11, 14). Although the shepherd was a common motif in pagan art (as here), this naturally became a prominent way in which Christian believers thought of Christ.

'[Jesus] said this while teaching in the synagogue in Capernaum' (John 6:59). View northwards towards the Capernaum synagogue (built between the 2nd and 4th centuries, but possibly on the site of the one mentioned in the Gospels); its white limestone forms quite a contrast with the local black basalt used for other buildings.

('I and the Father are one... I am in the Father and the Father is in me').

- We hear Jesus praying intimately to God, speaking of the glory he had enjoyed in his presence 'before the world began'.

However, John has yet further ways of highlighting this truth, some of which we might miss if we ignore their Old Testament background. For example, within biblical thought Jerusalem's Temple was the place where God truly dwelt (like the tabernacle in the wilderness: see p. 43). John now shows Jesus going up to the Temple during its various feasts (Passover, Tabernacles, the feast of its Dedication), but pointing to himself as the fulfilment of these festivals (as the true Passover lamb, the one ultimately dedicated to God and so on). Jesus truly *is* the Temple. That's why John recounts very early in his Gospel Jesus' puzzling words: 'Destroy this temple and I will raise it again in three days.' John explains that Jesus was referring to his own body (raised after three days) because he wants us to see that Jesus himself is God's true temple – which means, in the light of the Old Testament, that he is *the very presence of God* on earth. So John's special lenses, which see Jesus as the ultimate 'Holy Place', help us to see that Jesus embodied God's presence in his own person – or, to use the phrase coined by John, that he was God *incarnate*: 'The Word *became flesh* and made his dwelling [literally, his 'tabernacle'] among us.'

Finally, and famously, John recounts seven occasions when Jesus proactively used the phrase 'I AM' (see p. 210). This phrase, which echoes God's words to Moses at the burning bush (see p. 37), was identified with God's own name. Now Jesus uses it of himself: 'I AM the Light of the World... Before Abraham was, I AM!' For John, Jesus is the embodiment of God himself; he is, in *that* sense, the unique 'Son of God'.

Jesus' gift to believers: 'eternal life'

John also wants us, however, to see how this Jesus can give us 'life through his name'. His Gospel therefore contains numerous pictures of this life. The 'I AM' sayings themselves, for example, reveal a range of things that Jesus can give: bread (or spiritual sustenance), light (guidance) and resurrection life; Jesus can protect his people (as their shepherd), and they can live within him (as branches within a vine). Earlier, Jesus offered the Samaritan woman an endless supply of fresh (or 'living') water, explaining to his disciples that this was the gift of his own Spirit.

John's over-arching term for this gift of Jesus to his people is 'eternal life'. More literally this can also be translated as the 'life of the new age'. Jewish people were expecting the 'age to come', an era *within*

'God so loved the world that he gave his one and only son, that whoever believes in him shall not perish but have eternal life.'
John 3:16

John and the synoptics

As can be seen from the tables on p. 188–189, the content of John's Gospel is quite different from that found in the three synoptic Gospels. The first half of John's Gospel is largely set in Jerusalem, not Galilee; in the second half, five long chapters are devoted exclusively to the events of Jesus' last night (in the upper room and walking to Gethsemane). Almost certainly John knew the synoptic tradition (and presumed his readers did too), so he has consciously produced a different, complementary account. Yet this has involved him in making some surprising omissions (such as the Transfiguration and the Last Supper).

However, there are some further major differences. John has a more reflective style, so he focuses on Jesus' extended 'discourses', as well as on his encounters with individuals (such as Nicodemus, or the Samaritan woman) in which we can trace that person's growing response to Jesus. Other differences, however, are more puzzling: why are there so many revelations in *advance* about Jesus' identity in John's opening chapter, when in the synoptics these unfold gradually? And why in John's passion narrative does Jesus come across as such a 'glorious' figure?

'A new command I give you: Love one another. As I have loved you, so you must love one another.'
John 13:34

Christ Before Pontius Pilate, by Niccolo Frangipane (c. 1555–1600).

this world's history when God would be king. If for John Jesus has now established this 'kingdom of God' (a phrase used only twice in John), then the 'eternal life' of this kingdom is already available. And this life, though continuing beyond death, is available in the here and now.

In one of his final prayers, Jesus defines this eternal life: 'Now this is eternal life: that they may know you, the only true God, and Jesus Christ, whom you have sent.' For John this life is characterized by knowing God personally through Christ, and being drawn into a relationship with God which, though qualitatively different, is patterned on Jesus' own relationship with God. Jesus is uniquely the Son of God, but he can share something of that relationship with his followers – hence his remarkable instructions to Mary Magdalene after the resurrection: 'I am ascending to my Father and *your* Father, to my God

and *your* God.' Until this point God has been Jesus' 'Father' in a unique sense; but Jesus' disciples will now be able to speak of this God as *their* Father. This Jesus can evidently (in the words of John's prologue) give people the 'right to become children of God'.

This eternal life is also characterized, mysteriously, by people being 'indwelt' by God. 'Anyone who loves me will obey my teaching. My Father will love them, and we will come to them and make our home with them.' Here is a promise of a divine *indwelling*. Jesus then uses a different image to make the same point: 'you must abide [or 'dwell'] in the vine; abide in me, and I will abide in you.'

So John's Jesus offers a new kind of life, marked by knowing God and experiencing his presence. And, when we ask John how this gift can be received, his answer is clear: 'by believing you may have life'. Thus, when people ask Jesus what they must do 'to do the works God requires', his reply too is unequivocal: they must '*believe* in the one he has sent'.

John's Gospel is therefore designed to bring its readers to this point of belief in Jesus. And this belief is clearly not just a matter of intellectual assent to certain truths about Jesus; it involves developing an attitude of trust that warmly welcomes Jesus' person. Thus, in the words of his prologue, John carefully defines 'believing in his name' as more than just recognizing Jesus but also 'receiving' (or welcoming) him personally.

This then explains why the Gospel contains several examples of people within Jesus' lifetime who 'received' Jesus in this sense (for example, a Samaritan woman, a man born blind, Mary and Martha, the disciples). Yet there are also examples of those who did *not* receive him, remaining in their unbelief (Pontius Pilate). There is also the enigmatic example of Nicodemus, who seems to have left his interview with Jesus in a puzzled state but who later helps to bury Jesus' body. Is this an example of someone coming to faith in Jesus gradually? More clear is the powerful example of Thomas (which John uses as the climax of his story): when the risen Jesus appears to him, he abandons his previous insistence on putting his own hand on Jesus' wounds and simply exclaims, 'My Lord and my God!'

'Those who drink the water I give them will never thirst. Indeed, the water I give them will become in them a spring of water welling up to eternal life.' (Jesus' words in John 4:14.)

***

John's Gospel has proved remarkably powerful over the centuries, and has been the indispensable basis for all attempts to explain the phenomenon of Jesus. When the early Christians formulated their summaries of the faith (in the creeds), they were effectively seeking to express what they had found in John's Gospel. For here is vital teaching on the incarnation, on the cross and resurrection, and on the person and work of the Holy Spirit. Here too are important perspectives on

The restored remains of a wealthy home in Jerusalem's Upper City: the 'upper room' used by Jesus for his Last Supper and for his extended teaching (as recounted in John 13–17) may well have been somewhere in this quarter of the city.

both baptism (in Jesus' words to Nicodemus) and the Lord's Supper (in Jesus' discourse about the 'bread of life'). Thus, although John has given us a narrative story about Jesus, his text has also been read as a rich quarry for Christian doctrine.

To repeat the analogy above, John is offering us his finely crafted spectacles. And they are an incredible gift, which perhaps John alone was able to give. For, if John was himself the 'disciple whom Jesus loved' (and was lying down close to Jesus in the 'upper room': see John 13:23), then he had experienced a uniquely *privileged relationship with Jesus*. If so, when towards the end of his life he wrote down his memoirs, he may well have hoped that others might come to know this Jesus as intimately as he did. As one of the last survivors of the generation which had seen Jesus in the flesh, he wanted to help those who had *not* been so privileged – to help them *see Jesus as he had now come to see him*. Through the gift of his unique lenses, then, others too would be able to see Jesus – not physically, but in a way that was both spiritual and true. Truly, as Jesus said to Thomas, 'Blessed are those who have *not* seen and yet have believed!'

FOUR GOSPELS, ONE JESUS

The Gospels must rank as the most highly valued books of all time. No other books have been read out so regularly in worship nor studied in such detail by scholars; and no other books have been copied so meticulously.

When combined, the four Gospels give us a comprehensive and multi-dimensional portrait of Jesus. Contrary to those who see this as posing a difficulty (perhaps endlessly trying to solve the 'synoptic problem'), we should see this instead as offering us a rich resource – four distinctive perspectives with which to understand this unique figure (whose character was far more than any *one* human author could adequately convey). The evangelists are presenting us with four complementary angles on Jesus which mutually enrich each other. The following table gives an overview of these perspectives:

Gospel:	Written for:	Presenting Jesus, the Son of God, as:
Mark	Individuals	A powerful figure, who is also the Suffering Servant.
Matthew	A Jewish audience	Israel's Messiah, who is the true king and judge.
Luke	A Gentile audience	The authentic human, who is the friend of sinners and welcomes the outsider.
John	The whole world (or 'cosmos')	The eternal Word of God, the light of the world, who is God's 'incarnate' presence on earth.

Each evangelist has selected material which develops his chosen theme. This is then reflected in some of their preferred vocabulary: Matthew will often speak of righteousness or law; Luke will emphasize salvation or forgiveness; John will focus on more abstract ideas (such as light, love, truth). Becoming familiar with these different styles and perspectives will only enrich our appreciation of the Gospels.

In the second century some Christians became concerned about the existence of four Gospels and a man called Tatian tried to produce a single, conflated account. Yet Christians such as Irenaeus were soon stressing the great value of the four ancient Gospels because they retained each evangelist's individual concerns. Moreover, Irenaeus saw the four-fold Gospel as a sign of God's intention to reach the whole world – going out to the four points of the compass. And, intriguingly, recent scholarship has reverted to acknowledging that the Gospels had a universal audience in mind (rather than being focused on the local community in quite a parochial way). The evangelists thus wrote their Gospels for *all* people, for *all* time, to introduce them to this unique figure who, so they believed, stood at the centre of *all* human existence.

The next book of the Bible is the only book in the New Testament dedicated to telling the history of the early church. The Acts of the Apostles (normally abbreviated to 'Acts') tells the story of how Jesus' first followers spread the message about him in the first thirty years after his death and resurrection – travelling through numerous cities in the Roman empire and eventually reaching the imperial capital. So Acts is a dynamic book, full of action and adventure, and pulsating with vibrancy and energy.

Its author was Luke, the same person who wrote the Gospel. Luke was a companion of Paul and is mentioned by Paul in two of his letters (Colossians 4:14 and 2 Timothy 4:11), both written from Rome. This fits neatly with Acts' final chapter, where Luke describes how 'we came to Rome'. This is one of several episodes in the book where the author uses the first person ('we', 'us'), strongly suggesting that Luke was describing events in which he personally had been involved. So Acts was almost certainly written in Rome in the early AD 60s by a man with some first-hand memory of recent events.

This then explains why there is a slightly disproportionate focus on Paul (the apostle whom Luke knew personally). Paul is first mentioned at the end of Acts 7 and the story of his conversion on the road to Damascus is described in Acts 9. From Acts 13 onwards the narrative is then focused exclusively on Paul and his travels – his three so-called 'missionary journeys' and his eventual journey towards Rome. This gives readers of the New Testament a biographical portrait of Paul which nicely complements what can be gleaned from his letters (see pp. 233–69). Here in Acts we see his strategy and determination in his travels, the way he chose and built his team of companions, his courage in the face of repeated opposition; yet also his desire for some occasional solitude (going for a twenty-five-mile walk on his own: Acts 20:13) and his patience – when stuck in prison for two whole years (Acts 22–26).

Luke's close proximity to the events would also explain why his narrative shows strong signs of being remarkably reliable. Thus many of the details in Acts have been corroborated by modern research: for example, Luke consistently uses the correct terminology when referring to the local political authorities in various cities ('politarchs' in Thessalonica, 'rod-bearers' in Philippi, etc.); and his account of his sea voyage with Paul and their shipwreck off Malta (in Acts 27) is used by classical and maritime historians as primary and reliable evidence for ancient seafaring.

There are also signs that Luke consciously wrote Acts as a sequel to his Gospel. Thus, while his Gospel is structured with a strong sense of Jesus' journey up to Jerusalem, Acts tells a complementary story of how the message about Jesus went out 'from Jerusalem, through Judea and Samaria to the ends of the earth'. There are also some deliberate parallels drawn between Jesus and the apostles: for example, both Jesus and Paul go up and face hostile crowds in Jerusalem who clamour for their deaths; or again, the final picture of Paul (preaching the kingdom of God in Rome) echoes Luke's first picture of the adult Jesus (preaching the kingdom in his home town of Nazareth). Luke is thus showing how the story of Jesus did not finish in Jerusalem, but was launched into a new phase – because of the resurrection and the gift of God's Spirit. So these 'acts of the apostles' can also be seen as the continued acts of *Jesus*.

Date	Event
c. 5 BC	Birth of Jesus (in Bethlehem)
4 BC	Death of Herod the Great (March); leads to rebellion in Palestine crushed by Romans under General Varus
c. AD 5	Birth of Paul (in Tarsus)
6	Herod Archelaus deposed from Judea (now coming under direct Roman rule); revolt led by Judas the Galilean
c. 8	Jesus' visit as a 12-year-old to Jerusalem's Temple
14	Death of Augustus; reign of Tiberius (until AD 37)
c. 20	Paul sent to Jerusalem for his education
26	Pontius Pilate as governor of Judea (until AD 36)
27/28	Ministry of John the Baptist; start of Jesus' ministry
30	Probable date for Jesus' crucifixion (Friday 7 April)
31/32	Stephen's martyrdom; Paul's conversion on Damascus road
33	Alternative date for Jesus' crucifixion (Friday 4 April)
34/35	Paul's brief visit to Jerusalem and then to Tarsus
39	Fierce Jewish resistance to the attempt of Emperor Caligula (37–41) to install his statue in Jerusalem Temple
c. 40	Paul summoned by Barnabas to minister in Syrian Antioch
45	Paul and Barnabas' visit to Jerusalem for famine relief
46	Paul's first missionary journey (to Cyprus and Galatia) with Barnabas and Mark
49	The apostolic council in Jerusalem; riots in Jerusalem leading to a massacre
50	Paul's second missionary journey (through Macedonia to Athens)
50–52	Paul's 18 months in Corinth (July 51 – June 52) during Gallio's year of office as proconsul
52–55	Paul's three-year ministry in Ephesus
54	The opening five 'good years' of Emperor Nero (54–68); Jewish citizens' return to Rome
55–56	Paul's travels through Macedonia and Illyricum
57	Paul's winter in Corinth and journey up to Jerusalem for Pentecost (late May)
57–59	Paul's imprisonment in Caesarea (under Felix and Festus)
59	Paul's shipwreck on Malta (November)
60	Paul's arrival in Rome (April/May)
62	Martyrdom of James (Jesus' brother) in Jerusalem Temple
62	Destruction of Colossae by earthquake
63	Martyrdom of Peter and Paul in Rome (earliest possible dating)
64	Great fire in Rome (18 July)
67	Roman siege of Jerusalem under General Vespasian; flight of city's Christians to region of Pella in Galilee/Syria
68	Death of Nero and 'year of the four emperors'
70	Destruction of Temple (August) and sacking of Jerusalem (September) under General Titus
72/73	Roman siege of Masada (end of first Jewish revolt)
81–96	Reign of Emperor Domitian
96	Death of the apostle John, during early years of reign of Trajan (AD 96–117)

Key dates in the first Christian century.

Acts

'Thirty years that changed the world.' That is an apt summary of the book of Acts, as the message about Jesus spreads out from Jerusalem to Rome. The world of the Roman empire was being challenged with the surprising news of another kingdom and a different king – not the Roman emperor but a man named Jesus from a small village called Nazareth.

The early years in Jerusalem (chapters 1–7)

Acts starts where Luke's Gospel ended: with a repeated account of Jesus' final departure (known as his 'ascension'). While on the Mount of Olives, Jesus' disciples see him 'taken up in a cloud'. So ends a unique period of roughly 'forty days' in which the risen Jesus has met with his disciples and instructed them further in the kingdom of God. Now they are on their own.

These impressive breakwaters, built by Herod for his vast new harbour at Caesarea Maritima (the Roman capital of Palestine), would have been well known to the apostles as they set out from Jerusalem to other lands with the message about Christ.

Yet, in another sense, they are not. Acts 2 explains how ten days later, after returning to Jerusalem and appointing a replacement for Judas Iscariot, the first believers (numbering about 120) are suddenly empowered by a new divine presence – the Holy Spirit whom Jesus had promised would be sent to them by his Father. God's power, previously seen uniquely in Jesus, is now unleashed on his followers.

Yet this first church also had its problems: the noble ideal of sharing resources was open to abuse, with one married couple pretending they owned less than they did, and with disputes erupting over unfair food rationing. Even so, writes Luke, 'God's grace was powerfully at work in them all.'

Understandably, however, the local religious authorities begin to express their concern at this new phenomenon:

The Church of Saint Peter, carved into the mountainside above Syrian Antioch – the city where Peter, Paul and Barnabas preached and where believers were first called 'Christians' (Acts 11:26). Although its façade was rebuilt in 1863, the cave-church inside contains some floor mosaics and frescoes from the first centuries AD.

- Two of the apostles, Peter and John, are hauled before the Temple authorities to account for this new teaching about Jesus. When ordered to stop their preaching, they assert they must obey God first. Eventually they are set free, but things continue to be tense.

- Some apostles are then brought before the council, known as the Sanhedrin, who demand the death penalty. However, a leading Pharisee named Gamaliel persuades the council to have them flogged and then released.

Then a believer called Stephen is accused of blasphemy – not least because he is repeating Jesus' prophecies against the Temple. So he is put on trial and gives an extended defence. However, when he implicates the religious leaders in Jesus' death, this is too much. They drag him outside the city and stone him to death.

This then triggers a persecution, with all but the apostles fleeing for their lives. Any honeymoon period has now come to an end, after perhaps no more than a year or two.

'God has made this Jesus, whom you crucified, both Lord and Messiah.'
Peter speaking in Acts 2:36

'Jesus is "the stone you builders rejected, which has become the cornerstone." Salvation is found in no one else.'
Peter speaking in Acts 4:11–12

Paul's conversion

Illuminated medieval manuscript (c. 1320), depicting Paul's conversion.

'I was so obsessed with persecuting [the Lord's people] that I even hunted them down in foreign cities... I was going to Damascus with the authority and commission of the chief priests. About noon... I saw a light from heaven, brighter than the sun... I heard a voice saying to me in Aramaic, "Saul, Saul, why do you persecute me? It is hard for you to kick against the goads." Then I asked, "Who are you, Lord?" "I am Jesus, whom you are persecuting... I have appeared to you to appoint you as a servant and as a witness... I am sending you to [the Gentiles] to turn them from darkness to light."'

Acts 26:11–18

Paul's conversion is described three times in Acts (chapters 9, 22, 26), being seen as a remarkable event, in which Christ's hostile persecutor is humbled and then commissioned in his service. Paul himself describes it as an appearance of the risen Christ – similar to, though different from, those given to other apostles (1 Corinthians 9:1, 15:8). As such it was quite unique and so cannot be taken as a normal model for responding to Christ's message.

Many have speculated about the state of Paul's mind up to this point: was he burdened by a guilty conscience? However, Paul's language elsewhere suggests otherwise (1 Timothy 1:10, Philippians 3:6, Galatians 1:14). Instead, through this encounter he came to see Christ as God's 'Son', who despite fulfilling the Law had been 'cursed' for others and had opened up God's purposes to the Gentiles.

'"Saul, why do you persecute me?" "Who are you, Lord?" "I am Jesus, whom you are persecuting."'

Acts 9:4–5

The word spreads from Jerusalem (chapters 8–12)

Jesus' message spreads yet further:

• Through a man called Philip it reaches the Jews' historic enemies, the Samaritans; also an Ethiopian Jew who, while reading Isaiah 53 after a pilgrimage to Jerusalem, is persuaded that this prophecy points to Jesus.

• It has already reached people in Lydda and Joppa but now, through the ministry of Peter, it reaches a Roman centurion called Cornelius living in the provincial capital of Caesarea.

• And it reaches a young man named Saul (later known as Paul). Paul had seen Stephen's stoning, but now, as he approaches Damascus, he is stopped in his tracks, says Luke, by an encounter with the risen Christ.

Despite his impeccable Jewish credentials, Paul is immediately commissioned as Jesus' special messenger to the Gentiles. As seen in Peter's encounter with Cornelius, the Holy Spirit is being given to 'uncircumcised Gentiles'. As it spreads out from Jerusalem, the good news is breaking down long-standing social barriers.

Paul's first journey: Gentile mission and the council of Jerusalem (13 – 15:35)

The same is happening in a vast city in the north-east of the Mediterranean – Syrian Antioch. Paul and Barnabas have been teaching the city's various congregations here for some years when they are commissioned on their first missionary journey.

Taking Mark with them, they take a boat to Cyprus, landing at Salamis probably in the spring of AD 46. During the summer they travel on to Paphos, where the Roman governor is suitably impressed when Paul exercises some miraculous power over his court magician.

In the autumn they sail north to Pamphylia, but when Paul suggests travelling inland over the Taurus mountains, Mark decides to return home to Jerusalem. Paul and Barnabas then go up to the remote area of southern Galatia, preaching in the Roman colony of Pisidian Antioch, and other cities further to the east (Iconium, Lystra and Derbe).

Their strategy, if possible, is always to go first to the local synagogue. Invariably, however, this triggers a hostile reaction, especially when the synagogue authorities see some of their fringe members (the so-called 'God-fearers') being attracted to Paul's message. At this point Paul and Barnabas normally focus instead on the Gentiles. Sometimes they get a hero's welcome but more often they experience persecution. So on one occasion Paul is stoned and left for dead, only to get up and proceed to the next city for some more preaching! Eventually they sail back to Syrian Antioch, where they report with joy on 'how [God] had opened a door of faith to the Gentiles'.

An ornate column in the public square (or 'gymnasium') at Salamis, the first 'port of call' for Paul and his companions.

'God... raised Jesus
from the dead... that
he might bring Israel to
repentance and forgive
their sins.'
Acts 5:30–31

This rejoicing, however, does not last long. Some believers in Jerusalem have heard about Paul's work in Galatia (probably from Mark once he got home), and are concerned that these new Gentile believers will imagine they can belong to God's people without first becoming Jews through the rite of circumcision. News of this reaches Antioch and causes both Barnabas and even Peter to have their doubts about what should be demanded of Gentile believers. So an urgent meeting is convened in Jerusalem.

Paul and Barnabas go up for this apostolic council, aware that their missionary work is under severe scrutiny. The 'circumcision party' are allowed their say, but eventually James, Jesus' brother (by now the leader of the Jerusalem church), gives his ruling: the Gentile believers are acceptable to God *as Gentiles* and do not need to be circumcised.

This historic decision is a brave ruling: it will make James unpopular, not just with some in his own congregation, but also with Jewish nationalists in Jerusalem. The council then issues a short statement (the 'apostolic decree'), which is sent to 'the Gentile believers in Antioch, Syria and Cilicia'. After this crisis the Gentile mission can proceed in full confidence that it will not be undermined by people back in Judea.

Paul's second journey: around the Aegean (15:36 – 18:22)

Paul soon wants to return to Galatia, but when Barnabas suggests

One of several inland lakes
in the remote region of
Galatia, separated from the
Mediterranean sea by the large
Taurus mountains.

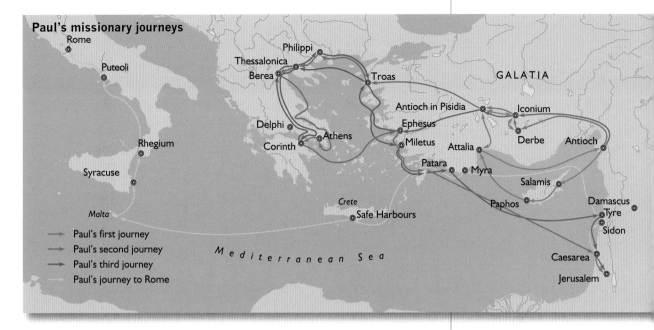

Paul's missionary journeys

Rome
Puteoli
Rhegium
Syracuse
Malta
Philippi
Thessalonica
Berea
Troas
Delphi
Athens
Corinth
Ephesus
Miletus
Attalia
Patara
Myra
Crete
Safe Harbours
GALATIA
Antioch in Pisidia
Iconium
Derbe
Antioch
Salamis
Paphos
Damascus
Tyre
Sidon
Caesarea
Jerusalem
Mediterranean Sea

→ Paul's first journey
→ Paul's second journey
→ Paul's third journey
→ Paul's journey to Rome

taking Mark again as their companion, Paul thinks this is too great a risk. So Barnabas takes Mark back to Cyprus. Paul sets out instead with Silas, and they are then joined by a young man called Timothy.

For Paul, however, Galatia is simply a springboard for going on to places yet further west. Eventually, after a dream featuring a man in Macedonian dress, Paul concludes they are being called to sail from Troas across to Macedonia. So the three missionaries travel through several key cities on the continent of Europe (Philippi, Thessalonica and Athens). In each place there are distinct challenges to their message from the secular authorities or the local synagogue; from the challenge of pagan religion or philosophy. Eventually Paul spends two winters in Corinth, establishing a vibrant young church; yet he is also dragged before the city's Roman proconsul, Gallio – who thankfully rules that these Christians are not doing anything illegal.

Paul's third journey: from Ephesus back to Jerusalem
(18:23 – 21:16)
After a brief visit back to Antioch, Paul sets out again and comes at last to Ephesus, where he stays nearly three years. He hires a lecture hall where he teaches each day during the midday siesta, enabling visitors from the 'whole province of Asia' to hear his message. The results are so significant that visitors stop buying the small figurines of Artemis at the ancient temple. The craftsmen, noting this drop in

Left: A large cult-statue of Artemis found in Ephesus.

Spectacular early morning view of Ephesus' theatre (seating capacity: 25,000), looking down the main street towards the ancient harbour (now silted up). Paul wanted to address the mob in the theatre but was persuaded by some of the city leaders not to do so (Acts 19:30–31).

sales, eventually stoke up a rioting crowd, which then storms the vast theatre, chanting, 'Great is Artemis of the Ephesians!' It is clearly time for Paul to leave.

So he heads off through Macedonia and eventually comes to Corinth – the agreed rendezvous point for the small team to take some monies collected for the Jerusalem church. Before embarking, however, they learn of a plot on Paul's life, so Paul decides to travel back by land. Eventually they take a series of boats southwards to ports such as Miletus and Patara, sailing across the Mediterranean to Caesarea. Throughout this journey there is a growing sense of foreboding, with

Paul and others being fully aware that danger lies ahead. Paul, however, like Jesus, is determined to reach Jerusalem.

Paul in Jerusalem and Caesarea (21:17 – 26:32)

The foreboding turns out to be justified. There is another riot – stirred up again by Jewish visitors from Ephesus (who accuse him of taking a Gentile into the Temple). Paul is rescued by Roman soldiers and is allowed, under guard, to address the crowd. When he mentions his calling to preach to Gentiles, however, there is another uproar. So a few days later, the Roman authorities escort him under guard down to Caesarea.

Paul is now a Roman prisoner – and will remain so for two long years. Felix, the Roman governor, plays for time – hoping for a bribe from Paul. He gives Paul some freedom, however, and permits his friends (such as Luke) to take care of his needs. When he is replaced as governor by Porcius Festus, Paul stands trial again; but when Festus suggests the trial should be reconvened in Jerusalem, Paul uses his right as a Roman citizen to appeal for a trial before the emperor. Faced with a choice of returning to Jerusalem (a virtual death sentence) or appearing before the young Nero in Rome, Paul opts for the latter. Ironically, however, when Festus asks for advice from King Agrippa, the two rulers conclude that Paul is doing 'nothing that deserves death': 'this man could have been set free if he had not appealed to Caesar'.

The final journey to Rome
(chapters 27–28)
So Paul (guarded by a Roman

Roman villa on Malta on the hills above the likely site of Paul's shipwreck; this may be where Publius, the local landlord, welcomed the survivors (Acts 28:7–10).

Paul and Luke entered Rome walking along the Appian Way, guarded by soldiers but surrounded by friends from the Roman church – who had walked out more than 20 miles to welcome them into the imperial capital (Acts 28:1–16).

centurion, but accompanied by Luke and Aristarchus) is put on a boat heading towards the Aegean. At Myra they find a boat heading towards Italy and set sail, but they are buffeted southwards to Crete. They manage to dock on Crete's southern shore but, ill-advisedly, they try to reach Phoenix – being a better place, they think, to spend the winter. A howling gale rips into them and they spend the next fourteen days being driven along westwards by a raging storm.

Yet Paul has received a vision from God, confirming that all on board will survive. At long last the crew sense they are approaching land and, as dawn breaks, the outline of a sandy beach comes into view. The ship hits some reefs, they jump into the water, and all 276 passengers safely reach the shore. The mysterious island that has prevented them drifting on hopelessly towards Tunisia turns out to be called Malta.

Malta then becomes Paul's winter home. In March they set sail and eventually reach the imperial capital. 'And so we came to Rome,' writes Luke with a sense of relief, yet also with a sense of fulfilment – this was the place where God had brought Paul. But what would happen next? Would Paul stand before Nero, and with what result?

Tantalizingly, Luke never tells us. Instead we read that Paul 'stayed for two whole years in his own rented house' (though presumably under guard) and was able to 'proclaim the kingdom of God without hindrance'.

✵ ✵ ✵

The book of Acts thus reveals how the kingdom of God, first announced by Jesus, spread far and wide as his followers proclaimed and lived out that kingdom. Its dynamic is relentlessly outwards, its scope universal.

Within the storyline of the Bible, Acts introduces us to the 'church age' (or Act IV: see p. 17) – that is, the era between Jesus' first coming and the ultimate End. This is the same era in which all subsequent Bible readers find themselves, so Acts is often a great inspiration, showing examples of God at work by his Spirit. Yet some events recorded here may be exceptional rather than normative (for example, the events at Pentecost marked the unique launch of the Christian church). Even so, the book encourages its readers to raise their sights to what God can do, and to be bold in working for the kingdom.

Equally, it is a warning – that there will be many hardships (as Paul states in Acts 14:22). The first Christians, then, did not have it all easy, nor were they morally perfect. So there is no point in attempting to turn the clock back to this supposedly golden era.

Acts also serves to give us the historical background to the New Testament's next books – the epistles. As we approach these letters, it is good to imagine them being written precisely to the kind of churches mentioned here in Acts. Luke has given us a useful storyline of the early church, but it will be up to Paul and the other letter-writers to convey the apostles' teaching for that church – then and now.

Paul at Miletus

'I served the Lord... with tears and in the midst of severe testing by the plots of the Jews... I have not hesitated to preach ... I have declared to both Jews and Greeks that they must turn to God in repentance and have faith in our Lord Jesus... my only aim is to finish the race and complete the task the Lord Jesus has given me – the task of testifying to the good news of God's grace... Be shepherds of the church of God, which he bought with his own blood. I know that after I leave, savage wolves... will not spare the flock. Even from your own number some will... distort the truth. ... You yourselves know that these hands of mine have supplied my own need... I showed you that... we must help the weak, remembering the words the Lord Jesus himself said: "It is more blessed to give than to receive."'

Extracts from Acts 20:19–35

In these words Luke summarizes Paul's farewell speech to the Ephesian church leaders gathered on the beach at Miletus. The speech gives us some key insights into Paul's priorities during his ministry in Asia (AD 52–55): preaching Christ to all kinds of people; training leaders to be faithful teachers and 'shepherds'; and himself modelling a servant leadership, reminiscent of Jesus'.

More personally, we see the acute cost of exercising this ministry, but also the strength which Paul drew from being commissioned by Christ with a lifelong task – to tell others of the 'grace' he himself had received.

Letters

The next section of the New Testament contains twenty-one letters (or epistles) written by the apostles. Some of these are addressed to individuals, but most were sent to church congregations. The first thirteen, all attributed to Paul, were collected together into the so-called 'Pauline corpus' at a very early stage (perhaps even by AD 100).

These letters of Paul have proved enormously influential. They were mostly written to address quite local specific situations (and sometimes in reply to letters which are now lost). Yet they have become a key foundation for subsequent Christian thought and practice – in situations quite different from Paul's own. For they not only provide an unparalleled insight into the way Jesus' message was being taught and applied around the Mediterranean very soon after Jesus' own ministry; they are also received as 'apostolic', thus having a lasting authority for the Christian church in any age.

Here we will find Paul's teaching on the person of Christ; his new understanding of God as Father, Son and Holy Spirit; his insights into the meaning of Jesus' death and resurrection; his proclamation of the good news and what this can mean for individuals; his vision for the community of believers in Christ; and his Christ-centred hope for the future and for God's renewal of the world.

As a former rabbi, Paul especially considers the way God's activity in Christ meshes with Israel's experience of God in the Old Testament period. So he devotes a good proportion of his writings to explaining the new relationships that should pertain between Jews and Gentiles, and also how the Law (or Torah) should now be understood in the light of Christ. In this connection he develops his key concept that men and women are 'justified' (or vindicated in God's sight) 'by faith' in Christ, not through 'works of the Law' (see Romans, p. 234). Above all, he sees the message about Christ as being all about grace – that is, God's undeserved love towards sinful human beings, shown supremely in Jesus' death.

Paul's letters, however, are also very personal. Unlike with most figures of ancient history, with Paul we are able to see into the person's inner world – his motivations and struggles. On several occasions (for example, in Galatians, Philippians and 1 Timothy) he reflects on his life before his conversion (p. 222). In 2 Corinthians we see someone who has come through a near-death experience, constantly burdened with anxiety over the various churches, and wrestling with what it means to live as an apostle whose message is focused on a Lord who suffered. And in several letters (such as 2 Timothy) we sense what it was like for Paul to be in chains, as a prisoner for the faith, articulating his convictions on paper, which he would soon have to defend in a public trial.

Paul's letters thus give us some of the inside story of the person we read about in Acts: we see the dedication that drove him around the Mediterranean; we see his love for his own people and yet his desire to make Christ known beyond the boundaries of Israel. And we are also taken into his social world – the network of first-century believers. For in almost every letter, he mentions some of his friends and contacts, as he greets them or gives them personal instructions – sometimes even adding a note in his own handwriting (rather than dictating through his secretary): 'see what large letters I use as I write to you with my own hand!' (Galatians 6:11).

This was a person, then, who was in live contact with real people, who suffered and struggled alongside them, and who taught them about Christ not from a detached, safe distance but from the front-line – as seen in his list of difficult experiences in 2 Corinthians 11. This gives his writing an earthed quality, and his theology, far from being abstract or theoretical, proves to be supremely practical – with a capacity to touch and transform real lives.

The precise dating of Paul's letters has, of course, been hotly debated. Indeed many wonder if all these letters truly come from Paul's own hand (questions have been especially raised about 1 and 2 Timothy, Titus and Ephesians: see pp. 264–68). However, as argued in my book *In the Steps of Saint Paul* (Lion, 2008), a strong case can be made for the suggested table of dates (p. 178). Within this table, the most disputed dates would be those of Galatians (some suggesting AD 55 instead) and the three 'pastoral epistles' (which, if accepted as authentic, are often dated to a period in the mid-60s when Paul had a further period of ministry before his eventual martyrdom in Rome).

Quite possibly the last four chapters of 2 Corinthians were penned shortly after the main bulk of the letter – when Paul received some further criticisms of his ministry. We cannot tell whether he received these criticisms *before* he had dispatched Titus with the main letter or only afterwards (with these chapters being sent with a later courier). Either way, they were soon 'filed' together and thereafter always appeared as one letter in the earliest manuscripts.

'I have worked harder, been in prison more frequently, been flogged more severely, and been exposed to death again and again... Once I was stoned, three times I was shipwrecked, I spent a night and a day in the open sea.'
2 Corinthians 11:23–25

ACTS REFERENCE	LETTER	LOCATION	DATE	
(Acts 13–14) (Acts 15:1–35)	Galatians	Antioch	Late AD 48 AD 49	**A. After first journey** Apostolic council
(Acts 15:36 – 18:22)	1 Thessalonians	Corinth	AD 51	**B. During second journey**
	2 Thessalonians	Corinth	AD 52	
(Acts 19:1 – 21:17)	1 Corinthians	Ephesus	AD 53/54	**C. During third journey**
	2 Corinthians (1–9)	Philippi?	AD 55	
	2 Corinthians (10–13)	Macedonia	AD 56	
	1 Timothy	Illyricum	AD 56	
	Titus	Illyricum	AD 56	
	Romans	Corinth	AD 57	
			May AD 57	**Arrival in Jerusalem**
			AD 57–59	**Caesarean imprisonment**
(Acts 21:17 – 28:29)			AD 59	**Final journey to Rome**
(Acts 28:30–31)			AD 60–?64	**D. During Roman imprisonment**
	2 Timothy	Rome	Early AD 60	
	Colossians	Rome	AD 61/62	
	Philemon	Rome	AD 61/62	
	Ephesians	Rome	AD 61/62	
	Philippians	Rome	AD 62/63	

Romans

The book of Romans is widely recognized as Paul's masterpiece. Composed during a winter stopover in Corinth (January to March AD 57), it is Paul's most systematic statement of his teaching, being designed to give an overview of his message to the Christians in Rome.

Various reasons can be given as to why Paul wrote this letter. First, because he had no direct knowledge of the Roman church, this was a good opportunity to start from a blank piece of paper, setting out his teaching in a logical order. Secondly he was about to set sail for Jerusalem: if things went badly – perhaps with him even being martyred there – it would be important to have committed his thoughts to paper as a theological 'last will and testament'. Alternatively, if he survived, he knew his Gentile missionary work would be closely scrutinized in Jewish Jerusalem, so it would be worth clarifying his exact position on Jew/Gentile matters in order to guard against any misinterpretation. And finally, if he did eventually arrive safely in Rome, he would want

Overview of Romans

God's gift of 'justification by faith'
(chapters 1–4)

A vision for the Christian life
(chapters 5–8)

Paul's prayer for his fellow Israelites
(chapters 9–11)

Being God's people (chapters 12–16)

Remains of the forum in Rome – the centre of the ancient world. By Paul's day the market area had been filled in with numerous buildings, but victorious generals would still process up the 'triumphal way' towards the Capitoline hill (off picture to the left). Paul had often wanted to visit Rome (Romans 1:13), but when he finally reached it, he was under guard and may never have seen this historic forum.

The righteousness of God

What does Paul mean by this key concept? In the Old Testament, Israel's God was described as 'righteous', not only because of his moral holiness but also because he faithfully fulfilled his covenant promises. Paul now sees Christ's faithfulness as the supreme instance of this same covenant faithfulness. So Christ's coming reveals God not abandoning his previous promises, but rather fulfilling them – Christ is the goal (or climax) of the covenant (Romans 10:4).

Yet, not coincidentally, God's righteous action in Christ brings about salvation – it enables sinful people to be deemed 'righteous' in God's sight. God's righteous activity thus brings about a righteous status for human beings. The progression of Paul's argument from chapter 3 to chapter 4 makes clear this vital second point: after highlighting human sin ('no one is righteous') he cites the example of Abraham, who had been 'credited with righteousness' (Genesis 15:6). Paul is thus showing how 'unrighteous' people can be credited with a righteousness that is not naturally their own.

This comes about – as seen in the pivotal, intervening passage (3:21–26) – through Jesus' death on the cross, which was a 'sacrifice of atonement', thus making it possible for those exercising faith in this Jesus to be forgiven. This, then, is the 'righteousness of God that is by faith' – an undeserved righteous status in God's sight. This great truth (known as 'justification by faith') was rediscovered by the Reformers in the sixteenth century and has been a key ingredient in people's understanding of the essential Christian gospel ever since.

the Roman Christians to have been introduced to him in advance, enabling them to support him with some confidence in his next round of missionary endeavour (possibly in Spain).

However, Paul may also have been aware of an issue troubling the church in Rome. Eight years earlier, the emperor Claudius had expelled all Jews from Rome (see Acts 18:2 and Suetonius, *Life of Claudius* 25.4); so any fledgling church would have been entirely Gentile. Then, after Claudius' death (in AD 54) the Jews had returned, so the church would again have been a mixture of both Gentile and Jewish believers. Perhaps the relationship between these two groups was proving awkward?

The good news of God's grace (chapters 1–4)

Paul begins by making it clear just how much he had long wanted to visit Rome and preach the gospel there. For through his resurrection, Jesus had been revealed as the Messiah and the Son of God. This was a message which Rome, as the imperial capital, needed to hear. Compared with the visible power of Rome, the gospel may appear quite a small thing, but Paul, however, is 'not ashamed of the gospel' because it has the power to bring salvation to *anyone* who believes; for in it is seen God's '*righteousness*'. What Paul means by this word is much debated (see box, left). Yet, essentially, Paul is about to argue that, in Christ, God has acted faithfully to his covenant promises in order to bring about forgiveness for his people's sins: because of Christ's death they can be declared righteous in God's sight.

Paul then starts explaining this great truth: Jew and Gentile are all 'under the power of sin' and so under God's judgment (or 'wrath'); they do not glorify the creator but exchange God's truth for a lie; those who claim to obey God's Law still break that Law in many ways. It is a bleak picture, and the Law itself cannot offer any rescue: 'no one will be declared righteous merely by observing the Law'; for 'all have sinned and fallen short of God's glory'.

But now a new righteousness has been made available. On the cross God has 'presented Christ as a sacrifice of atonement', so that anyone can be 'justified freely by his grace'. Paul sees the cross as the moment when God both *revealed* his judgment on human sin and, simultaneously, *removed* it – by himself dying for that sin. So God has 'demonstrated his justice' and yet also made it possible, without contradiction, to 'justify those who have faith in Jesus'.

So faith in Christ becomes the critical factor – not relying on the marks of circumcision, nor trying hard to please God. This righteous status before God comes about simply through faith in Christ's death. Paul finds this biblical principle of 'justification by faith' in the example of Abraham: 'Abraham *believed* God,' Genesis had said, 'and it was credited to him as righteousness'. Clearly, then, Abraham had been saved, not by circumcision or by arduous morality, but simply by his faith.

New life in Christ (chapters 5–8)

Paul then lists the great blessings believers experience through the gospel; in particular, the cross is an extraordinary demonstration of God's love and a clear sign that God will not abandon those reconciled to him at such great cost. Yet might this mean that if people sin more often, they will also experience grace more often? 'By no means!' Paul replies. For baptism is the mark of dying to sin and the sure sign of believers being raised to lead a new resurrection life: so 'count yourselves dead to sin but alive to God in Christ Jesus'. Sin is no longer to be their master. Instead they are to see themselves as 'slaves to righteousness' and 'betrothed' to Christ. Sin will always pose a problem but believers will eventually be delivered from this through Christ. And even now believers can experience the power of the Holy Spirit.

Romans chapter 8 is one of the Bible's most powerful chapters, describing this new life lived in the power of God's Spirit. The Spirit of the risen Christ now truly dwells within each believer, bringing an awareness of God as 'Abba' ('Father') and a confidence in eventually sharing in God's glory. Yet the Spirit's presence also makes believers aware of the frustration now inherent in creation and makes them yearn for God's future, of which as yet they have only a tantalizing foretaste.

Even so, 'we know that in all things God works for the good of those who love him'. Despite all the frustrations, 'God is for us.' He has already given his most precious gift – his own Son – so he will give his people yet further gifts of grace. So Paul concludes in praise: 'I am convinced that... *nothing* will be able to separate us from the love of God that is in Christ Jesus our Lord.'

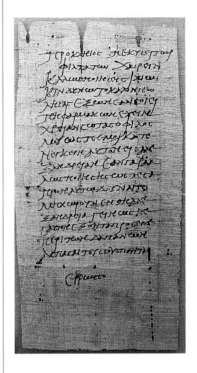

'I, Tertius, who wrote down this letter, greet you in the Lord' (Romans 16:22). Almost all of Paul's letters would have been dictated by him to an *amanuensis* (secretary). In the Greco-Roman world, letter writing using ink on papyrus was a painstaking task. Here, a man called Prokleios writes to his good friend Pekusis on a personal matter.

God's purposes and the people of God (chapters 9–11)

There is a sudden change of tone, however, as Paul, who has just spoken of the deep love found in God's heart, begins to speak of some 'unceasing anguish' in his own heart – namely, his great sorrow that his fellow Jews do not recognize their Messiah and are thus missing out on all those blessings. This urgent issue needs a response. How could those promised so much now miss so much? And given that, according to his own argument, the gospel reveals the 'covenant faithfulness' of Israel's God, why then are so many people in that original covenant now rejecting it? Has God not been faithful? Or has God got some alternative plan for Israel? Or, going the other way, does Israel's rejection of the Messiah mean God has totally abandoned them – rejected them, as it were, beyond the point of no return?

Paul's answer on this last point is 'By no means! I am an Israelite myself, a descendant of Abraham...' In other words, if God really had rejected his former people and was now totally debarring them from the gospel, *there would not be any Jewish believers at all*. But there are. God's desire to call people within Israel to himself has not changed. And

Paul likens God's people, going back through history, to an olive tree. Olive trees can indeed last through many generations: these olive trees in Jerusalem's garden of Gethsemane (even if not there in Jesus' day) may be over 1,500 years old.

there remains a sense in which Jewish people will always be 'loved on account of the patriarchs' – that is, there will always be a special place in God's heart for those who are the physical descendants of his servant Abraham.

Yet God's desire for them is clearly that they should now find their Messiah. There are not now two tracks – one for Gentiles (focused on Christ) and another for Jews (focused on the Law). No, Christ is himself the 'end of the Law' – the very goal to which the Law was pointing. So there cannot be any salvation through the Law alone, apart from Christ – which would overturn all Paul has argued for. So Paul continues to long for his fellow Israelites to confess Jesus as Lord: 'my heart's desire is that they may be saved'. Until they do so, Paul argues, they remain strangers to God's salvation. After all, if this were not their situation, why was Paul feeling so anguished?

So, paradoxically, the people previously considered to be the 'people of God' now find they have fallen outside. To explain this, Paul compares the historic people of God – the 'stock' of Israel, if you like – to an olive tree; but now, because of their non-belief in Christ, some branches have been broken off. Yet Paul longs that they be grafted back in. This will happen if they do not 'persist in their unbelief' but turn to receive God's mercy through the gospel. Meanwhile, Gentile believers, quite undeservedly, have been brought into God's people – like 'a wild olive shoot… grafted in' to the ancient olive tree, 'and now share in the nourishing sap from the olive root'. They should be filled with gratitude – as well as an appropriate fear, lest they too fall back into a state of unbelief.

Paul's answer, then, to the big question about God's faithfulness is that God himself has been fully faithful to his promises. If there has been faithlessness, this has been found, not in God, but in his people Israel. That's why, even in Old Testament times, the prophets had

236

spoken of a faithful 'remnant' *within* Israel. If God in Jesus has placed a 'stumbling-stone' in their path which has revealed the scope of the problem, then God is not to be blamed for having brought this matter to a head.

Paul closes this section by reasserting his confidence that – despite appearances, despite Israel's present unbelief, and even if the precise details are unclear – at the end of time God will surely achieve his intended purposes through Christ. 'Oh the depth of the riches of the wisdom and knowledge of God!... To him be glory for ever! Amen.'

Living together as God's new people (12:1 – 15:13)

Paul now outlines a powerful vision for God's new people in Christ. The members of this new community are to:

- see their whole lives as 'living sacrifices' offered to the God who has shown them such mercy;

- see themselves as each playing a valuable part within the 'body' of Christ, depending on how God has gifted them;

- love one another, living in peace, and not repaying 'evil for evil';

- be submissive before the secular authorities, paying their taxes and respecting those who govern;

- put aside any deeds of darkness (such as drunkenness, immorality or dissension) and instead clothe themselves with Christ's own character.

In particular, if there are differing viewpoints among them on matters of religious scruple or conscience, they must not fall into judgmentalism but treat each other as someone 'for whom Christ died', making 'every effort to do what leads to peace'. They should remember the gracious welcome each person has received in Christ and offer that same hospitality to one another. In particular Jews and Gentiles need to extend this welcome to each other in Christ. For Jesus was himself Jewish, a 'servant of the Jews' acting to confirm God's promises to Israel; but Jesus' coming was all about God's opening the door towards Gentiles. As a result the two people groups are to come into one, glorifying God 'with one heart and voice'.

Paul's plans and closing greetings (15:14 – 16:27)

Paul closes with some personal remarks and greetings. He restates his calling to be a 'minister of Christ to the Gentiles' and speaks of his pioneering evangelistic work, which has taken him from Jerusalem round to Illyricum. He asks his readers to pray for him during his forthcoming visit to Jerusalem and then commends to them a woman

---

Romans 11

'I do not want you to be ignorant of this mystery... Israel has experienced a hardening in part until the full number of Gentiles has come in, and in this way all Israel will be saved. As it is written: "The deliverer will come from Zion; he will turn godlessness away from Jacob."'
Romans 11:25–26

These crucial verses can be taken as predicting some future mysterious events (often associated with some special 'End Time' events located within the nation of Israel), in which suddenly every physical descendant of Abraham will be 'saved'.

Yet Paul is describing here the 'mysterious' events of the present gospel age (not the future), in which God has allowed Israel to experience a hardening of heart – seen in their rejection of their Messiah, Jesus. He asserts that this is all within God's sovereign plan and so discourages any looking down on Jewish people; instead God is mercifully wanting as many people as possible to respond to the gospel.

'All Israel' does not refer to every last Israelite but to *all within Israel whom God intends* to receive salvation (similar to the 'full number of Gentiles', which equally does not refer to *every* Gentile). So, even if many in Israel remain in unbelief, God will fulfil his promises. And he will do this through the gospel of Christ, not by some other method. For, as predicted by Isaiah, Jesus is the deliverer whose message is ringing out from Jerusalem. So Paul's readers should trust that God will 'turn godlessness away, and bring people in Israel to faith.

Model of Rome showing the Colosseum (built AD 80: centre), the Circus Maximus athletics stadium (extreme left) and the bridges over the River Tiber (top left). The model portrays the city at the time of Constantine (AD 312–37); amazingly, within 300 years of Paul's ministry, the emperor himself was now confessing Christ as the ultimate 'Lord' (cf. Romans 1:1–7).

called Phoebe, who will be acting as the courier bringing this letter from Corinth to Rome. The letter closes with a final blessing, preceded by a long list of greetings: Paul knows the personal names of over twenty-five different believers already in Rome. So this great letter ends in a way that reminds us that, despite its deep theology, it was written for ordinary people living out their lives in the first-century world.

***

Romans takes us to the heart of Paul's thinking. As we read his other letters, we will see them complementing Romans in various ways, but here we can see the essential components of his thought: his wonder at the cross and his delight in the Spirit; his convictions about God's faithfulness and the power of the gospel; his focus on God's gifts of forgiveness and righteousness, which are available to all, but only through faith in Christ; and his desire that the great barrier between Jew and Gentile should now be broken down – with a new community (the church) being formed out of the two as they both focus on Jesus, the Messiah and Lord.

This letter has had a dynamic effect in subsequent history. It has transformed the lives of communities and of individuals. Great minds such as Augustine of Hippo (AD 354–415), Martin Luther (1483–1546) and Karl Barth (1886–1968) have built their theologies upon it.

Romans sometimes seems too lofty to attain. Yet its overall theme – that God's forgiveness is freely available for those who put their faith in Christ – is the perfect message to address those who have failed to live up to its ideals. For here its readers can come back to basics and be restored, ready to serve Christ afresh as his forgiven people: indeed 'all have sinned', but all can be 'justified freely by his grace'.

1 Corinthians

Paul stayed eighteen months in Corinth (Acts 18:11). When he left, a vibrant young church had been established – perhaps numbering several hundred believers, meeting in different houses in the city or its neighbouring ports. This Corinthian church was thus a test case for the quality of Paul's ministry. So when he received a letter from the believers, asking for his advice, and then further reports of some major problems, Paul had to respond as a matter of urgency.

He had already written them a short note. Now he responds by sending Timothy to them from Ephesus with a longer letter (which we know as 1 Corinthians); in this he addresses five major topics one after the other (see below). After this, with the problems not satisfactorily resolved, he himself crosses the Aegean for what he later describes as a 'painful visit' (2 Corinthians 2:1). Later, after leaving Ephesus for good, he writes what we now call 2 Corinthians (see p. 245). In these two lengthy letters we see into Paul's apostolic heart, his passionate concern for these young Christians, and his pastoral skill in bringing the great truths of Christ into life-changing contact with their difficult issues.

The seven columns of the temple of Apollo (originally built c. 550 BC) stand in the centre of ancient Corinth – set against the impressive backdrop of Acro-Corinth (1,887 ft or 575 m).

Divisions and party spirit (chapters 1–4)

Though well aware of some major problems in the church, Paul begins by positively thanking God for the believers. Then he goes straight to one of the reported issues – their quarrelling: some are saying 'I follow Paul', and others follow Apollos (an eloquent Christian preacher who had recently visited Corinth). This jealousy and party spirit must stop – they are to follow Christ, not Paul!

They need to remember:

The 'Erastus' pavement near Corinth's theatre is the only surviving archaeological find that names a Christian believer known to us from the New Testament. Paul describes Erastus as the 'city's director of public works' (Romans 16:24). This is confirmed by the pavement's Latin inscription: 'Erastus laid this pavement at his own expense in return for his aedileship' (the name for a public office involved with buildings).

- God is the source of all wisdom, and they should only 'boast in the Lord'. God's wisdom is different from the world's – coming through God's Spirit and forming within them the 'mind of Christ'.

- Jesus' cross, which seems so foolish in the world's eyes, truly manifests God's power and wisdom, and Paul's own preaching – focused on 'Christ and him crucified' – has not been marked by the persuasive words of worldly wisdom.

- Both himself and Apollos are simply servants of Christ, equally accountable to God alone for their work done in building God's church – which is also to be seen as God's temple, the place where he truly now dwells.

Their new position in Christ is all due to God's generosity, yet they are in danger of abusing this and becoming arrogant. Throughout this, Paul's tone, while firm, has also been tender, seeing himself as their 'father' in Christ, not wanting to shame them, but warning them as his 'dear children'.

'The message of the cross is foolishness to those who are perishing, but to us who are being saved it is the power of God.'
1 Corinthians 1:18

'We [the apostles] have become the scum of the earth, the garbage of the world.'
1 Corinthians 4:13

Lawsuits and sexual lifestyles (chapters 5–7)

Yet there are other reported problems: believers are taking their disputes with each other before the civil law courts; worse still, one believer is in an incestuous relationship with his father's current wife. Paul says that they should settle their own disputes privately and should exclude this 'immoral brother' from their gatherings until he repents. Although they themselves have previously been involved in dishonest dealings and sexual immorality, they are to turn their backs now on all this – if they want to remain within the kingdom of God.

'I have the right to do anything!' some might reply. Yet this is a total misunderstanding of freedom in Christ, which is never a freedom to do evil. This is particularly so in the area of sexual relations. For what believers do with their bodies is far from irrelevant: those bodies will one day be raised with Christ, and are even now 'temples of the Holy Spirit'; so having sex with prostitutes, for example, is out of order. No, believers belong to the Lord and have been 'redeemed at a price', so they are to 'honour God with their bodies'. 'Flee from sexual immorality' (a command that would need special underlining here in Corinth, a city famous for its sexual licence).

In response to their specific questions about sex and marriage, there are some basic ground rules which they should follow: married sexual relations are good and should be marked by mutual consent; singleness is to be seen as a good option, but there is nothing wrong with believers getting married; and divorce from an unbelieving spouse is never necessary (however, if the non-believer insists on a divorce, the believer is free to remarry).

'"I have the right to do anything" – but not everything is beneficial... not everything is constructive. No one should seek their own good, but the good of others.'
1 Corinthians 10:23–24

Sacrificial food and Christian worship (chapters 8–11)

Then there are their questions about food: can they eat meat that has earlier been used in a sacrificial ceremony at a pagan temple? Paul responds with the clear assurance that pagan demons and idols are powerless compared to the one true God; so eating such meat is permissible, involving no spiritual risk. However, if the conscience of some 'weaker' believers is still troubled, the 'stronger' believers should not act proudly or force believers to sin against their own conscience. Instead they should themselves refrain from eating, if necessary. For love is more important than vaunting one's own 'knowledge' or rights.

Paul illustrates this principle from his own life. He does not insist on his 'right' to be married, or to be supported financially by others; he does not always express his 'freedom' but often surrenders it, adapting his behaviour for others: 'to the weak I became weak'. So they too should put the larger concerns of the gospel above their own wishes, seeing the Christian life as like an athletic race which requires discipline in order to win the prize. Moreover, in pursuing their freedom they may suddenly fall into temptation and commit the sins of idolatry and immorality (like the Israelites in the wilderness).

Then there is the issue of their irreverent approach to Christian worship – especially the celebration of the Lord's Supper. Some turn up late, and others arrive early and eat all the good food; some women are looking like prostitutes because they are praying without covering their hair in the customary way; many are failing to see that to eat this bread and drink this cup is genuinely a 'participation' (or 'communion') in the 'body and blood of the Lord'. Instead they should recognize the spiritual importance of this meal, and examine themselves; if they do not, they may experience God's judgment.

Spiritual gifts and love (chapters 12–14)

Overall their corporate worship is rather chaotic. So even if each believer should come ready to contribute – perhaps with a song, or a prophecy, or a 'word of instruction' – things should be done in an orderly way: 'God is not a God of disorder but of peace.' In particular, the spiritual gift of being able to speak in tongues (a Spirit-inspired utterance that involves using a prayer language different from one's own mother tongue) needs to be used with discernment within corporate worship – with any message spoken in a 'tongue' always being interpreted and then evaluated. If it promotes Jesus' lordship, fine; but if its content is effectively that Jesus is 'cursed', then this utterance has not come from the Spirit. And there are other gifts which, even if less dramatic, may ultimately be more important – not least the gift of love.

For the Christian community is like a human body – made up of many parts, but recognizably a unity. There are different gifts, but they all come from the one Spirit who sovereignly distributes them 'as he determines'. Similarly, there are many believers but they all make up the one 'body of Christ'. And each part of that body – even if it looks less important – is vitally important. So believers are to value each other and the gifts that God has given to others; they are not to be filled with envy or pride, but are to value their differences.

Paul's teaching on the Lord's Supper

'The Lord Jesus… took bread, and when he had given thanks, he broke it and said, "This is my body, which is for you; do this in remembrance of me."… For whenever you eat this bread and drink this cup, you proclaim the Lord's death until he comes.'
1 Corinthians 11:23–26

The Corinthians' unruly worship meant Paul had to spend some time describing his vision for the Lord's Supper. This is our earliest description of the meal which over the centuries would become a central act within Christian worship. Paul recounts Jesus' famous words spoken at his Last Supper with disciples and urges the Corinthians to see their serious meaning. They are remembering Jesus' death, 'participating' in his body and blood.

The Corinthians evidently came together on Sunday (the 'first day of the week'). They celebrated this meal frequently (even weekly?), apparently just after a 'bring and share' supper (sometimes known as an *agape* meal). References in Acts (2:46; 20:7) confirm that the first Christians 'broke bread' frequently – a significant contrast to the *annual* celebration of Passover.

This meal, celebrated in many different ways, has come to be known by various names. Although the word 'Mass' is related to the words of dismissal (from the Latin *missa*), the word 'Eucharist' (from the Greek *eucharista*) picks up Paul's language here of 'thanksgiving', and 'Communion' builds on his reference to 'participating' (or sharing) in Christ.

Resurrection and conclusion (chapters 15–16)

Finally, some believers are denying the future resurrection of the dead. (Some may have misunderstood Paul's teaching about believers *already* being 'raised with Christ' while others may have been influenced by pagan ideas – either that there is no conscious after-life *at all*, or that it is only the *soul*, not the body, which experiences immortality.) To come to a true perspective they should remember:

- Jesus was raised bodily 'on the third day' and was seen by his apostles; this is a non-negotiable part of Christian preaching;

- this physical resurrection shows that Jesus has defeated the great enemy of death;

- his risen body acts as the prototype (or 'first-fruits') for the resurrection of believers, who will similarly be clothed with a Spirit-animated body – 'glorious' and 'imperishable'.

'For we were all baptized by one Spirit so as to form one body… you are the body of Christ.'
1 Corinthians 12:13, 27

'I tell you a mystery… the trumpet will sound, the dead will be raised imperishable… "Death has been swallowed up in victory." '
1 Corinthians 15:51–52, 54

Paul's hymn to love

'If I speak in human or angelic tongues, but do not have love, I am only a resounding gong or a clanging cymbal.'
1 Corinthians 13:1

So begins one of the New Testament's most famous passages – what is sometimes known as Paul's 'hymn to love'. Though possibly developed some time before, this hymn is very closely related to Paul's specific argument in 1 Corinthians and so may well have been written specially for this occasion. For he is arguing that love is so much more important than the things valued in Corinth ('prophecy', 'tongues', 'knowledge', etc.) and showing how their corporate worship would be transformed if marked by such love.

Paul uses a word (*agape*) that was coined by the first Christians to reflect the love they glimpsed in the life of Jesus himself – the love which they also were now experiencing among themselves in the Christian community. Paul offers some key definitions of this new kind of Christ-like *agape* love: it is 'patient and kind'; it does not 'envy or boast'. It always 'protects, trusts, hopes and perseveres'. The Corinthians are to test their actions by this new demanding standard.

Paul finishes with a poetic flourish. 'Imperfect' things (such as prophecy and knowledge) will fade to nothing when believers see Christ face to face: 'now I know in part; then I shall know fully, even as I am fully known'. He then identifies three qualities which will endure for eternity – faith, hope and love; 'but the greatest of these is love'.

Even though this future remains hard to imagine, believers are to have confidence in this ultimate victory, not living only 'for this life', but being assured that their 'labour is not in vain'.

Paul gives some final greetings and discusses his future travel plans, but the note that would have continued resounding in the Corinthians' ears is this one of confident hope in the resurrection: 'But thanks be to God! He gives us the victory… Therefore, my dear brothers and sisters, stand firm. Let nothing move you.'

2 Corinthians

This resurrection hope, outlined so positively in 1 Corinthians 15, is precisely what Paul himself would soon need. For, by the time he writes 2 Corinthians (perhaps a year later), he has apparently been through a near-death experience.

Paul's subsequent response (chapters 1–7)

'We were under great pressure... so that we despaired of life itself... But this happened so that we might not rely on ourselves but on God, who raises the dead.' Paul's resurrection hope has strengthened him, so he gives praise to the 'God of all comfort' who has delivered him through this critical period.

This letter is therefore marked with a raw honesty as Paul describes his ministry: 'We are... persecuted, but not abandoned... We always carry around in our body the death of Jesus...'; 'But we have this treasure in jars of clay...' He lists many of his hardships (beatings, imprisonments, riots and so on), yet he does not lose heart; he is 'sorrowful, but always rejoicing', because these 'momentary troubles are achieving an eternal glory'. Though his human body seems like a 'tent',

The Bema (or tribune-seat) in the agora at Corinth: the Roman proconsul would try legal cases here in the open air – as did Gallio, when Paul was brought before him (Acts 18:12–17).

'And we all, who with unveiled faces contemplate the Lord's glory, are being transformed into his image with ever-increasing glory,...'
2 Corinthians 3:18

'...the one who raised the Lord Jesus from the dead will also raise us with Jesus...'
2 Corinthians 4:14

he knows God will provide him with an 'eternal house'. All this is based on the resurrection.

This, then, is the context in which Paul pens some of his greatest lines on the nature of the Christian faith:

- The 'new covenant' in Christ, unlike the temporary covenant associated with Moses, is marked by a 'surpassing glory' because it is eternal and releases the 'transforming' power of the Holy Spirit.

- The gospel helps people to become a 'new creation', because they encounter 'God's glory in the face of Christ.'

- Through the cross the gospel achieves reconciliation between God and human beings, for 'God was in Christ reconciling the world to himself, not counting people's sins against them'.

So Paul, believing that Jesus has died for all, sees himself as now 'compelled by the love of Christ': 'he died for all, so that those who live should no longer live for themselves, but for him who died for them'.

It is also the context for Paul's careful response to the outstanding issues between himself and the Corinthians. Apparently some have complained about Paul changing his travel plans. So he explains some of his reasons, assuring them he has not been making fickle promises. His ministry is transparent, not marked by 'secret and shameful ways'; instead, knowing his work will be reviewed before the 'judgment seat of Christ', he aims to keep a clear conscience. Though sharply criticized here about his ministry and its motivations, Paul's response is to 'open wide his heart' and to appeal to them to do the same in return. It is a powerful appeal, but one which leaves Paul quite vulnerable and exposed.

Paul's particular fear is that they might have reacted badly to Titus' visit and Paul's accompanying letter. Almost certainly Paul's note had focused on the continuing issue of the 'immoral brother', which had not been properly resolved by Timothy (when he had delivered 1 Corinthians). By the time Paul writes 2 Corinthians chapter 7, however, Titus has just returned with good news: Paul's note had triggered a 'godly sorrow' and a change of heart – both in the individual concerned and in the wider church. So Paul insists this is the time for them to 'reaffirm their love' for that brother and to 'forgive and comfort him'. Even though it shows the acute strains on Paul, as he pastors a young church so many miles removed, 2 Corinthians is thus written with a sense of great relief.

Paul thus concludes this section on a positive note – with an extended discussion of the money he is raising for the impoverished Jerusalem church. He reminds them of their generous promises and commends to them the Macedonian believers for their active involvement in this project. His tactful words include many

The temple of Apollo was one of the few buildings to survive the Roman destruction of the Greek city in 146 BC. After the city was refounded by Julius Caesar in 44 BC, the temple was surrounded by numerous shops – especially butchers selling meat from animals used for temple sacrifices (see p. 242).

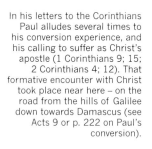

In his letters to the Corinthians Paul alludes several times to his conversion experience, and his calling to suffer as Christ's apostle (1 Corinthians 9; 15; 2 Corinthians 4; 12). That formative encounter with Christ took place near here – on the road from the hills of Galilee down towards Damascus (see Acts 9 or p. 222 on Paul's conversion).

encouragements to give: 'whoever sows generously will also reap generously'; 'God loves a cheerful giver.' The deepest reason, however, is Jesus' own example: 'though he was rich, yet for your sake he became poor, so that you through his poverty might become rich'.

Further problems (chapters 10–13)

Suddenly, however, there is a dramatic change of tone. Paul speaks out once more in defence of his ministry, vigorously responding to some specific charges. Evidently Paul has received some further criticisms from the Corinthians (on the dating issue here, see p. 245). One accusation is that he has come across as rather authoritative in his letters, but rather *timid* during his actual visits to Corinth – 'weighty in his letters but unimpressive in his speaking'. Another (ironically) is that Paul is compared unfavourably with other apostles who have recently visited Corinth (perhaps from Jerusalem?), yet unlike them he has not charged them financially for his services!

Paul responds forthrightly. He will certainly be bold on his next (third) visit, if that is what they prefer! He will use godly weapons to 'demolish every pretension' opposed to Christ. He may not be a 'trained speaker' but he *does* have 'knowledge'; and if he finds any wrong-doing, he will not hesitate to speak out. Yet he will continue his practice of making the gospel available free of charge – this is a sign of love, not weakness! He will not exploit them, but rather spend himself for them – just as parents do gladly for their children. Deep down he has a 'godly jealousy' for them, because he was the very first to preach the gospel to them. Yet he fears they are now receiving teaching from those whom he sarcastically terms 'super-apostles' – a false teaching which is leading them astray from their 'pure devotion to Christ'.

Moreover, Paul senses he has been dismissed as a fool. So he deliberately takes up the mantle of a jester and starts boasting of all his weaknesses. In the course of this extended jest, he mentions some of his key credentials (as a true Hebrew, as one granted great revelations and so on), but he also lists his more embarrassing experiences (for example, being lowered in a basket over the wall in Damascus). He also speaks of a recurring 'thorn in the flesh' (what precisely this was we do not know – an illness of some kind?); yet Paul sees it as God's way of teaching him that 'God's grace is made perfect in weakness.'

In this way, Paul parodies the pretensions of these other preachers. If the believers want some 'proof that Christ is speaking through him', Paul's deepest reply is that the Christ who himself was 'crucified in weakness' manifests his power precisely through those who, when judged by worldly standards, might appear weak and foolish. Thus authentic Christian ministry is cross-shaped. However, it is not to be dismissed as powerless. For, just as Christ was raised to new life, so true apostles have a legitimate 'authority' given them by the Lord – which Paul will surely exercise, if necessary.

On this strong note he comes to quite a sudden halt, concluding with a short prayer (which has been repeated ever since and is known simply as 'the grace'): 'May the grace of the Lord Jesus Christ, and the love of God, and the fellowship of the Holy Spirit, be with you all.'

'For when I am weak, then I am strong.'
2 Corinthians 12:10

Paul's Shorter Letters

Galatians

Galatians is probably Paul's first letter. It is also his most heated, for he has just heard that his converts in Galatia have been disturbed by Jewish Christian teachers (probably from Jerusalem) insisting that they must be circumcised: only so, by effectively first becoming Jews, can they fully enter the Christian family. Paul is incensed at this interference and alarmed by this teaching, which runs counter to his vision of the Christian message – that man and woman, Jew and Gentile, can *all* equally experience God's grace through exercising repentant faith in Jesus Christ. There are no other entrance requirements.

The cities visited by Paul in Acts 13–14 were in the southern end of the large province of Galatia, which covered much of central Anatolia – a remote area with numerous plateaus and some inland lakes.

Paul knows that his work among Gentiles is severely under threat, so he writes this impassioned letter to make clear his calling to be Christ's 'apostle to the Gentiles'. He probably also senses that this issue will need to be resolved in a face-to-face meeting in Jerusalem. This apostolic council indeed took place during AD 49 (see p. 224), so we can read Galatians as Paul's opening salvo in that forthcoming debate. At that council Paul's position would be vindicated, and he would subsequently visit the Galatians to tell them so (Acts 16:1–6). But at the time of writing the issues hang precariously in the balance – hence Paul's passionate defence.

Explaining some recent events

Paul's opening greeting (probably the first written words of the New Testament) gives us a fascinating window into early Christian belief: already Jesus is identified both as God's divine Son – not merely 'human' – and as the risen Lord; already his death is 'for our sins'. Yet Paul goes on immediately, without any thanksgiving for the Galatians, to voice his astonishment that they have turned to a 'different gospel – which is really no gospel at all'. These teachers are trying to pervert the gospel of Christ – an activity upon which Paul pronounces a strong anathema (or 'curse').

He then affirms the authenticity of his own calling. God alone brought about his dramatic conversion, commissioning him to preach to the Gentiles. This commission did not come from the Jerusalem-

Locating the Galatians

Galatia was a large province, recently created by the Romans, lying in Asia Minor's central heartlands. Some have therefore questioned whether Paul's visit (to Pisidian Antioch: see Acts 13–14) was really a visit to 'Galatia'. If not, then Paul must have visited these Galatians some time later. On this reading Paul could not have written this letter before the mid-50s; and the meeting in Jerusalem (described in Galatians 2) must be the apostolic council mentioned by Luke in Acts 15 (in AD 49: see pp. 219 and 224).

There is evidence, however, that the area visited by Paul in AD 47–48 was indeed within Galatia – even though inhabitants used more regional names for themselves (such as 'Pisidian'). And the meeting Paul describes evidently refers to a much smaller private meeting with just *three* of Jerusalem's church leaders – probably during his visit when offering some famine relief (in AD 45–46: see Acts 11:28–30).

So Galatians was probably written in the period between those private and public meetings. This would make good sense. Paul would be encouraged by that private agreement to do more work among the Gentiles (going to Cyprus and Galatia). Those not at the meeting, however, would want the issue to be re-examined – this time in public and with the 'circumcision group' representing their views in person. On this reading, Peter's hesitations (described by Paul in Galatians chapter 2) are more explicable: he is not disagreeing with the apostolic council, but vacillating in the interim period when the matter is still requiring resolution.

based apostles – though he had had appropriate contact with them a couple of times when they had fully recognized the validity of his work. Yet in recent months, this issue about what is expected of Gentile believers has indeed caused a rupture between himself and these other apostles. For, during his recent visit to Antioch, even Peter, being troubled by the viewpoints of James and others in the 'circumcision group', had stopped eating with 'unclean' Gentile 'sinners'. So Paul had publicly disagreed with Peter, contending that both Jews and Gentiles could only be 'justified' (or forgiven by God) on the basis of faith; that other requirements (obeying the Jewish dietary laws or undergoing circumcision) were not necessary; and that this was, surely, the very purpose of Jesus' death – to open up access to God's grace. So Paul had exclaimed, 'If righteousness could be gained through the law, Christ died for nothing!'

'No one will be justified by observing the law… I have been crucified with Christ … I live by faith in the Son of God, who loved me and gave himself for me.'
Galatians 2:16, 20

Arguing for faith in Christ alone

Paul then turns back to the 'foolish Galatians', who have also been bewitched by this same false teaching, and rebuts it with some overlapping arguments:

- God's call to Abraham was based on his faith alone; it also preceded God's giving of the Law at Sinai. The Law was thus never intended as a means of salvation but instead had revealed human sin and pointed forward to the Christ who would be the one to take away the 'curse' of that sin.

- Through their faith in Christ, the Galatians are the heirs of the Abrahamic promises – indeed they are now God's 'children'. They are truly 'children of the promise' (like Abraham's son Isaac) – unlike those emanating from Jerusalem, who fulfil the opposite role (like Abraham's son Ishmael, a child born in slavery).

- If the Galatians are circumcised, they will be obliged to fulfil the whole Law. Believers, however, are free from all this. Yet this is *not* a 'freedom to indulge the sinful nature', but rather a freedom to live out the 'law of love', to crucify evil desires, to 'live by the Spirit' and bring forth the 'fruit of the Spirit'.

Throughout these chapters Paul pleads with the Galatians in quite personal ways, urging them to remember their former delight in his ministry and to stand up against the false teachers, whom he sees as opposed to Christ's cross. For Paul the cross is central, so he adds a final paragraph in his own handwriting, which puts the issue in a nutshell: 'May I never boast except in the cross of our Lord Jesus Christ, through which the world has been crucified to me, and I to the world.'

Ephesians

Ephesians is a masterpiece, distilling Paul's thinking towards the end of his life. Paul describes himself as a prisoner 'in chains', probably awaiting trial before Nero in Rome (see p. 227); yet, despite his own circumstances, Paul's vision soars as he sees all the 'spiritual blessings' that believers now have 'in the heavenly realms'.

This was also a circular letter, designed to be read in as many as possible of the Christian communities in the province of Asia – not just in the provincial capital, Ephesus. (Hence the opening greeting to the saints 'in Ephesus' is not found in some early manuscripts.) So Paul avoids any specific references to local problems being encountered by his potential readers. Instead he focuses on the great universal truths of the Christian message, portraying the glories of Christ on a grand scale.

The letter breaks down into two halves. The first three chapters focus on God's blessings 'in Christ' (a much-used phrase in this letter); the final three on what this means in practice. This shift has been summarized in different ways: as a move from theology (or 'doctrine')

This large temple was built in Ephesus in honour of the Emperor Domitian (c. AD 90). Domitian's insistence that his subjects acknowledge him as 'Lord and Saviour' led to some severe persecution of Christians. After his assassination, however, honouring Domitian's memory was officially condemned.

'You also were included in Christ, when you heard the word of truth, the gospel of your salvation.'
Ephesians 1:13

'I pray that you may have power to grasp how wide and long and high and deep is the love of Christ.'
Ephesians 3:17–18

to ethics; or as a move from teaching about God's *grace* to a focus on the proper response of *gratitude*. This, then, is a book that can refresh its readers with vision but also resource them for action.

God's riches in Christ: a new life

In the opening chapter Paul lists these blessings: God's initiative to adopt people as his children and to lavish on them his grace; to redeem them and to reveal to them his purposes in Christ; to include people in Christ and to give them his Holy Spirit as a foretaste of their future inheritance. So he prays for believers' spiritual eyes to be opened to see this hope, and for their hearts to be strengthened by God's mighty power – that same power seen when God raised Jesus and exalted him to his 'right hand'.

Paul then reminds them of their former way of life and how God has rescued them 'because of his great love': though they were dead in their sins, God has made them to be 'alive in Christ' and 'seated with him' – not due to their own effort or works, but only 'by grace'. Moreover, those who had been Gentile pagans – dismissed as uncircumcised and as foreigners to God's promises within Israel – have now been brought within God's people; again this is only due to Christ, who has opened up

Paul and the first Christian believers would often have walked along this main road in Ephesus (Curetes' street). Although the temple of Hadrian (left) was only built later (c. AD 130), there would have been numerous other reminders of the inhabitants' commitment to paganism and the growing imperial cult.

'access to the Father' for *all* people – whether Jew or Gentile. All believers are now part of God's new family (or 'household') and have a place within God's new Temple – built on Christ and indwelt by God's Spirit.

Paul now interrupts himself. Seeing his own imminent trial before Nero as a test case of his ministry among the Gentiles, he wants his audience to know what he is risking on their behalf: 'I am a prisoner for the sake of you Gentiles.' So he reminds them of his unique calling to 'preach to the Gentiles the unsearchable riches of Christ' and to announce the newly revealed 'mystery' of how Gentiles are now 'heirs together' with Jewish believers, brought into 'one body'. He closes by praying that Christ will truly dwell in their hearts, and they will know the full measure of his love and power.

God's calling in Christ: a new lifestyle

Paul now addresses practical implications, urging them to live a life worthy of their calling (or, literally, to '*walk* worthily'). Believers are called:

• to be humble and patient, seeking unity within this new body (of which Christ is the head), and valuing the different gifts given by Christ to his people;

255

'You were taught to put off your old self, to be made new in the attitude of your minds and to put on the new self, created to be like God in true holiness.'

Ephesians 4:22–24

- to turn their backs on their former pagan lifestyles, turning instead towards truth, godliness, love and peace, and to rid themselves of any hint of greed, impurity or sexual immorality;

- to live a life of love and to be 'children of the light', remembering Christ's love shown on the cross.

This should then affect every aspect of life: all their relationships are to be marked by a reverence for Christ and a willingness, where appropriate, to submit to one another. This is to be seen between husbands and wives, between parents and their children, and indeed even between slaves and their masters.

Finally, Paul develops a picture of believers each putting on the 'whole armour of God' (the 'shield of faith', the 'helmet of salvation' and so on). Thus equipped, they are to take their stand against the spiritual forces of evil. With this stirring picture in their minds, Paul's audience can now sense the progression that has developed through the letter: they have been called to *sit* with Christ in the heavenly realms, to *walk* before him in holiness of life, and now, finally, to *stand* firm against evil. This is a Pauline masterpiece indeed – skilfully crafted, comprehensive in its scope, and powerful in its effect.

Philippians

Philippians is one of Paul's most personal letters. Writing from prison in Rome, and awaiting his trial, he thanks the believers in Philippi for their recent gift, which has been so encouraging to him. Paul has fond memories of the believers there, so he does not need to focus on any problems in their community – except for one reported clash between two women. Instead Paul expresses openly his feelings of Christian affection for them; he gives thanks for their shared 'partnership in the gospel' and prays that God will continue his 'good work' in them.

Paul also speaks honestly about the pressures he himself is under: the discouragement he felt when some believers in Rome stirred up trouble for him during his imprisonment; but, above all, the concern about his own death – possibly quite soon. Paul does not know which way things will go, but he prays that, whatever happens (whether 'by life or by death'), 'Christ will be exalted.' For, in his memorable motto, 'to me, to live is Christ; to die is gain'. We are encountering here a man on the point of death, evaluating his own life and making his final appeals.

'I pray that your love may abound more and more, so that… you may be pure until the day of Christ.'
Philippians 1:9–10

The Philippians' conduct
After his opening greetings and prayers, Paul reports on recent events in Rome – how his arrival has 'really served to advance the gospel'; in particular, the whole palace guard knows he is in chains for Christ. Paul rejoices whenever Christ is preached and hopes things will work out for his own deliverance. Even if they do not, however, the Philippians must 'conduct themselves in a manner worthy of the gospel'. In particular, they should be like-minded, 'standing firm in one spirit', and not doing anything out of selfish ambition. Instead they should have the same mindset as Jesus himself, who had made himself nothing and become 'obedient to death'. There is to be no more arguing, because the quality of their community life must shine out before others 'like stars in the universe'.

Paul then moves on to practical matters, talking warmly about two recent visitors, Timothy and Epaphroditus: the latter (one of their own number, who had probably delivered their gift) he will send back

The 'cup of Augustus' (c. 10 BC) shows the seated emperor being surrounded by 'lictors' (or 'rod-bearers') – the name used for the magistrates in the Roman colony of Philippi (see Acts 16:20). In Philippi Paul encourages believers to see themselves as belonging to a different colony – as 'citizens of heaven' – and as 'bowing the knee' to a different ruler, Christ the 'Lord' (Philippians 2:11; 3:20).

The hymn to Christ

'... *being in very nature God, [Jesus] did not consider equality with God something to be used to his own advantage; rather, he made himself nothing by taking the very nature of a servant, being made in human likeness. And being found in appearance as a human being, he humbled himself by becoming obedient to death – even death on a cross! Therefore God exalted him to the highest place and gave him the name that is above every name, that at the name of Jesus every knee should bow, in heaven and on earth and under the earth, and every tongue confess that Jesus Christ is Lord, to the glory of God the Father.'*
Philippians 2:6–11

Almost certainly these are the words of a very early Christian song which expresses exactly what Paul wants to say about Jesus. The song appears to have had two verses (each containing three smaller sections), into which Paul has dramatically inserted the phrase 'even death on a cross!' – presumably to underscore his amazement at the degradation Jesus endured in his death.

The song provides very early evidence for Christians believing in Jesus as both human and divine ('in very nature *God*'). It speaks of the humility involved in the incarnation but also of Jesus as Lord. Intriguingly the song-writers have adapted words from Isaiah 45:23, where 'every knee' was to 'bow' before *Yahweh*, the unique God of Israel. Now people are bowing down to Jesus – a remarkable act of worship when set against the backdrop of Old Testament monotheism.

View westwards across the Roman forum towards the tall remains of a basilica (built for Christian worship c. AD 550).

to Philippi with this letter, but he wants to keep Timothy with him a little longer.

The letter seems to be drawing to a close ('Finally, rejoice in the Lord!'), but Paul suddenly warns them about some who 'live as enemies of the cross' and, in particular, some Judaizing believers who may disturb them with the demand for circumcision. This triggers in Paul a quite personal account of his own life: despite all his Jewish privileges, he now reckons them to be as 'dung' compared to the 'surpassing greatness of knowing Christ'. The supreme goal is to 'be found in Christ', and 'pressing on towards the goal' of meeting the risen Christ, who will return from heaven to transform believers' bodies to be 'like his glorious body'.

Paul then returns to the theme of 'rejoicing in the Lord', and how this can keep believers' hearts and minds at peace. Once again we expect the letter to end, when suddenly (so it seems) he remembers he has not properly expressed his thanks for the Philippians' gift! This he does warmly and with heartfelt gratitude. So this is not a carefully ordered letter, but a personal note, in which Paul is choosing his final words to these dear friends. If he never sees them again, what lasting impression does he want them to have? The answer, repeated at several points, is that key command: 'Rejoice in the Lord.' This is the upbeat vision Paul wants them to hear, ringing in their ears, whenever in the future they think of him.

Below: View within Philippi, looking northwards along the Via Egnatia. This road linked Philippi to Rome via Dyrrachium on the Adriatic coast and had played a vital role in the military campaigns leading to the battle of Philippi (42 BC). It was also used by Epaphroditus and other couriers for the exchange of gifts and letters between Paul and the Philippians. The journey from Rome to Philippi might take up to two months.

'I have no one else like him… Timothy has proved himself… as a son with his father.'
Philippians 2:20, 22

'Our citizenship is in heaven, from where we eagerly await a Saviour.'
Philippians 3:20

Colossians

Paul's letter to the believers in Colossae shares some remarkable similarities with Ephesians. Written also from prison in Rome, it has a broadly similar pattern: after opening greetings and prayers, there are some bold visionary statements of theology followed by a more practical section on Christian lifestyle (this last section being often identical word for word to Ephesians). Yet there are differences: it is shorter and sounds more personal. Paul has received news of the Colossians through Epaphras (through whom they had first heard the gospel); thus, although Paul has never met them, he speaks into their particular situation with some personal knowledge.

The similarities between these two letters have probably come about because Paul takes the opportunity of Tychicus' intended visit to Colossae to write a second letter (known to us as Ephesians) in which he simply works up some of his fresh ideas in Colossians into a more magisterial piece – intended as an 'encyclical' sent to all the churches of Asia, starting in Laodicea (see p. 290). Hence his encouragement at the end of Colossians that they should also read this second letter (which Paul has sent to neighbouring Laodicea).

In Colossians Paul speaks quite personally about his own ministry,

Main image: View looking northwards to the mound of Colossae (middle distance). The city was destroyed by an earthquake later in the AD 60s and has never been excavated.

Inset: This symbol (looking like a 'P' superimposed on an 'X') combines two Greek letters (Chi and Ro) which are the first letters in the name of 'Christ'. From the time of Constantine onwards, this became one of the most common symbols for Jesus.

'Just as you received Christ Jesus as Lord, continue to live in him, rooted and built up in him.'
Colossians 2:6–7

'For in Christ all the fullness of the Deity lives in bodily form.'
Colossians 2:9

wanting them to know that, though imprisoned far away in Rome, he is 'struggling for you and for those in Laodicea'. He is constantly presenting to people God's newly revealed 'mystery' – which he summarizes in the pithy phrase 'Christ in you, the hope of glory'. '*Him* we proclaim, so that we might present everyone perfect in Christ.' Colossians turns out to be just that – a proclamation of the glorious Christ, designed to develop in his followers a deep, spiritual maturity.

In his opening prayers Paul rejoices in the Colossians' response to the gospel ('God's grace in all its truth') – seen in their faith, hope and love. Now that they have experienced redemption and have been brought into the 'kingdom of God's Son', they should grow in their 'knowledge of God' and live a life worthy of him, 'bearing fruit in every good work'.

His chief goal, however, is to promote a vision of the glory of Christ:

- 'He is the image of the invisible God,' God's agent in creation, who is 'before all things' and in whom 'all things hold together'; in him 'are hidden all the treasures of wisdom and knowledge'.

- Through his death God has reconciled to himself all things and triumphed over all evil powers and authorities, and his resurrection reveals that 'God was pleased to have all his fullness dwell in him.'

This is a powerful vision – of Christ's person and work – and the rest of the letter is an encouragement to the believers to live their lives guided by it. Through faith in him they have 'died with Christ' and have 'died to the basic principles of this world' (with its petty religious rules and its hollow and deceptive philosophies). Through his resurrection they have been 'made alive in Christ'. Through his own fully divine nature, they themselves have been given 'fullness in Christ': 'for you died and your life is now hidden with Christ in God'.

As a result, they must set their minds 'on things above', focused on Christ's return in glory; they are to 'put to death anything that belongs to their earthly nature' and to put on the 'new self, which is being renewed in the image of its creator' – marked by virtues such as love, peace and patience. In every sphere of life they are to 'serve the Lord Christ'; and, in their relationships with those outside their community, they are to be both wise and gracious.

Paul then closes with some personal greetings, listing some of those in Rome with him, and adds a final note in his own hand: 'Remember my chains.'

1 and 2 Thessalonians

The return of Christ

Already by AD 50 Paul's message evidently included clear teaching that Christ would return to visit his people. This teaching almost certainly was rooted in Jesus' own teaching. For in his parables Jesus had spoken of a master *returning* to find his servants asleep; he had also spoken about the '*coming* of the Son of Man in glory'.

Some of this teaching may in the first instance have referred to Jesus' *first* coming (when he arrived in Jerusalem as its king or was vindicated as God's Son in the resurrection). Yet any such confusions could well have been sorted out in the forty-day period after the resurrection (Acts 1:3). Certainly, according to Luke's account of the ascension (Acts 1:11), when Jesus finally departed from them, the apostles were assured he would one day *be coming back*.

This return is known as Christ's *parousia* – a word which, though often translated as 'second coming', refers to Christ's royal *presence*. One of the potential early confusions was whether this *parousia* might coincide with Jerusalem's destruction (as predicted by Jesus: see p. 194) – which might explain why the Thessalonians wonder whether *this* 'day of the Lord' has already happened. Books written after Jerusalem's destruction in AD 70 (such as Revelation) clarify this, however, emphasizing *still* this hope for Christ's return. So, although the apparent delay of the *parousia* caused some concern (such as in 2 Peter 3), this hope remains undiminished. Thus almost the last words of Revelation are a prayer: 'Come, Lord Jesus.'

Paul first writes to the believers in Thessalonica shortly after his visit (around May AD 50?). According to Acts chapter 17, Paul had been forced to leave the city by cover of night, after being there for only a few weeks. So, understandably, he was anxious to know how the few believers were faring; and, after a few months of hearing nothing, he sent Timothy back for news. Paul feared the Thessalonians might have been tempted away from the faith and his own efforts might have been in vain. The first letter to the Thessalonians is written when Timothy returns to Paul, now in Corinth and with a great sense of relief: 'Timothy has just now come to us and has brought good news about your faith and love!'

Paul's joy is felt throughout this letter: 'now we *really live*, since you are standing'. He is so grateful that they responded positively to his preaching, receiving it as the 'word of God': and that they had not listened to his critics, seeing Paul's visit as a failure or his ministry as selfish. He is so encouraged that they have stood up to some fierce opposition – especially from the city's synagogue. 'How can we thank God enough for all the joy we have because of you?' 'For what is our joy, or crown in which we will glory…? Is it not you? Indeed, you are our glory and our joy!'

So Paul longs to see them again soon. Meanwhile he writes to encourage them. He reminds them of his time spent in Thessalonica (his motivations, his labours, his lifestyle) and of the instructions he has passed on – namely that they should be holy, avoiding sexual immorality and pursuing brotherly love; they are also to be prepared for Christ's return, and to live in ways which earn others' respect. After some other brief instructions, he closes with a prayer: 'May God himself, the God of peace, sanctify you… May your whole spirit, soul and body be kept blameless at the coming of our Lord Jesus Christ. The one who calls you is faithful, and he will do it.'

A few months later, however, Paul, Silas and Timothy send a second (shorter) letter in response to some disturbing reports: some of the Thessalonians are apparently becoming idle; others are confused about Christ's return, believing that perhaps the day of the Lord has already come. Both these matters had been touched on in 1 Thessalonians. Paul had clearly indicated there that the day of the Lord would come 'like a thief in the night'; now, however, he reiterates that Jesus will be seen in his majesty and will judge the disobedient, overcoming any who oppose him (including a mysterious figure known as the 'lawless one'). Similarly, Paul had clearly stated that believers should 'work with their own hands'; but now he presses the point, warning them against 'idle busybodies' who should be 'earning the bread they eat'. Whatever the precise cause (were they abusing their fellow Christians' hospitality or simply waiting for Christ's return?) Paul's teaching is clear, and he cites as an example his own hard manual labour during his visit.

Macedonia

RHODOPE MTS

PINDOS MTS

Thessalonica Philippi

Berea

Pinios

Troas

Aegean Sea

Nicopolis

Athens

Ephesus

Corinth
1 Thessalonians, AD 51
2 Thessalonians, AD 52

Rhodes

KEY

———— Route of Paul, Silas and Timothy
———— Route of Silas and Timothy
———— Route of Paul and Silas
———— Route of Timothy
———— Route of Paul

Above: The Roman forum in Thessalonica showing its underground store-rooms. According to Acts 17 Paul's opponents dragged a believer called Jason into the forum and told the city authorities that these Christians were acting 'against the decrees of Caesar' with their proclamation of an alternative 'king' – called Jesus (Acts 17:5–9).

Left: Journeys of Paul's companions (AD 50–51).

Below: The first Greek word (top left) on this stone inscription reads 'politarchountos'. This 19th-century discovery (from an arch in Thessalonica later destroyed) confirms that Luke was correct to describe the city's authorities as 'politarchs' (Acts 17:6, 8).

Paul closes with a few words in his own handwriting – presumably so they could spot any fraudulent letters in the future. 'I, Paul, write this greeting in my own hand, which is the distinguishing mark in all my letters. This is how I write.' It's a pity that that signature has not been preserved!

The 'Pastoral' Letters

The last four Pauline epistles are addressed to individuals, not to church congregations. Three of these (1 Timothy, 2 Timothy and Titus) have for many centuries been referred to as the 'pastoral epistles' because (unlike the small letter to Philemon: see p. 268) they were written to individual *pastors* who were responsible for leading local churches.

The title is helpful, as long as we remember that, within the New Testament church, pastors were not only involved in pastoral care but had important roles as teachers and managers. Indeed this is a key point learned from these epistles. Thus Paul encourages these church leaders to devote themselves to preaching and teaching, and lays down clear guidelines for the way they should seek to manage their congregations.

This is particularly true of 1 Timothy and Titus, which read somewhat like management memos. But 2 Timothy is quite different. It is acutely personal, as Paul, waiting to stand trial, writes to his trusted young colleague, beseeching him to join him in Rome (see p. 266).

1 Timothy

Paul has left Timothy in charge of the congregations in Ephesus. This is a big assignment for a young man, who must now carefully 'guard what has been entrusted to your care'. So Paul encourages him, 'Don't let anyone look down on you because you are young;' and he writes in such a way as to strengthen his hand, placing his own apostolic authority behind his young protégé. For Paul knows how congregations can fly apart following individuals with strong agendas. What is needed is strong, godly leadership.

Some examples of Paul's detailed advice to Timothy are:

- Oppose those who promote controversy with false doctrine, godless chatter and false claims to knowledge. This unhealthy teaching may take various forms: focusing on myths and genealogies; offering over-strict interpretations of the Law which do not allow for God's grace; or even inventing new rules (forbidding marriage or eating certain foods). In every case, the antidote is healthy teaching ('sound doctrine').

- Build your ministry on certain trustworthy sayings, reliable truths that will stand the test of time; for example: 'Christ Jesus came into the world to save sinners.'

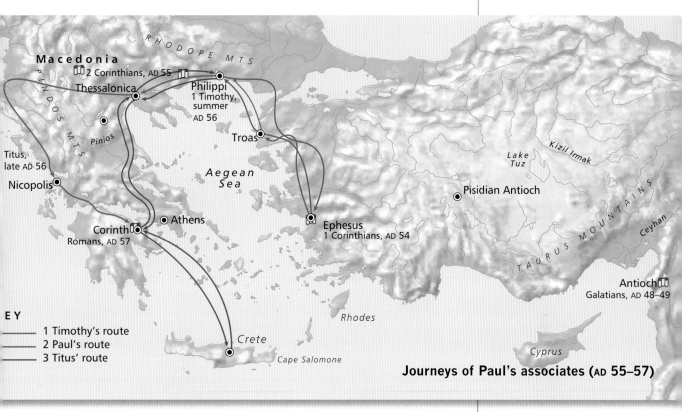

Macedonia
2 Corinthians, AD 55

Thessalonica

Philippi
1 Timothy,
summer
AD 56

R H O D O P E   M T S

Troas

Lake
Tuz

Kizil Irmak

P I N D O S   M T S

Pinios

*Aegean
Sea*

Titus,
late AD 56

Nicopolis

Pisidian Antioch

Athens

Corinth
Romans, AD 57

Ephesus
1 Corinthians, AD 54

T A U R U S   M O U N T A I N S

Ceyhan

Antioch
Galatians, AD 48–49

KEY

— 1 Timothy's route
— 2 Paul's route
— 3 Titus' route

Rhodes

Crete

Cape Salomone

Cyprus

Journeys of Paul's associates (AD 55–57)

- Remember that God wants *all* people to come to a knowledge of the truth, so encourage his congregations, when they gather, to pray for *everyone* – including their rulers. (It is in this context that Paul gives his controversial ruling that women should 'learn in quietness [and full submission]': see p. 281.)

- Ensure that believers do not act in ways that tarnish the reputation of the 'church of the living God', which is truly God's household and the 'pillar and foundation of the truth'.

- Work within appropriate guidelines when appointing church leaders – whether 'overseers' (later translated as 'bishops') or 'deacons' (literally, those who 'serve'); these are to be people with a known track record of appropriate behaviour.

- Do nothing out of favouritism, showing a proper respect to those in the congregation who are older (but only adding widows to the church's list of those it supports if they are of a certain age and really in need); conduct yourself with absolute purity when relating to women in your congregation.

- Finally, keep an eye on your own life and teaching, pursuing 'godliness with contentment' and avoiding the love of money.

1 Timothy's route: Ephesus (summer AD 55) to Macedonia and back to Ephesus (spring AD 56).

2 Paul's route: Ephesus (autumn AD 55) to Corinth (January AD 57).

3 Titus' route: Corinth (autumn AD 55) to Macedonia and back to Corinth (spring AD 56) followed on by summer visit to Crete and back (summer AD 56).

'… the overseer must be above reproach… temperate, self-controlled… able to teach.'
1 Timothy 3:2

265

Below: Paul describes himself in 2 Timothy and elsewhere as a 'prisoner', 'in chains' for the gospel. Paul was continuously under guard for more than four years (AD 57–62) – in Caesarea and then Rome. This relief (of Roman soldiers dealing with barbarian captives) highlights Rome's brutality; Paul, however, was a Roman citizen and was treated well, being effectively only under 'house arrest' for much of that time.

While encouraging others to be 'rich in good deeds' and to 'lay up treasures for themselves for the coming age', you yourself are to pursue righteousness, godliness, faith, love, endurance and gentleness, keeping a pure heart, a good conscience and a sincere faith.

To encourage him in all these tasks, Paul reminds Timothy of the incredible grace which he, Paul, has received (as a former 'blasphemer, persecutor and a violent man'); but also of the 'prophetic words' spoken over Timothy before he took up this daunting assignment. All these are to stir him up so he can 'fight the good fight' and keep the faith.

2 Timothy

Unlike the other pastoral epistles, 2 Timothy is evidently written from prison in Rome (some time after Paul's arrival in March AD 60). He comments that only Luke is with him, so he asks Timothy to come quickly – before winter, if possible. He also refers to his first defence (presumably an initial court hearing, which registered his case).

Paul focuses much on Timothy, giving him encouragements, despite his innate timidity, to 'guard the good deposit entrusted to him'; this is the good news of the grace of God, who in Christ's resurrection has

'destroyed death and brought immortality to light'. Timothy is to be strong, like a soldier or athlete, and prove himself a reliable worker. He is to flee the evil desires of youth and to avoid stupid arguments. Instead he must 'correctly handle the word of truth', taking his stand on the 'God-breathed' nature of Scripture, and 'preach the word in season and out of season'.

Yet Paul is also thinking about his own death: 'the time is near for my departure.' The letter has an incredible poignancy as he asks Timothy not to be ashamed of him (though now he is 'chained like a criminal') and as he looks back on his own ministry with a sense of finality: 'I have fought the good fight, I have finished the race, I have kept the faith.' Yet he is looking into the future with confidence: 'Now there is in store for me the crown of righteousness... The Lord will bring me safely to his heavenly kingdom.'

Titus

Paul's memo to Titus is slightly shorter than 1 Timothy but essentially very similar. (Conceivably Titus was more experienced than Timothy and so did not need such detailed instructions.) Paul wants Titus to rendezvous with him in Nicopolis for the winter, but in the meantime he asks him to stay on in Crete for a while in order to 'straighten out what is unfinished'. In particular this involves appointing elders (or 'overseers') in every town where there are believers. Again there are clear guidelines about the qualities desirable in making these appointments. And again there is an emphasis on their capacity to teach 'sound doctrine' – so they are able to refute those who are deceiving people with falsehoods (here especially focused on Jewish myths of some kind). Meanwhile, Titus himself is to 'avoid foolish controversies and genealogies and quarrels about the law'; he is to warn divisive people, teaching what accords with sound doctrine. He is to 'encourage and rebuke with all authority'. And Paul gives him an outline of key things to stress for particular groups of people (that is, older or younger men, older or younger women, slaves relating to their masters or subjects relating to their rulers).

Throughout we see Paul's conviction that authentic Christian truth always leads on to godliness. Twice Paul summarizes what God has done in Christ – seeing it as a revelation of his grace, kindness and love – but both times this summary is followed by a key challenge: 'the grace of God that brings salvation has appeared and teaches us to say "No" to ungodliness'; or again, all those who have 'trusted in God' should now 'devote themselves to doing what is good'. For Paul is convinced that God's purpose, seen in the cross, is to redeem people from evil and to 'purify for himself a people that are his very own, eager to do what is good'. It is imperative, therefore, that the redeemed community should be godly. Indeed God's own reputation is tied up with the reputation of the church! Believers should be peaceable and humble in

'In everything set them an example by doing what is good. In your teaching show integrity, seriousness and soundness of speech that cannot be condemned, so that those who oppose you may be ashamed because they have nothing bad to say about us.'
Titus 2:7–8

their relationships, productive in their lives, and so make the teaching about God their Saviour attractive. Paul is thus laying down a challenge that those who claim to know God must ensure their actions do not undermine that claim.

Philemon

Paul also sends a short personal note to one particular believer in Colossae – a man called Philemon. Paul had led Philemon to faith in Christ (while in Ephesus?) and now has an important favour to ask.

A young man called Onesimus (meaning 'useful') has met up with Paul in Rome and has become a believer. However, he is actually a runaway slave – who had previously worked for Philemon! Onesimus is now returning to Colossae (with Paul's courier, Tychicus); so Paul writes to Philemon, urging him to give his former slave a good welcome.

We see here the quality of Paul's relationships: he describes Onesimus as his 'son' (indeed as his 'very heart') and appeals to Philemon by reminding him that he owes to Paul 'his very self'.

We also see the radical effects of the Christian message on society. Runaway slaves could be executed, but now there is a call to forgive. Paul gives guidance in Colossians about how masters and slaves should behave. Yet what if *both* the master and his slave were now believers (as here, where Philemon is to consider Onesimus as a 'brother in the Lord')? Former barriers might come tumbling down.

So this short memo places a ticking bomb under ancient slavery – challenging it with the Christian message of the equal worth of each human being. We do not know how Philemon responded to Paul's appeal, but, if he welcomed Onesimus back with open arms, this small step would have marked a quantum leap forwards in human society.

'Manumission' was a formal process in which slaves were given their freedom. Often they became Roman citizens, taking on the family name of their former master (as happened perhaps to Paul's own parents?). On this stone stele (c. 50 BC) a slave (standing, wearing a Phrygian hat as a symbol of freedom) touches his master's hand in the presence of a witness (a 'lictor': see p. 257).

269

Other Apostolic Letters

After Paul's writings we come to eight further letters. The first of these, the letter to the Hebrews, is quite long, but the remainder are much shorter (three of them having only one chapter). These last seven letters are known as the 'catholic epistles', in the sense that, though they are small and focused on particular situations, they belong to the Christian community throughout the world ('catholic' comes from a Greek phrase meaning 'across the world').

Precisely because none of them were placed securely within the defined Pauline corpus in the first century, these non-Pauline letters were inevitably put through a lengthy process of scrutiny when the early church drew up its definitive list of New Testament books. The smaller ones in particular were naturally vulnerable to being questioned. So the fact that it was several centuries before the *whole* church received all these letters is not a sign of the letters' original inauthenticity but rather of the extreme care Christians showed – not wishing to lose anything (not even a tiny, personal letter) that God had truly given in the apostolic age.

In modern scholarship the document most questioned for its authenticity is 2 Peter (because its style seems quite different from 1 Peter). Perhaps, then, it was written by one of Peter's followers? If so, this would be an example of pseudepigraphy – a convention which some think was widely accepted in the ancient world, where followers of a religious leader might write in the 'name' of that leader. The other smaller letters are normally received as truly written by the named person (on 2 and 3 John, however, see p. 284).

The story of Hebrews' acceptance within the canon is quite distinctive. Almost certainly it was written to Rome in the AD 60s (see p. 272), with the Roman church knowing it had *not* been written to them by Paul (but rather by one of his trusted leaders). In that sense it *did* come from the apostolic company, but not actually from one of the 'apostles' in the narrower sense of that word. Many centuries later, when the test of apostolic authorship was applied in that narrower sense, it was conveniently assumed that perhaps it *had* been written by Paul after all: only so would the church receive it into its canon. Most people today, however, have little difficulty in recognizing its apostolic credentials, even if the precise name of the writer remains a complete mystery: as Origen aptly said back in the early third century, 'As to who wrote Hebrews, *God only knows!*'

** This phrase, which picks up the Old Testament imagery of the twelve tribes of Israel, is being used metaphorically to refer to Christian congregations (perhaps even including Gentiles?), whom James sees as now the true inheritors of Israel's destiny. Peter's use of the Old Testament term 'elect' will also have included Gentiles. Note too how both James and Peter see the believers as 'scattered' (picking up the imagery previously used of the 'scattered' Jewish dispersion).

	From	To	Date
Hebrews	Outside Italy	Jewish believers in Rome	Early 60s
James	Jerusalem	'Twelve tribes scattered among the nations'**	c. 45–50
1 Peter	Rome	'God's elect scattered throughout Pontus, Galatia, Cappadocia, Asia and Bithynia' (modern-day Turkey)	Early 60s
2 Peter	Rome?	Not specified	Early 60s?
1–3 John	Ephesus	Local Christian communities (and individuals) in the surrounding province of Asia	75–90
Jude	Palestine?	Not specified: local Christian congregations?	50–70

Hebrews

The book of Hebrews is the longest letter in the New Testament outside the Pauline corpus. It was probably written to Christians in Rome in the AD 60s by someone who knew the Roman church well, but who was temporarily travelling elsewhere: hence his final comment that 'those from Italy send their greetings' (suggesting that he was travelling with some Italian believers to churches in other provinces). The book's style strongly suggests that Paul himself was *not* the author. Yet it remains possible that Paul, who arrived in Rome in March AD 60, was one of those who *encouraged* the author to write. For the believers in Rome were evidently facing a severe crisis and they needed the strong counsel of someone they knew well (unlike Paul) and who had himself been with them through good days and bad.

The precise nature of the crisis is a little harder to determine. Evidently the threat of persecution was not far away. The author reminds his audience of 'those earlier days' when they faced persecution and encourages them to persevere – presumably because another spate of persecution is looming. This would fit well with the situation in Rome in the early 60s as the emperor Nero became increasingly unpredictable, eventually scapegoating the Christians for the great fire in Rome (18 July AD 64).

Yet the author evidently has a more specific concern that relates to the *Jewish* Christians (hence the title later given to his letter: 'to the *Hebrews*' – that is, the Jewish believers in Jesus). At one point he notes that some of them have 'given up meeting together'. So perhaps the Jewish believers were no longer meeting together with Gentile believers or, worse still, were reverting to meeting only with their non-Christian fellow-Jews – either for regular sabbath worship or for special festival meals. Such a reversion to the Jewish synagogue might have been very tempting – not just because of prior family loyalties, but also because the Roman authorities recognized the legitimacy of Judaism as an ancient 'permitted religion' (*religio licita*). So, if persecution was in the air, it would be very tempting to hide under the umbrella of Judaism rather than be exposed as a member of a new-fangled religion easily categorized as illegal: for it was far safer to be known as a Jew than as a Christian.

The writer passionately urges them not to do this. He senses that this may lead eventually (whether initially intended or not) to their abandoning their faith in Jesus. So he mounts a powerful presentation of the unique glory of Jesus, arguing that he is much greater than anything they possessed through their Jewish background. So Hebrews is a passionate, Christ-centred sermon, full of encouragements and warnings, as the writer seeks to woo them back from the brink of apostasy.

Jesus: his incarnation and demanding call (chapters 1–4)

In the past God spoke to our ancestors through the prophets... but in these last days he has spoken to us by his Son, whom he appointed heir of all things, and through whom he made the universe. The Son is the radiance of God's glory and the exact representation of his being... After he had provided purification for sins, he sat down at the right hand of the Majesty in heaven.

Hebrews 1:1–3

Hebrews begins with a clarion wake-up call – an opening salvo in which we see immediately some of the author's chief convictions:

- that the God who spoke in the Old Testament is identical to the God who has now sent Jesus (so his audience cannot revert back to faith in an 'Old Testament only' God);

- that Jesus' coming is God's definitive speech-act (so people must listen carefully and not ignore this vital message);

'Therefore, since we are surrounded by such a great cloud of witnesses... let us run with perseverance the race marked out for us' (Hebrews 12:1). The author may have been drawing on the imagery of contemporary athletics tracks – such as the Circus Maximus in Rome (see p. 238) or this spectacular one in Aphrodisias (capacity: 30,000).

'For the word of God is alive and active. Sharper than any double-edged sword... it judges the thoughts and attitudes of the heart.'
Hebrews 4:12

- that Jesus is eternally God's 'Son' – and indeed the creator, sustainer and future 'heir' of the world (so to abandon faith in Jesus is to abandon faith in God as he really is);

- and that recently Jesus has successfully accomplished an incredible task, described as the 'purification for sins' (so he can offer to human beings a divine forgiveness not previously available – even through God's appointed Temple in Jerusalem).

These themes will recur throughout the letter. For now the author develops the third point, showing how Jesus is in quite a different category from that of the angels: angels are God's servants, but Jesus is God's Son, who instead is worshipped by those angels and who sits on God's throne. As such, 'we must pay careful attention, so that we do not drift away'.

Next the author emphasizes the incarnation – that in coming into the world this divine Son was, paradoxically, truly human; he became like one of us – sharing in our flesh and blood, in suffering and even in death. So he can help us when we are being tempted, be merciful to those who need forgiveness, and greatly encourage those 'in slavery by their fear of death'. If the opening chapter focused on the divinity of Christ, here now we see his full humanity. Yet the point is the same – that Jesus' followers, those who 'share in the heavenly calling', should 'fix their thoughts' resolutely on Jesus.

Jesus, he continues, is even greater than Moses. This then leads on to a reflection on how the Israelites, when under Moses, rejected God's voice and so did not 'enter God's rest' (that is, the Promised Land). Those now under *Jesus'* leadership must not repeat their mistake, falling into unbelief and disobedience, and so failing to enter the 'sabbath rest' God still offers to his people (see box, right). Instead they should accept the challenges of receiving God's sharp and powerful word. Yet, if this challenge might provoke some appropriate fear of the 'God to whom we must give account', they should note that Jesus, because of his own sufferings and testings, is uniquely able to 'sympathize with our weakness'. 'Let us then approach God's throne of grace with confidence, so that we may receive mercy and find grace to help us in our time of need.'

Jesus the great 'high priest': access into God's presence through his death (5:1 – 10:25)

In speaking of Jesus here the author repeats a key description of Jesus – that he is a 'great high priest'. This distinctive imagery (not used by any other New Testament writer) is drawn from the Temple – itself based on the instructions given to Moses concerning the tabernacle in the wilderness (see p. 43). The author now develops this imagery at some length, arguing that Jesus, this new high priest, offers people something much richer than what the Temple offers.

To build his argument, the author quotes from Psalm 110 (the most frequently quoted psalm in the New Testament, which Jesus himself discussed just days before his crucifixion): 'Sit at my right hand until I make your enemies a footstool for your feet... You are a priest for ever, in the order of Melchizedek.' He sees this as fulfilled in Christ now seated 'at God's right hand', where he eternally acts as a priest, representing God's people and bringing them forgiveness. The text, however, also requires him to explain what is meant by the 'order of Melchizedek'.

Melchizedek (literally 'king of righteousness') was a mysterious figure mentioned in Genesis 14, when he went out from Salem/Jerusalem to greet Abraham and blessed him. The author of Hebrews deduces from this that he was greater than Abraham (because he blessed him) and that he was a mysterious pre-figurement of Christ himself, the ultimate king. In any event, the psalmist had clearly predicted that an alternative priesthood would eventually be introduced – not based on the Levitical priesthood (the priestly order named after Abraham's descendant Levi), but somehow patterned on Melchizedek.

The journey of faith

The author of Hebrews regularly describes faith as a journey. He compares his audience to the Israelites wandering through the desert towards the Promised Land (chapters 3–4). Individuals are to follow the example of Abraham, who left his homeland for that 'land of promise', and who, having arrived, was still 'longing for a better country' and for God's true city (chapter 11).

So (in chapter 12) believers are to 'throw off everything that hinders and run the race with perseverance'; they are to keep their eyes 'fixed on Jesus', who as a 'pioneer' is leading the race, setting an example to those who follow. The author here may well have been imagining the Roman stadium, when he portrays believers as 'surrounded by such a great cloud of witnesses': it is as though all God's faithful servants from the past are now seated in the sports arena, cheering on the marathon athletes as they run their final lap! And, once over the finishing line, they will be in the 'heavenly Jerusalem', surrounded by 'thousands of angels in joyful assembly'.

Hebrews is thus a sustained encouragement to persevere in this race. Yet, paradoxically, the author teaches that believers have *already* arrived: 'you *have come* to the heavenly Jerusalem'! Even more striking, through Jesus they can have confidence – here and now – to *enter* into the Most Holy Place. Thus, uncertainty on the journey is offset by the assurance of having already arrived! Or, as Hebrews puts it, 'faith is the assurance of things hoped for'.

Model of the Jerusalem Temple, looking towards the Holy of Holies – the place, in biblical thought, of God's holy Presence. At the time of Jesus' death the protective curtain had been 'torn in two from top to bottom' (Mark 15:38). Now the author of Hebrews teaches that there is no longer any need for the Temple. A few years later (August AD 70) the Temple was indeed destroyed by the Romans.

So believers can legitimately refer to Jesus as a high priest – even though, humanly, he was 'descended from Judah' (not Levi) and thus was not eligible to be the high priest in Jerusalem. 'Now the main point of what we are saying is this: *We do have such a high priest, who serves in… the true tabernacle.*'

This in turn, however, requires an explanation of the 'true tabernacle'. This tabernacle, which God commanded Moses to build, was essentially patterned on a heavenly reality; it depicted in structural and visual format the truth that human beings could only approach God on the basis of an acceptable sacrifice.

This sacrifice, however, is precisely what Jesus has now offered – when he 'offered himself once for all'. As a result, believers can enter into God's presence and be assured of their forgiveness. All this then means that there is no need for any physical tabernacle (nor for its successor, the Jerusalem Temple) because Jesus has fulfilled all that it was intended to signify. His death and now his priesthood offer the most profound spiritual reality, of which the physical tabernacle was only a 'copy and shadow'.

The argument gets quite detailed. Inevitably it presumes a basic sympathy with Old Testament teaching and a knowledge of the Temple cult (which modern readers may find more difficult). The author also expounds Old Testament passages (such as Jeremiah 31 and Psalm 40) as prophecies pointing forward to Christ. His overriding purpose, however, is plain, especially when he reaches his resounding conclusion:

> *We have been made holy through the sacrifice of the body of Jesus Christ once for all… Therefore… since we have confidence to enter the Most Holy Place by the blood of Jesus, let us draw near to God with a sincere heart in full assurance of faith… Let us hold unswervingly to the hope we profess.*

Hebrews 10:10, 19, 22–23a

Persevering in faith (10:26 – 13:25)

In all this the author has shown how many are the 'good things that are already here' in Christ. Compared to the Old Testament, Jesus offers his people a better covenant and makes them better promises. How, then, can they be tempted to return to a *pre*-Christian era or act as if it would have been better that Christ had *not* come? They are in serious danger of committing apostasy. Yet the author is a skilful pastor and his predominant tactic is to encourage them, to spur them on to follow Christ faithfully to the end:

- He devotes one whole chapter to commending the many individuals within the Old Testament who showed great perseverance – despite living in an era when the full scope of God's goodness had not yet been revealed in Christ.

- He encourages them to 'run with perseverance the race marked out' for them and to 'fix their eyes on Jesus', who himself had endured such opposition from sinful human beings.

- He reminds them that suffering can sometimes be a form of discipline which God uses for those who are truly his children.

- And he gives a mouth-watering vision of their journey's ultimate goal – the 'heavenly Jerusalem', where multitudes are praising God, all focused on Jesus.

So his sermon ends with an urgent appeal: 'do not refuse him who speaks... since we are receiving a kingdom that cannot be shaken, let us be thankful, and so worship God acceptably with reverence and awe, for our God is a consuming fire'.

After this powerful climax, the final chapter (13) reads like an afterthought – like a gentle conversation after the end of the sermon, deliberately written in a quieter tone. In it he sends some personal greetings and mentions other more practical instructions – some of which (for example, on marriage, leadership, hospitality) have proved remarkably important over the years. It also contains some compelling descriptions of Jesus.

Moreover, there is arguably quite a carefully worded allusion to the precise issue which has triggered the entire sermon: for he urges them not to be 'carried away by strange teachings' and by eating 'ceremonial foods' (which seem to be connected in some way to the Temple cult). No, instead of being focused on the Temple, they are to remember how Jesus put Jerusalem behind him when he walked out to be crucified: so, 'let us go to him outside the camp, bearing the disgrace he bore'. The author wants them to give up their former loyalties and to follow Jesus wholeheartedly – even if it means disgrace. And he then concludes, as his own heartfelt prayer for those believers facing tough choices – with a final blessing which has rung down the centuries:

Now may the God of peace, who... brought back from the dead our Lord Jesus, that great Shepherd of the sheep, equip you with everything good for doing his will.

Hebrews 13:20–21

'You no longer try to understand... You need milk, not solid food!'
Hebrews 5:11–12

'Jesus Christ is the same yesterday and today and forever!'
Hebrews 13:8

277

James

*'Everyone should be quick
to listen, slow to speak
and slow to become angry,
because our anger does not
produce the righteousness
that God desires.'*
James 1:19–20

The letter of James was probably written by the James who, as described in Acts, became the leader of the church in Jerusalem. Josephus records that this James was martyred in AD 62: the Jewish religious leaders took advantage of the absent Roman governor and threw James over the edge of the Temple. This letter does not give any hint of those rising tensions in Jerusalem during the AD 50s and so may have been written much earlier – perhaps in the 40s – thus making it one of the earliest New Testament texts.

James is described in Acts as the 'Lord's brother'. Jesus' family were initially sceptical about his ministry but, according to Paul, the risen Jesus 'appeared to James' (1 Corinthians 15:7); and James soon after emerges as a Christian leader. Intriguingly he introduces himself here, not as Jesus' brother, but rather as a 'servant of God and of the Lord Jesus Christ'; and later he describes Jesus as 'our glorious Lord'.

One of the letter's notable features is its close resemblance to Jesus' own teaching. Jesus used everyday images to illustrate his message; so too does James. He mentions scorched plants, shifting shadows and deadly poison; water springs, fig-trees and grapevines; autumn and spring rains; harvesting forest fires; horses' bits and the taming of animals; ships' rudders and being tossed on the waves of the sea.

Again, Jesus' teaching reflected Israel's longstanding wisdom tradition, giving practical guidance for everyday life; so too does James' letter. He raises issues such as helping the poor and appropriate seating arrangements at believers' meetings; or proper attitudes to commerce, and employers needing to pay staff their wages. So the overall tone is remarkably down to earth. Moreover, there are phrases which sound uncannily like Jesus' Sermon on the Mount (see p. 191): 'anyone who listens to the word, but does not do what it says, is like a person who…' Evidently James has been deeply influenced by Jesus' personal style. So his letter comes across as offering the homely advice of *Jesus himself* for those who, after his departure, are seeking to be his followers.

The letter encourages believers in the face of 'various trials': they need to persevere, seeking God's wisdom in any difficulty, and not blaming God for these temptations. After they have 'stood the test', they will receive the 'crown of life that God has promised to those who love him'. Yet James also warns them against various things: the arrogance that can come from being wealthy; anger and all 'moral filth'; disobedience to the 'royal law' of love (which is the true source of freedom); living in luxury and self-indulgence; claiming to have faith, but not letting that shape one's practice; showing favouritism or using their tongue (so tiny, but so

'Those who listen to the word but do not do what it says are like people who look at themselves in a mirror and immediately forget what they look like' (James 1:23–24). Hand-mirrors were quite common, but normally made (as here) of silver, not glass.

278

James and the gospel

James can appear quite different from other New Testament letters. It contains very little doctrine and refers to Jesus only twice. There is also no explicit teaching about Jesus' death and resurrection.

Presumably, however, this is because James took all this for granted. So he defines his audience as 'believers in our glorious Lord Jesus Christ' (revealing his own faith in Jesus as Lord – raised and exalted). A close reading reveals how much of this basic Christian faith he is assuming. Thus he talks of salvation, of God as 'our Father', and of God's future kingdom. Indeed, in language similar to Paul's, he even speaks of new birth: 'he chose to give us birth through the word of truth, that we might be a kind of first-fruits'. James assumes all this and now focuses instead on faith's practical implications.

Moreover, despite his criticisms of those who brag about being 'justified by faith', James evidently does not think that believers enjoy these blessings because of their own works or moral perfection. No, humans need mercy before God, the judge who can 'save and destroy'. He humbly admits his own shortcomings ('we all stumble in many ways'), teaches that no one can obey the 'whole law', and calls his readers to repent before God. So he also criticizes those who claim to have no faith but only deeds; mere works are *never* sufficient. He insists, however, that all true faith involves more than mere mental assent and always reveals its true character in lives transformed – through 'faith in action'.

dangerous!) to slander others; giving way to envy, selfish ambition or conflicting internal desires (which only leads to quarrels).

Instead believers' lives are to be marked by humility and wisdom; by honesty in speech and an attitude of peace-making; above all, by a faith which manifests itself in action, showing practical care and concerned prayer. 'But the wisdom that comes from heaven is... first of all pure; then peace-loving, considerate, submissive, full of mercy and good fruit, impartial and sincere.'

Many of James' images reflect his agrarian culture: 'Can both fresh water and salt water flow from the same spring? Can a fig-tree bear olives, or a grape vine bear figs?' (James 3:11–12).

1 and 2 Peter

This vast statue outside St Peter's basilica in Rome (the probable location of Peter's burial after his martyrdom in the 60s AD) reminds us of the authority Jesus gave his leading apostle ("I will give you the keys of the kingdom of heaven": Matthew 16:19). Peter's letters, however, are remarkable for their emphasis on humility, submission and commitment to service.

These two letters give us an important insight into the thinking of Simon Peter, the man whom Jesus called to lead his disciples. After Jesus' departure Peter took up this challenge, preaching boldly to the crowds at Pentecost and leading the young church in its mission (Acts 2–15). We have little idea, however, of what he did in the intervening years: he attended the apostolic council in AD 49 and possibly visited Corinth in the early 50s (1 Corinthians 1:12 and 9:5), but what else was he doing?

The silence is then broken in 1 Peter. It is a general letter written for circulation among five provinces in Asia Minor (modern Turkey), indicating that Peter has visited some (or all) of these provinces, perhaps quite recently. Peter is now in Rome with Silas and Mark (two people who also have accompanied Paul at different points on his travels). We learn this from Peter's final greetings – though he actually speaks here of being 'in Babylon' (almost certainly a codeword for Rome, the imperial capital which was proving so hostile to God's people). According to early church tradition Peter was indeed martyred in Rome, when persecution of Christians broke out under Nero (see 1 Clement and Tacitus' *Annals*). So this letter was probably written in Rome in the early to mid-60s.

Certainly the atmosphere is one in which Peter is bracing his readers for a time of suffering: he describes himself as a 'witness of Christ's sufferings', and encourages his hearers to ponder Christ's own example and 'to arm themselves with the same attitude'. They are not to be 'surprised at the painful trial' but rather to rejoice that they are 'participating in the sufferings of Christ'. Yet on at least three occasions he also encourages them, by suggesting that suffering – as for Christ, so now for his followers – is the necessary prelude to glory. The second letter, by contrast, as we shall see, breathes a different air and gives no hint of the author's situation, so it may have been written in a different context.

Peter addresses the people

After his initial greeting Peter launches into a positive, upbeat focus on the resurrection. Believers now have a sure hope, an 'imperishable inheritance' awaiting them; this future salvation is to be the source of their joy – despite various trials which are now testing their faith.

The risen Christ is a living Lord whom they can know and love – even though they (unlike Peter) have never set eyes on him. All this, Peter affirms, is fully in accord with God's eternal purposes: it was foreseen by Old Testament prophets, but even they would be amazed to see the 'glories' of what has been now revealed in Christ.

Peter is strengthening his audience for an uncertain future: 'prepare your minds for action'; 'be holy, because I am holy'; 'set your hope fully on the grace to be given you when Jesus Christ is revealed'. Yet they must also remember God's unchanging command that they should obey him and live transformed lives. Just like the Israelites in the Exodus story, so those who have been redeemed through the 'precious blood of Christ' are called to be holy, ridding themselves of evil and being responsive to God's enduring word. Individually and collectively they are to keep coming to Christ, the 'living Stone', and see themselves as being built up into a 'spiritual house' in which they serve as a 'holy' and 'royal priesthood'. Because of God's mercy their baptism signals that they have been rescued (like those kept safe within Noah's ark); they have now become God's own 'chosen people', who are to 'declare God's praises' and show forth his 'wonderful light'. Echoing Jesus' words (in Matthew 5), they are to live such good lives that their pagan neighbours 'see their good deeds and glorify God'.

This will involve developing a submissive attitude to those in authority and especially not paying back evil for evil. Instead they are to 'seek peace' and to be a 'blessing' to others. And if persecution does come, it should not be because they deserve this, but simply because they are 'Christian' (the only time this term is mentioned in the epistles). They are to 'commit themselves to their faithful creator and continue to do good'. Above all, they are to follow in the steps of Christ, who did not retaliate, but 'entrusted himself to him who judges justly'. They should remember the incredible reality of the cross: 'Jesus bore our sins in his body on the tree... the righteous for the unrighteous.' So Jesus' followers are to 'die to sin' and live for God.

Peter closes with instructions to those called to be elders in their congregations. He appeals to them to be good 'shepherds of God's flock', looking to the day when they will meet the 'Chief Shepherd'. One can almost hear Peter passing on the same words which he has heard from Jesus himself by Lake Galilee: 'if you love me, feed my sheep' (John 21:15). This is just one instance of many where one senses that the writer has been radically transformed by his encounters with Jesus thirty years before. Indeed there are numerous signs that Peter is now wiser, and has learned what Jesus had tried to teach him. So there is a new emphasis on 'reverent submission' to those in authority; on being considerate, sympathetic, compassionate and humble; on speaking with gentleness and respect; on being clear-minded, self-controlled, and not lording it over people. The impulsive young man we saw in the Gospels – over-confident and too hasty in his judgments – has clearly mellowed!

Women in the New Testament

Strikingly, Peter's vision of Jesus' suffering leads on to his teaching about marriage: 'wives, be submissive to your husbands... husbands, in the same way be considerate with your wives'. Peter wants all of life – but especially this vital relationship – to be transfigured by a vision of what Christ suffered: this should motivate his followers to give up playing proud games of power or manipulation.

His teaching on marriage, like Paul's (see p. 255), upholds distinct roles for the husband and wife but set within a context of fundamental equality: both are *equally* 'heirs of the gracious gift of life'. This surprising combination (different *roles* but equal *value*) seems contradictory to many but, arguably, underpins other texts – not least those where Paul specifies some gender roles during public Christian worship (see 1 Corinthians 11–14; 1 Timothy 2). The important debate is then whether those roles are universally essential or whether they were specific to that first-century culture (and thus can be adapted to fit modern cultures which are critical of gender-specific roles).

New Testament Christianity, even if an expanding movement largely driven by men, was something which proved especially attractive for women – not least because this teaching on sexual equality offered them such a marked improvement in their status, when compared with the prevailing non-Christian culture. Today's challenge is to reiterate this biblical vision of equality in ways that are similarly attractive, while not ignoring other biblical teaching which may provide important principles for ensuring good patterns of relating between the sexes.

The letter of Jude

Jude introduces himself as the 'brother of James'. As James was known as 'the Lord's brother', Jude may have been part of Jesus' family. Yet, humbly, he describes himself only as a 'servant of Jesus' and distinguishes himself from the 'apostles of the Lord Jesus'.

Jude's short letter is very similar to 2 Peter. He is warning believers about certain people who have been attending the believers' 'love feasts' and causing division: they are like 'clouds without rain', 'autumn trees without fruit' or 'wild waves of the sea'. And, as in 2 Peter, numerous Old Testament examples (such as Cain, Balaam and the sons of Korah) are cited to teach that they are liable to God's judgment. Once again these people are 'slandering celestial beings'; they 'follow their mere natural instincts' and 'pollute their own bodies'; they 'reject authority' and 'speak abusively'; they grumble, find fault, boast and flatter. Above all, they 'change the grace of our God into a licence for immorality and deny Jesus Christ our only sovereign'.

Jude urges the believers simply to 'contend for the faith entrusted to the saints', to 'build themselves up in their most holy faith', and to 'keep themselves in God's love'. They should be 'merciful to those who doubt' but extremely cautious in trying to rescue people such as these 'dreamers' and 'scoffers'. He closes with a (now famous) blessing which begins: 'To him who is able to keep you from falling and present you before his glorious presence... with great joy.'

Near the end, Peter expressly charges any young men to 'clothe themselves with humility' (or, in some translations, 'put on the apron of humility'). This may well reflect another Gospel episode (described in John 13) when Jesus took a towel and washed his disciples' feet – much to Peter's initial annoyance. One can almost hear Jesus saying to him, 'Well done, my good and faithful servant!' Peter here is not so much impressive as deeply *impressioned* – that is, the character of Jesus has been pressed deeply into his own.

Peter writes again

Peter's second letter is quite different. Yes, there is the same focus on believers living holy lives: they are to 'grow in the grace and knowledge of the Lord Jesus Christ', not being 'ineffective'; they are to develop qualities such as goodness, self-control, perseverance, brotherly kindness and love. Yet there is a much more outspoken criticism of 'false teachers': these teachers have apparently wheedled their way into Christian meetings, exploiting the believers with 'invented stories', and even 'blaspheming celestial beings' and 'denying the Lord who bought them'. Moreover, they entice people from the 'straight way', promising freedom when they themselves are 'slaves to depravity'. They are like characters in the Old Testament (such as Balaam, the contemporaries of Noah, or the inhabitants of Sodom and Gomorrah), all of whom experienced God's

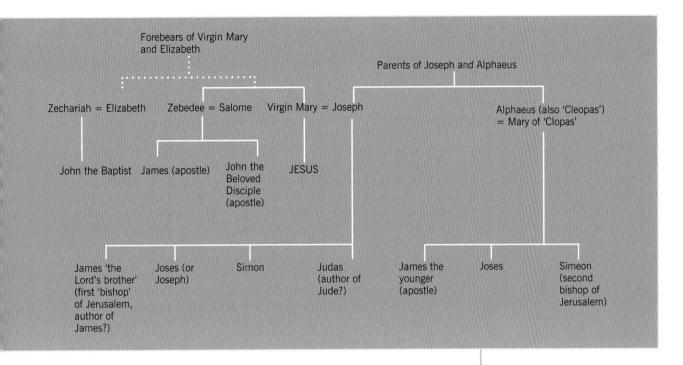

judgment; the line from Proverbs ('a dog returns to its vomit') serves as an indictment of the way they have returned to a life of corruption after briefly following the way of righteousness.

There are also strong warnings against those who scoff at the notion of the Lord coming to judge the world. Any delay is not due to God's slowness but because he is being patient, wanting everyone to 'come to repentance'. That day will assuredly 'come like a thief' and will usher in God's new age – with a 'new heaven and a new earth' (see also Revelation 21–22).

Some suggest this change of tone reflects a different author – that this letter comes not from Peter himself but from one of his followers (see p. 270). However, it could reflect Peter's urgency as he sees the young church being polluted by unhealthy influences. It becomes his unpleasant apostolic task to adopt a different tone and to pronounce God's judgment. His purpose remains a positive one – to stimulate people to wholesome thinking – but he achieves this by being very firm, reminding them of the prophets' teaching and the apostles' commands. For there is a real danger these believers will 'fall from their secure position'. So he encourages them to trust the words of the prophets, inspired by the Spirit; to believe his own testimony (as one who saw Jesus glorified on the mount of transfiguration: see p. 189); and to heed the letters of Paul (even though they 'contain things that are hard to understand'). Overall, he wants them to 'make their calling and election sure' and thus to 'receive a rich welcome' into Jesus' 'eternal kingdom'.

'These people are springs without water and mists driven by a storm.'
2 Peter 2:17

'His divine power has given us everything we need for a godly life.'
2 Peter 1:3

'... we were eyewitnesses of his majesty. He received honour and glory from God the Father when the voice came to him... saying, "This is my Son."'
2 Peter 1:16–17

1, 2 and 3 John

The three letters attributed to John are known as the 'Johannine epistles'. Both 2 John and 3 John (see p. 287) are very short notes from 'the elder' to personal friends; in the much longer first letter (1 John) the author is not given a name or a title. However, the traditional view is that all three letters were written by the elderly apostle John, who died 'in the reign of Trajan' (some time after AD 98).

'Whoever claims to live in him must live as Jesus did.'
1 John 2:6

Yet reliable ancient sources (discussed in Eusebius' *Ecclesiastical History*) also refer to a second person called John in Ephesus (known as 'John the elder') and suggest that this *other* John was the author of Revelation and perhaps also of 2 and 3 John (see further p. 288). What is clear, however, is that all three letters share a common style – both with each other and indeed with John's Gospel (see p. 209) – and thus probably reflect the teaching of the apostle John and his colleagues in the final decades of the first century.

Indeed, 1 John bears the hallmarks of having been written by an elderly person, giving mature teaching arising from many years of reflection. He addresses the 'dear children', 'young men' and 'fathers' in the churches in a way which indicates his own perspective was more that of a *grand*father. He also repeats these instructions in a repetitive, cyclical way, which may also reflect the thought processes of an older person. Indeed this is one of the distinctive features of the whole letter: John touches on only three or four main themes but keeps coming around to them from slightly different angles.

Right: View westwards across Ephesus towards the two-storeyed Celsus library (built c. AD 200) and the main commercial agora (right). According to early tradition the apostle John was one day in Ephesus' public bath-house when a 'heretic' called Cerinthus entered: John immediately left the building. His letters too, though emphasizing love, show the importance of defending Christ's truth against error.

John is concerned with both Christian belief and behaviour. Within this, his major themes are as follows:

- 'God is light; in him there is no darkness at all': so Jesus' followers must confess their sins, seeking to 'do the truth' and 'walk in the light' – just as Jesus did himself.

- 'God is love... and sent his Son as an atoning sacrifice for our sins': believers should 'love one another' (Jesus' 'new commandment'), showing this in practical ways and not falling into any hatred.

- Jesus is truly God's Son who 'came in the flesh', whom the author saw with his own eyes and even touched with his hands: those who either deny Jesus' divine sonship or, conversely, question his real humanity are opposed to Christ (that is, 'anti-Christ') and must not be allowed to lead believers astray.

These three themes are woven – like three strands in a rope – throughout 1 John (they also appear briefly in 2 and 3 John). They function as three vital questions which John is posing to test the health of any Christian congregation. Is there moral obedience and a readiness

to walk in the *way* of Christ (the ethical test)? Is there a commitment to show one another the *love* of Christ (the community test)? And is there a faithful receiving of the *truth* of Christ (the theological test)?

John's teaching boils down to these three questions. And John's returning to them repeatedly alerts his readers to their inescapable importance. Thus, maturity for the church will come not by departing from these simply stated truths, but rather through constantly being tested by them: they provide the safe framework, the essential coordinates, within which to conduct the Christian life. A close reading of 1 John, therefore, will reveal these repeated cycles – as the author glides artlessly through these themes of Christ's truth, his way and his love.

The letter begins (like John's Gospel) with a proclamation of truth: that Jesus is the 'word of life' which was 'from the beginning'. John has had the privilege of knowing this Jesus (what he calls 'having fellowship' with him), and writes to encourage others that they too can have a share in this profound relationship, both with the Son and with the Father. Yet they must always remember that God is holy and can only be approached through the 'blood of Jesus'. Human darkness is to be dispelled through entering into God's light and receiving his forgiveness. In response, those who claim to know this God must obey his commands, renouncing any love for the world (with its desires and arrogant boasting) and instead being committed to loving one other.

John then starts the cycle again. He warns them against the many 'anti-christs' who have spread false teaching about Christ. They should continue to live in Christ and prepare for the day of his coming when they 'shall see him as he is'. With this hope in mind, believers are to seek Christ's purity and to turn away from sin, remembering that Christ expressly came to deal with sin and to 'destroy the devil's work'. Thus, as God's beloved children, born of God, they should not continue to sin but have a new desire to 'do what is right'. This will be seen supremely when they renounce hatred and pursue a life of love – shown both in words and in actions. This love, modelled on the love shown by Jesus when he 'laid down his life', will be the result of God's Spirit at work in their life.

Coming round for a third time, John asserts that this divine Spirit is the 'Spirit of truth' and is quite different from the false spirits which deny God's truth – especially seen in those who deny Jesus has 'come in the flesh'. Believers are to stand against these worldly viewpoints, focusing instead on the way God has shown his love for the world through sending his Son. 'This is love, not that we loved God, but that he loved us and sent his Son…' This divine love is thus not dependent on humans first loving God; it precedes all such love, which only occurs once this divine love has been received. Those who have received this divine love, however, can know and rely upon this love for themselves and must share it with others.

'If we claim to be without sin, we deceive ourselves… If we confess our sins, he is faithful and will forgive us our sins.'
1 John 1:8–9

'And this is his command: to believe in the name of his Son, Jesus Christ, and to love one another as he commanded us.'
1 John 3:23

2 and 3 John

John's second and third letters are short notes written to two individuals (one an unnamed woman, the other a man called Gaius). In both he says he would prefer not to be using 'pen and ink', hoping instead to visit them soon and talk face to face. As personal memos, they are not doctrinal but instead provide us with a very human insight into the life of the first Christians: in particular, how they kept in touch by letter and offered hospitality to each other.

The early Christians became famous in the ancient world for their hospitality, being part of a growing international movement which crossed political and social boundaries. Yet this could easily be abused. So John warns about certain 'deceivers' who do not bring with them the 'teaching of Christ' (instead denying Jesus' true humanity) and who should *not* be welcomed. John is also aware that in Gaius' region there is a certain leader, called Diotrephes, who is gossiping maliciously about John and refusing to welcome some 'brothers' whom John has sent. Instead John expressly commends these men – especially Demetrius, who is 'well spoken of by everyone'.

Meanwhile John rejoices that both his recipients are themselves still faithful to Christ: 'I have no greater joy than to hear that my children are walking in the truth.' Yet he cannot resist repeating his teaching (see p. 286) about the new command to love one another: 'And this is love: that we walk in obedience to his commands.'

John sums this up by saying that those who believe in Jesus as the Son of God are gladly able to obey God's commands, expressing their love for God through also loving his children. He repeats his insistence on the physical reality of Jesus' coming and urges people to accept God's own testimony about his Son – only through this Son can eternal life be found. 'I write these things so that you may know that you have eternal life.' His readers are therefore to be confident in their praying to God, to help others not to fall into sin, and to be content with the true understanding which God has given to his children through Christ: 'We are in him who is true – even in his Son Jesus Christ. He is the true God and eternal life.'

'Perfect love drives out fear.'
1 John 4:18

Apocalypse

The Bible's last book takes us by surprise, as we are presented with a completely different style of literature – what is known as 'apocalyptic'. 'Apocalypse' is from the Greek word for an 'unveiling' and is in the first sentence of this final New Testament book: 'the *revelation* of Jesus Christ which God gave'.

Such apocalyptic literature had developed as a form of prophecy in the later periods of the Old Testament, being seen in the book of Daniel (see p. 156). Numerous apocalypses had then been composed in the 'inter-testamental' period (see p. 176), but Revelation is the only New Testament book to be given over entirely to this genre. Jesus himself had clearly spoken in apocalyptic terms (when predicting the Temple's destruction and the future 'coming of the Son of Man' in Mark 13), so the New Testament includes this book to show what the future holds within God's prophetic purposes – now that God's full revelation of himself has been given in Christ.

Apocalypses often took the form of a narrative of events in heaven, now revealed by an angel to a human recipient, and containing well-known symbols. One key point (better understood then than now?) was that these heavenly events were not meant to be understood literally, nor to give a detailed account of some spiritual realities only in the distant future. Instead they were metaphors describing *a real situation in the present*: they helped readers to see their own circumstances from God's perspective – a view of the present from the vantage point of heaven. So apocalypses use figurative language, not to describe the end of the space–time universe, but rather to invest events in this world with a cosmic significance (just as today we speak metaphorically of 'earth-shattering' events which 'turn our world upside down').

The opening verse of Revelation indicates that this 'apocalypse' was given to Christ's 'servant John' – possibly not John the apostle but a different person, known to us as 'John the Divine' or 'John the Seer' (see p. 284 on 2–3 John). He was 'on the island of Patmos because of the word of God' – possibly a reference to some enforced imprisonment. He writes to encourage believers back on the mainland to have 'patient endurance' in the face of persecution. He senses the stark possibility of Christian martyrdom and knows the opposition which 'Babylon' (normally taken as a codeword for Rome) is giving to believers – perhaps especially in Asia Minor with its strong advocacy of emperor-worship.

Dating Revelation is problematic: there may be allusions to the recent death of Nero in AD 68 (in Revelation 13:3; 17:8), or to the (imminent or recent) fall of Jerusalem in AD 70 (in Revelation 11:1–10); some, however, prefer a later date within the reign of Domitian (AD 81–96), on the grounds that this emperor explicitly demanded his subjects to recognize him as 'Lord and Saviour'.

Even more difficult is the book's interpretation. In particular, how should we understand the dramatic pictures of God's judgment in chapters 6 to 19? In reading these visions you will soon sense how they are deliberately repetitive (see pp. 292–97). They clearly do not describe a linear sequence of historical events, but show how human history is always under the threat of divine judgment – a judgment which, even if foreshadowed in various ways throughout history, properly belongs to the 'End Time'. Moreover, some of the pictures appear mutually contradictory (they are multiple images designed to build a cumulative case); and some of the images seemingly have multiple applications (though 'Babylon' probably refers to Rome, it can equally be applied to *all* subsequent human ideologies opposed to God).

Even so, some of Revelation's main themes are clear:

- The Lord God Almighty is sovereign over his world. He is the transcendent creator, the Alpha and Omega, 'who was and is and is to come'; he is the holy one, who 'sits on the throne' and who has authority to exercise final judgment.

- Jesus Christ shares in this sovereignty. He too is the Alpha and Omega, who does what God does, and who may rightly be worshipped. Twice John is tempted to worship an angel, but both times he is told that God alone is to be worshipped; however, there is no such bar on the worship of Jesus, who in Revelation chapter 5 (when portrayed as the Lamb) receives the same worship as that given to God in chapter 4. He is revealed in his majesty in the opening chapter and, at the moment of final victory, appears on a white horse as the 'Lord of lords.'

- Finally, this same Jesus will truly bring about God's purposes in the world. Though he died, Jesus was raised from the dead as the 'living one'. So he has already won the decisive battle that will lead to his ultimate victory. As the true Messiah he will defeat God's enemies; like Moses he will bring God's people through a new exodus. Above all, he will bring the 'kingdoms of this world' to be instead the 'kingdom of Christ'.

Key chapters in Revelation

John's vision of the risen Christ
(chapter 1)

Looking in on heaven's throne room
(chapters 4–5)

The mystery of the 'little scroll'
(chapters 10–11)

The fall of Babylon (chapter 18)

The new Jerusalem (chapters 21–22)

'Jesus Christ… is the 'faithful witness… the ruler of the kings of the earth… To him who loves us and has freed us from our sins by his blood…'
Revelation 1:5–6

John's vision, given on the island of Patmos, is particularly for the benefit of the seven churches in the Roman province of 'Asia Minor'. The postal courier service between these major cities (also possibly used for Ephesians: p. 253) would have helped the distribution process. Fascinatingly, each letter alludes to distinctive aspects of that particular city's geography and history.

Revelation

The opening words of the book announce that this is a 'revelation of Jesus Christ'. Thus, though also described as a prophecy, its readers are primarily to focus on what is 'unveiled' about Christ himself. It is an awesome picture.

Christ's seven letters to the churches (chapters 1–3)
The book was triggered by John receiving a dramatic revelation of Christ (given to him one Sunday): he saw 'one like a son of man' with eyes of fire, a voice that sounded like the 'rushing of many waters' and a face that 'shone like the sun'. This powerful figure, though he had died, is now 'alive for ever'. So John is clearly here meeting Christ in his risen glory.

The figure also describes himself as the 'First and the Last', echoing the words already used to describe the 'Lord God' ('I am the Alpha and Omega, who was, who is, and who is to come'). So this risen Christ is to be identified with Almighty God. This then is strictly a *theophany* (that is, a revelation of *God himself*), similar to that experienced by Moses and Isaiah (see pp. 37 and 132). John responds, as did they, by prostrating himself on the ground – 'as though dead'. However, he is

The seven churches of Asia Minor (Revelation 2–3)

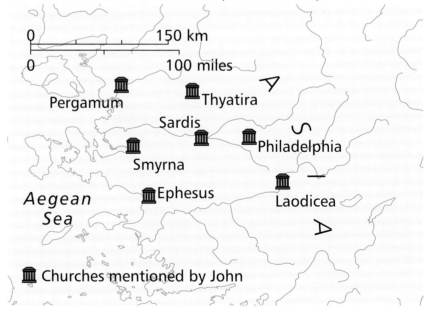

0   150 km
0   100 miles

Pergamum   Thyatira
Sardis
Smyrna   Philadelphia
Ephesus   Laodicea

Aegean Sea

🏛 Churches mentioned by John

A small Byzantine church, built in the south-east corner of the massive temple of Artemis in Sardis. Rich king Croesus had famously been caught off-guard at night, through believing his stronghold (on the neighbouring acropolis: not in view) was impregnable. So the risen Christ warns the believers there: 'If you do not awake, I will come like a thief...' (Revelation 3:3).

In John's vision the risen Christ stands in the midst of 'seven golden lampstands' (Revelation 1:12) – reminiscent of the frequently used symbolism of the menorah candlestick found in the Jerusalem Temple. This menorah medallion is from the synagogue door lintel in Aphek, Israel.

'I know your deeds, your love and faith, your service and perseverance.'
Revelation 2:19–20

'I will write on them the name of the city of my God, the new Jerusalem.'
Revelation 3:12

told not to be afraid, but to write down what he has just seen and, in particular, the messages and visions that he is about to witness.

Immediately Christ dictates to him seven letters, one for each of the main churches in the province of Asia (see p. 290). They all have a similar seven-fold pattern, which is roughly as follows:

- 'To the church in...' (the city's name)
- Speaks 'the First and the Last...' (an attribute of Christ)
- 'I know some good things about you...' (some compliments)
- Yet I also 'have a few things against you' (some criticisms)
- 'So repent!'
- 'The victor will...' (a promise)
- 'So hear what the Spirit says to the churches' (a final command).

Christ is assuring each church that he knows them intimately, seeing all their strengths and weaknesses, and is their judge. So he urges them to deal seriously with what is wrong – sometimes their lethargy or spiritual arrogance, but sometimes their tolerance of sexual immorality, deceptive prophets or false teaching. Yet, above all, Christ encourages his followers to persevere. In some cases he mentions some imminent persecution (or alludes to problems they may expect from secular or Jewish sources), but each time he makes a promise to those who 'overcome', for example: 'I will give the right to eat from the tree of life.'

Worship of Christ in the midst of suffering: seven seals opened (4:1 – 8:1)

John then looks up and sees in his vision an open door. He goes through and is ushered into a heavenly courtroom centred on a throne, around which are twenty-four elders and four 'living creatures' (described in terms similar to the cherubim seen by Ezekiel: see p. 147): all of them are giving glory to the one seated on the throne. As in Isaiah's vision of God (p. 132), the creatures cry out, 'Holy, Holy, Holy is the Lord'; and the elders lay down their crowns, crying out, 'You are worthy, our Lord and God, to receive glory and honour and power!'

John sees that the one on the throne is holding a scroll, sealed with seven seals, and is distressed that seemingly no one can open the seals; but then he is told that the authority to do so rests with the 'lion of Judah'. He turns and, contrary to his expectation, sees not a lion, but rather a 'lamb'! – indeed a 'lamb looking as if it had been slain'. The lamb moves forward to take the scroll and, as he does so, a new wave of praise peals around the heavenly court (now thronging with thousands of angels): 'You are worthy to open the seals, because you were slain and with your blood you purchased for God people from every tribe and language!' Indeed, every creature in heaven and on earth breaks into praise. The lamb is evidently a dramatic revelation of Christ – a picture of the Jesus who had been described, back in the opening chapter, as bringing forgiveness of sins through his death. Now, dramatically, it is revealed that he truly shares in the worship due to God alone.

All eyes are now on the lamb as he proceeds to open the seals. The first four unleash four differently coloured horses (white, red, black and pale) that go out into the world bent on conquest, war, famine and death. The fifth seal reveals a number of Christian martyrs crying out for justice; and the sixth brings about apocalyptic events, which cause everyone on earth to run for cover, fearing the 'wrath of the Lamb'. These seals speak of God's imminent judgment, especially as he avenges those martyred because of the 'word of God' and of their testimony to Christ.

John's vision of heaven includes twenty-four elders praising a 'lamb that had been slain', which evidently stands for Christ. Here Christ is depicted as seated on God's throne surrounded by some of his apostles and saints. Christ the Pantocrator (the 'all-creating') is very common in Greek iconography.

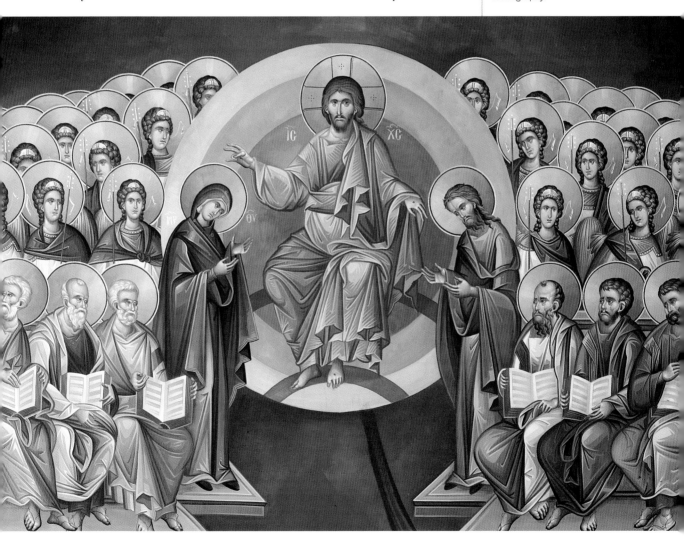

Yet, as we wait for the opening of the seventh seal (presumably to inaugurate the actual judgment), there is a dramatic pause. Angels request a delay so they can put a protective seal on the foreheads of God's servants. These are made up of 144,000 people – 12,000 from each of the ancient twelve tribes of Israel. This number is clearly symbolic; for what John then sees is a *countless* multitude of people, derived from *every* tribe and language (not just Israel). All these servants of God from throughout human history praise God and the lamb. Meanwhile survivors of the 'great tribulation' serve God day and night, enjoying the lamb as their shepherd and protector. At this moment the seventh seal is opened – and there is suddenly silence in heaven for about half an hour. The suspense is unbearable. What *will* happen next?

Judgment on the world: seven trumpets sounded (8:2 – 11:18)

Essentially we go through a repeat. Like taking off layer after layer of an onion, we are presented again with a series of seven dramatic actions, that rehearse once more God's judgment of the world. John sees not seven seals being opened, but seven angels sounding seven trumpets. Again the first four are grouped together, resulting in judgment being enacted, respectively, on the earth, sea, rivers and sky. The final three are aptly described as the 'three woes'. Thus the sounding of the fifth trumpet brings a torment of locusts on those without the protective seal on their foreheads. The sixth brings destruction to a third of humankind (though those who survive still will not repent of their idolatry and immorality). Just then, as we wait for the seventh trumpet, an angel appears, holding a small scroll, who announces that the seventh trumpet will without delay 'accomplish the mystery of God'.

Yet, at this critical moment, there *is* a delay, with John being told to *eat* the scroll! Initially it tastes sweet but then turns sour, and he is told to prophesy. His prophecy is set in an imaginary Temple (presumably modelled on Jerusalem) and concerns two 'witnesses', loyal prophets of God, who are eventually killed by the 'beast that comes up from the Abyss'. For three and a half days their enemies gloat over the corpses, but God makes them stand upright and then exalts them to heaven. Then, at last, the seventh trumpet is sounded – the 'time of judging' has arrived; now the elders say that his anointed one (the Christ) will reign over the 'kingdoms of the world' and bring reward to his 'saints'!

Cosmic upheavals in history: seven scenes of conflict (11:19 – 15:4)

At this moment, however, we are taken still deeper into the inner workings of God's judgment. John sees in the heavenly temple the ark

'Now have come the salvation and the power and the kingdom of our God, and the authority of his Messiah.
For the accuser of our brothers and sisters,
who accuses them before our God day and night,
has been hurled down.
They triumphed over him by the blood of the Lamb and by the word of their testimony.'
Revelation 12:10–11

of the covenant, surrounded by flashes of lightning, and from which emanate a series of dramatic conflicts:

- A dragon fights a woman, who gives birth to a son who will 'rule the nations' and is taken up to God's throne (presumably a reference to Jesus and his mother Mary).

- Michael and his angels fight back against the dragon (now identified as 'that ancient serpent called the devil, or Satan, who leads the whole world astray').

- The dragon, having failed to devour the woman, makes war against the rest of her offspring (identified as those who 'hold to the testimony of Jesus').

The Woman Clothed with the Sun and the Dragon (Revelation 17:3–4), as depicted in this apocalypse commentary of Beatus de Liebana (1498).

Identifying the 'beast'

'The beast... once was, now is not, and will come up... the seven heads are seven hills... They are also seven kings.'
Revelation 17:8–10

Who or what is this mysterious 'beast'? Between chapters 12 and 18 there is a series of evil figures: a dragon (identified with 'the devil'), a 'prostitute' (identified later as the 'great city') and two 'beasts' (one arising 'out of the sea', one 'from the earth'). The second beast has only two horns, but the first beast has 'ten horns and seven heads' (identified as various 'kings', one of whom strangely is recovering from a 'fatal wound') and is 'worshipped' by everyone apart from the lamb's followers.

John's frequent references to 'Babylon the Great' strongly suggest that these figures all represent different facets of any human rule and dominion which stands opposed to God and his people – epitomized previously by Babylon (see p. 143) and now by imperial Rome. Thus there is a discreet allusion to the 'seven hills', on which Rome was famously founded. Moreover, the eighth 'king', who seemingly returns from the dead ('who now is not, and yet will come'), may allude to the widespread fear that Nero, even after his death (in AD 68), might return to haunt the empire.

The 'prostitute' may highlight Rome's economic power, the 'beast' its military aggression. Yet John does not identify 'Babylon' with Rome totally, leaving modern readers able to see in Babylon's fall God's enduring judgment upon *all* human institutions which stand opposed to his purposes.

- The dragon cedes authority to a seven-headed beast, who in turn blasphemes God and is able – for a limited season only – to conquer the 'saints', being worshipped by all those whose names are not written in the 'lamb's book of life'.

- A second beast appears, forcing people to worship the first beast.

- John sees the one who is going to fight the beast – the lamb standing on Mount Zion, surrounded by 144,000 saints. Three angels call people to worship God at this critical hour, announcing judgment upon 'Babylon the Great' and those who worship the beast, but God's blessing upon those who 'die in the Lord'.

- And then, at long last, it happens – the seventh and ultimate conflict – a crowned figure 'like a son of man' wields his sickle to 'reap' the earth, and an angel gathers the grapes into the 'great winepress of God's wrath'.

Judgment for the world: seven bowls poured out (15:5 – 16:21)

We are then taken yet further *inside* this act of judgment. We see the saints singing the victory 'Song of Moses', while seven angels appear with the 'seven last plagues – last because with them God's wrath is completed'. The plagues are in seven bowls, filled with God's wrath, which are poured out: on the land, the sea, the rivers, the sun; on the 'throne of the beast', on the River Euphrates and, finally, 'into the air'. Torment and destruction give way to this last cataclysmic event, in which an earthquake and a hailstorm bring about the collapse of the cities of the world (including Babylon the Great) and the disappearance of all islands and mountains.

The end of Babylon the Great: seven descriptions of evil and its overthrow (16:22 – 19:10)

So yet deeper still, at the heart of all reality, there is a conflict between the lamb and 'Babylon the Great' – identified as 'the city that rules over the kings of the earth'. The city is portrayed, symbolically, as a prostitute sitting on the seven-headed beast; and she is 'drunk with the blood of the saints'. The angel then explains to John the mystery of the beast's seven heads and ten horns: these are ten kings who will 'make war against the lamb'.

The next descriptions are of Babylon's fall: 'she will be consumed by fire, for mighty is the Lord God who judges her'. Kings, traders and sea captains all mourn her loss, but eventually John sees the city in a state of eerie silence – thrown down, never to be found again. He also hears praise rising from those gathered around God's throne: 'Hallelujah, for our God has condemned the great prostitute and avenged the blood of his servants.' Moreover, having removed Babylon, God now introduces

Left: Babylon's destruction, mourned by kings and merchants: an illustration of Revelation 18, from the first edition of the Luther Bible (1530).

the 'wedding of the Lamb'. This will be the climax of history; the bride is getting herself ready. 'Blessed are those invited to the wedding supper of the Lamb!'

Reality behind the scene: seven visions of ultimate reality
(19:11 – 21:8)
At last John is able to see the ultimate reality deep down at the heart of the universe: 'I saw heaven standing open.' And what does he see?

- A figure riding a white horse. The figure is described in terms identical to those used of the risen Jesus back in chapter 1: 'his eyes are like blazing fire… and out of his mouth comes a sharp sword'. Yet now he is given various new names: 'Faithful and True'; the 'Word of God'; the 'King of kings and Lord of lords'.

- An angel inviting birds to be like vultures at this 'great supper'.

- God's enemies (the beast and the false prophet) being thrown into a fiery lake of burning sulphur.

- The devil being imprisoned in the abyss for a thousand years.

- Christian martyrs being raised to life and 'reigning with Christ for

'Great and marvellous are your deeds,
Lord God Almighty.
Just and true are your ways,
King of the nations.'
Revelation 15:3

'You mighty city of Babylon!
In one hour your doom has come… such great wealth has been brought to ruin!'
Revelation 18:10, 17

a thousand years' as 'priests of God and of Christ' – until, that is, the devil is released from prison; whereupon he entices the nations to gather against God's people, but is himself thrown into that fiery lake.

- All the dead standing before God's throne for judgment. 'Books opened' (which reveal all they have done) but so too is another book – the 'book of life'. Those whose names do not appear in this second book are also thrown into the lake.

- And finally, a 'new heaven and a new earth'. 'I saw the Holy City, the new Jerusalem, coming down out of heaven, prepared as a bride…' God dwells among his people, removing all death and mourning, and making everything new – a renewed creation.

The goal of the heavenly Jerusalem (21:9 – 22:21)

Within the book's overall scheme we are now deep within its 'seventh seven', the place of ultimate perfection. Not surprisingly, at the culmination of this long journey, there is a great sense of arrival. So we join John on a grand tour around the holy city, guided by an angel.

First John is shown its four high walls (made of jasper) and its twelve gates (made of pearls), named after Israel's twelve tribes. There are also twelve foundation stones, decorated with precious jewels – named after the lamb's twelve apostles. The city shines like a jewel with God's glory.

Next he notes there is no temple in the city, because the Lord Almighty and the lamb are already its temple. In other words, the whole city – not just a prescribed sanctuary – is filled with God's presence. Then he sees a river, crystal clear, flowing from God's throne through the city's great street; on each side is the 'tree of life', yielding fruit every month for the 'healing of the nations' – a sign of the whole world coming under God's saving rule. This is a place where there is no more cursing and no more night, because God's light continuously blesses his people.

John's attention is then redirected by the angel to the total revelation he has been receiving. The angel repeats the importance of human beings turning from evil and preparing themselves for the coming of him who is the 'Alpha and the Omega'.

And then *Jesus himself* speaks – to confirm that the book's revelation has truly come from him. To this the saints respond by saying, 'Come, Lord Jesus!' There is a final blessing (on those who 'take the free gift of the water of life') and a final curse (on any who add to or subtract from this 'prophecy'); and then John closes, in his own voice, with his own prayer: 'Come, Lord Jesus! The grace of the Lord Jesus be with God's people. Amen!'

'God's dwelling place is now among the people… They will be his people, and God himself will be with them and be their God. He will wipe away every tear from their eyes.'

Revelation 21:3–4

Right: Medieval depiction of the Heavenly Jerusalem, inspired by Revelation 21–22: from a manuscript of Augustine's *De Civitae Dei*.

The Ultimate Goal:
the Renewal of Creation

The final four chapters of Revelation provide a climactic conclusion –
both to John's vision and to the whole Bible. Now we see God's great goal
for human history: the vindication of Jesus as the 'King of kings'; God's
judgment upon evil and its removal from his presence; God's people
rejoicing in him and enjoying his eternal presence. And we see creation,
no longer under any curse, no longer the scene of tears and frustration,
but gloriously renewed and reflecting the glory of its Creator.

Ever since they were first written, these chapters have inspired
hope and purpose, giving human beings a confidence that God is
sovereignly in control and that human history, despite all its tragedy
and uncertainty, is not a meaningless journey but rather is truly going
somewhere: what does not make sense now, one day will.

These chapters, however, precisely because they describe future
realities which are unknown to us and unprovable, have also inevitably
led to differences of interpretation. For example, what is meant by the
'thousand-year' reign of Christ (the 'millennium') in 20:6? Will this
occur before Christ's return or, instead, immediately after it? Or does
it refer to the whole of the 'church age' (this present era in which
Christ *even now* truly reigns over his world)? Or perhaps it is simply an
evocative image, not to be taken literally?

Then again, what will this 'return' of Christ look like (see also p. 262)? In particular, how does it relate to John's vision of the 'new Jerusalem coming down out of heaven'? And what does it mean for there to be a 'new heaven and new earth', with the first heaven and earth 'passing away'? Some readers conclude that God will destroy this present creation, replacing it with something entirely new. Others, however, see such a wholesale destruction as contrary to the Bible's emphasis on God's commitment to his creation; after all, the Old Testament is a very 'earthy' book, and the resurrection of Jesus shows God's commitment to renewing created matter in resurrection power.

Many therefore see the 'new earth' in terms of a *renewed* earth; they also highlight how the new Jerusalem 'comes down *from* heaven' to earth – not the other way round (with human beings being taken up to some alternative reality in heaven). If so, John's vision looks forward, not to creation's abandonment, but rather to its renewal. Hence it picks up the imagery of the Garden of Eden in Genesis 3, showing how God's people are no longer under God's curse or banished from his presence. As such the new Jerusalem can be seen as Eden revisited, paradise regained, creation renewed and, indeed, humanity redeemed – a powerful climax to the Bible's great story and a fitting goal to inspire all its readers.

Looking back on the New Testament

Looking back now over these twenty-seven books, one can sense that the New Testament is far from being a monochrome document. It is full of variety, pulsating with energy. In its pages we have discovered history and poetry, practical instructions and mysterious visions. Is it possible, then, to pull such diverse material together into a coherent whole?

The Christian church has always answered that question positively: yes, despite this diversity, the New Testament is marked by a fundamental unity. The apostles' authoritative witness to Jesus Christ, though multi-coloured, is deeply coherent. This, however, has naturally been questioned by many, who urge that the New Testament is instead a motley collection of writings that contradict one another at various points: for example, is not James' attitude to 'justification by faith' different from Paul's (see p. 279)? More generally, are there not some quite divergent attitudes on such matters as the role of the secular state, marriage and singleness, or the return of Christ?

Those involved in New Testament theology seek to answer these questions. My own strategy is to imagine the various New Testament writers being seated around a four-sided conference table (see diagram, left). Around the four sides are the four evangelists who themselves 'represent' four different geographical regions: Matthew writing from near Jerusalem; Mark from Rome; John writing from Ephesus; and Luke from the wider Mediterranean world (because Luke travels from Philippi to Jerusalem and then to Rome). Associated with each evangelist are various other writings which come from a similar perspective or school of thought.

This model, while valuing the New Testament's diverse perspectives, simultaneously portrays the truth

A possible 'conference table' for the New Testament writers, focused on the four evangelists and their geographical location. Hebrews and Revelation are associated with Rome and Ephesus respectively, but more loosely. The numbers in brackets indicate the number of chapters within the New Testament written by that author (Paul and Luke, together, contributing 53 per cent of the whole).

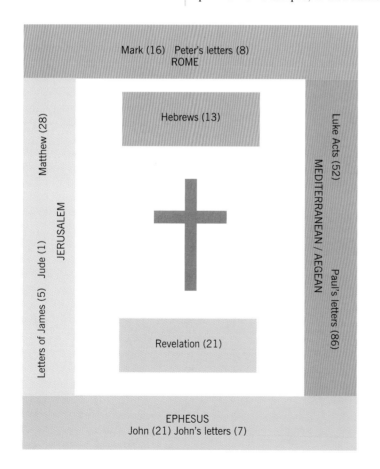

Mark (16)   Peter's letters (8)
ROME

Hebrews (13)

Matthew (28)

JERUSALEM

Letters of James (5)   Jude (1)

Luke Acts (52)

MEDITERRANEAN / AEGEAN

Paul's letters (86)

Revelation (21)

EPHESUS
John (21) John's letters (7)

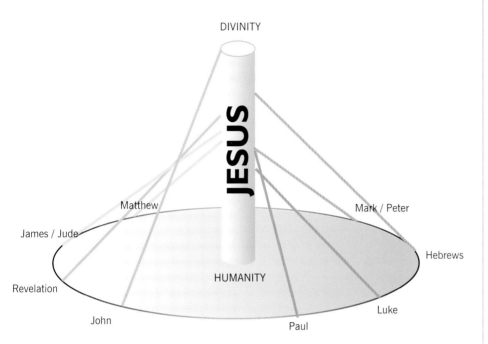

that its authors are all gathered around the *same* table: they do not have their backs turned to one another, nor are they heading off in vastly different directions! The diagram above makes the same point, emphasizing that in the centre stands the figure of Jesus himself: the New Testament writers are then giving us their own unique perspective on the phenomenon of Jesus who (if, as they asserted both human and divine) was inevitably more than any *one* writer could adequately convey.

These models are also true to first-century practice: the apostles gave an incredible emphasis to unity. So, when they encountered the divisive issue about the Gentiles (see p. 224), they regathered in Jerusalem to reach a resolution: James and Paul (representing, respectively, the Jewish and Gentile schools of thought) reached a full agreement. So we would do well not to pit their writings against one another but to discover the essential harmony between them – a harmony which they themselves would have sought and found.

The Nature of the Bible:
Revelation and Inspiration

Epilogue

At the end of this *Guide* it is worth looking back over our journey. Having traced our way through sixty-six books, we might well want to ask: what precisely *is* this collection of books known as 'the Bible'?

The Bible's own central claim is that the coming of Jesus was the supreme act of God in human history: Jesus, so it is claimed, was not just a human being commissioned by God for a certain task but was *himself* the embodiment of *God at work* in his world. He was the supreme example of *divine activity* operating in the human sphere. Moreover, this divine activity did not come entirely out of the blue but had been preceded by *other* acts of God among his people: his calling of Abraham, his revelation of his Law on Mount Sinai, his work in inspiring prophets and teachers. If so, then the Bible should be seen, at the very least, as the 'book of the acts of God' – as the book uniquely placed to pass on to future generations these important examples of divine action.

Those who go this far, conceding that these *have* been examples of God working in his world, often then go further. For is the Bible *only* a human and fallible witness to divine activity? Surely, if God was thus acting in human history, it would be important to ensure that there was also a *reliable account* of that activity? Otherwise future generations could not know for sure what God had done, thus causing God's activity to be wasted. The most important example of this is the cross, which would have been utterly pointless if no one had written down what Jesus was doing and why. Divine *activity* thus requires, so they argue, an equally divine *account* – an account which gives to future generations a reliable interpretation. Only when these two factors (of event followed by interpretation) are joined together, can people receive God's 'revelation'.

On this model, then, the Bible is more than enlightened human projection, dreamed up by religiously minded people wanting to assert apparent 'truths' about God without any foundation. On the contrary, it is God's own *authorized account* of his actions; it is an act of divine 'self-testimony', God's own witness to himself and his deeds.

This might be a laughable idea were it not that the Bible clearly portrays its God as a 'speaking' God, well able to communicate through words with human beings. It is the 'idols of the nations' who 'have mouths but cannot speak'. Israel's God, by contrast, is seen frequently encountering individuals, giving laws (such as the Ten Commandments) and inspiring prophets with messages. Old Testament religion was therefore quite different from ancient paganism because it was a 'religion of the *word*': Israel had been given divine messages and was called to treasure 'every word that proceeds from the mouth of the Lord' (Deuteronomy 8:3). The God portrayed in the Bible is thus a God who both *acts* and *speaks*. So, the Bible itself can be seen not just as describing God's action, but as a *summary of his speaking*. More than that, the Bible *itself* becomes the prime instance of God's continued speaking to his people. It not only contains the *words* of God but becomes the *Word* of God.

All this becomes possible because of yet another important biblical theme – the reality of God's Spirit. God is able, so the Bible claims, to speak with people by means of the Holy Spirit; for example, the prophets are 'moved by the Spirit' and Jesus is 'filled with the Spirit'. As a result, New Testament writers such as Paul and Peter (see 2 Timothy 3:16; 2 Peter 1:20–21) can see all the previous biblical writings as 'in-*spired*' (or, more literally, 'God-breathed). The biblical authors, they assert, had not been following their own, human interpretations but rather had 'spoken from God as they were carried along by the Holy Spirit'.

Such teaching has led to the Bible being seen as inspired by God's Spirit. Much debate then ensues as to what this means. Does this mean that *every* point of detail within the Bible is factually and precisely accurate? Or should this reliability be limited only to that which the biblical writers were evidently aiming to communicate about eternal, spiritual truths? Whatever the case, this process of inspiration clearly did not entail each author being reduced to a dictating machine. On the contrary, the biblical writers, even though inspired by God, evidently preserved their own distinctive characters, producing a body of literature that is very varied in its style. As a result, this inspiration is sometimes described as 'concursive' (literally, 'running together'): God's activity (in inspiring) and human activity (in researching, praying and committing to paper) *run together* in parallel. In this way, it is claimed, God worked in the circumstances of each biblical writer and thus enabled their writing to be simultaneously both the writer's work and God's work.

For these and numerous other reasons, many people receive the Bible as a book quite unlike any other: despite its obvious humanity, they find in its pages the word of God – an inspired revelation from the same God who, in its pages, is seen to act and speak powerfully to his people.

The Nature of the Bible: Authority and Story

If, as just suggested, the Bible can be received as an inspired revelation from God, its readers have to reckon with its unique authority. For, if the Bible is the book in which we are given a reliable witness concerning God's actions in the past, then we must turn to the Bible if we wish to learn more about this same God today. Moreover, if it is also an inspired text through which God has revealed himself, then these are the words to which we must pay the closest attention if we are to hear God's voice speaking today.

The Bible has therefore always been given a position of great authority by those who are convinced by its portrait of its central character, Jesus Christ. Throughout the centuries Christ's followers have found this book to be that through which they are not only first introduced to Christ, but also then strengthened in their faith in him.

What is true for individuals is also true at the corporate level. The Christian church receives the Bible like a foundation charter, setting out the principles which should govern its existence. More than that, the Bible serves as a benchmark by which to test that which is authentically Christian. Thus, when new ideas or practices are presented, the church goes back to the Bible to assess whether they are a valid outworking of biblical principles. Finally, the Bible is also received by the church as a living text through which God continues to address his people: hence the priority given in many churches not only to the public reading of Scripture but also to its exposition – where biblical passages are 'expounded' or explained and applied to the present context.

The Bible thus gives the church its life and vitality, providing it with a perennial supply of instruction, challenge, vision and encouragement. Through the centuries the church has sometimes turned a deaf ear to biblical teaching or allowed other things (even its own traditions) to muddy the waters, but sooner or later the Bible's voice is rediscovered.

So, ever since its final compilation, the Bible has exerted a phenomenal authority over its readers. Yet in our modern climate many feel uncomfortable with such notions of authority. Authority is heard as signalling repressive domination, as that which limits our human freedom. True biblical authority, however, turns out to be genuinely liberating, for several reasons.

First, those who submit to the Bible's authority do so not because they are tying themselves to an ancient *text,* but because they have freely chosen to follow a *person,* namely Christ. They are not 'bibliolaters' (people who worship the Bible) but those who worship Christ; they go back to the Scriptures because here they learn about *him*. And, if they find there any commands to obey, they respond to them as part of their obedience to Christ. This obedience is not blind but part of an ongoing relationship marked by faith and trust.

Second, the biblical God exercises his authority in some surprisingly anti-authoritarian ways. Yes, he is the transcendent, holy God, the creator and judge of his creation. Yet at the mid-point of the biblical drama, he enters that creation as a helpless baby and, thirty years later, experiences a horrendous death. This God knows weakness from the inside; this God subverts the power ploys of worldly authorities by a chosen act of wounded love. Those who submit to his authority thus find it to be one marked by compassion and grace.

Finally, the Bible is far more than a series of commands. Yes, it does give instructions about belief and practice, but a vast proportion of it (as we have seen in this *Guide*) is given over to narrative. The Bible is more truly a long story. Indeed (as we saw on p. 17) it is essentially a story told in five great episodes or acts. As such, the Bible often exercises its authority over us by inviting us to join in this story ourselves.

To use an analogy, we are invited to stop watching the game from beyond the touchline and to become players – getting involved in the action, helping to move the story forward to the best possible outcome. And, when we start to play the game, we find there is plenty of space for creativity. The game's essential rules have been agreed, but they merely provide the safe framework within which to develop our skills. Or, to change the picture, it is as though a great playwright has left us an unfinished script, and we are now invited to act out some final scenes in a way which is true to the original instalments.

Yet there is one key difference. The Bible also provides us with a clear summary of the last act (God's restoration of the 'new creation' as seen in the final chapters of Revelation). So we know the direction in which the author wants to take the play; that's one way he exercises his 'authority' over us. It is our task, then, to know what has happened before, to know where things ultimately will end, but in the meantime to play our own part as faithfully as we can. The Bible is God's story for the world; and we are invited to join in that story praying (as Jesus taught us) that through us, God's 'kingdom may come' and God's will be done 'on earth as it is in heaven'.

Index

Scripture Index

Acknowledgments

Alamy: pp. 66–67, 116 Israel images; p. 108 Frans Lemmens; p. 172 Trevor Smithers ARPS; p. 233 Adam Eastland; p. 256 UK City Images
Corbis: p. 42 Michal Czerwonka/epa; pp. 46, 114, 150–51, 202, 212 Richard T. Nowitz; p. 63 Peter Guttman; p. 79 Elio Ciol; pp. 206, 215 Hanan Isachar; p. 99 Alaa Badarneh/epa; pp. 111, 142 Shai Ginott; p. 118 Yannis Behrakis/Reuters; pp. 122–23 Carlos Hernandez/Aurora Photos; p. 124 Frans Lemmens; p. 134 Charles & Josette Lenars; p. 145 Peter M. Wilson; p. 158 (main and inset) Gianni Dagli Orti; p. 164 Gregor Schuster; p. 167 Brooklyn Museum; p. 169 Robert Landau; p. 170 Shepard Sherbell; p. 196 Con Tanasiuk/Design Pics; p. 204 Alan Carey; p. 211 The Gallery Collection; p. 213 Araldo de Luca; p. 214 Arte & Immagini srl; p. 225 Nik Wheeler; p. 247 Bettmann; pp. 250–51 Murat Taner; pp. 272–73 Warren Faidley; p. 280 Kazuyoshi Nomachi; p. 285 Michael Nicholson; pp. 288–89 Frans Lanting; pp. 300–01 Dex Image; pp. 304–05 John Lund/Blend Images
David Alexander: pp. 47, 51, 60tl, 68–69, 93, 148, 169, 208, 209, 235
Getty Images: p. 29 National Geographic; p.154 The Bridgeman Art Library
Sarah Hayes: pp. 8–9, 76
Todd Bolen: p. 228
Zev Radovan: pp. 74, 120, 160, 161
Images research by Zooid: pp. 22 The Hubble Heritage Team/STScI/AURA/NASA, 23 NASA, 25 Erich Lessing/akg-images, 26 Erich Lessing/akg-images, 27 Georg Gerster/Panos Pictures, 28 The Trustees of the British Museum, 30 Nathan Benn/Alamy, 31 Zev Radovan, Jerusalem, 33 © Look and Learn/Bridgeman Art Library, 36 Liu Liqun/Corbis UK Ltd., 37 Robert Harding Picture Library Ltd/Alamy, 38 Alex Timaios Egypt Imaging/Alamy, 39 Richard Nowitz/Getty Images, 40 Photolibrary Group, 43 Erich Lessing/akg-images, 53 Zev Radovan, Jerusalem, 54/55 Photolibrary Group, 56 Photolibrary Group, 58 Photolibrary Group, 60/61 dfwalls/Alamy, 65 Egyptian/Getty Images, 68 Israel images/Alamy, 71 Hanan Isachar/Corbis UK Ltd., 73 Caroline Penn/Panos Pictures, 77 Zev Radovan, Jerusalem, 78t Zev Radovan, Jerusalem, 78b Vladimir Khirman/Alamy, 81/82 Hanan Isachar/Alamy, 85 PhotoStock-Israel/Alamy, 87/88 Cameraphoto/akg-images, 88 akg-images, 89 The London Art Archive/Alamy, 90 Dagli Orti/Museo Barracco Rome/Art Archive, 91 Erich Lessing/British Museum/akg-images, 92 Spectrum Colour Library/Heritage Images, 96 Assyrian/Getty Images, 98 Dagli Orti/Archaeological Museum Teheran/Art Archive, 102/103 Erich Lessing/akg-images, 106 Erich Lessing/akg-

Maps and Illustrations
HL Studios:150
Richard Watts of Total Media Services: front and back endpapers, 37, 77, 81, 192, 195, 225, 263, 265, 290
Tony Cantale Graphics: p. 30, 67, 71

Lion Hudson

Commissioning editor: Paul Clifford
Project editor: Miranda Powell
Proofreaders: Rachel Ashley-Pain, Lizzie Clifford, Olivia Warburton
Book designer: Jonathan Roberts
Jacket designer: Jonathan Roberts
Production manager: Kylie Ord

DALMATIA

MOESIA SUPERIOR

ITALY

Rome

Three Taverns

Forum of Appius

Fundi

Formia

Capua

Puteoli

MACEDONIA

Philippi

Neapolis

Dyrrachium

Thessalonica

Berea

Apollonia

Tyrrhenian Sea

Aegean Sea

EPIRUS

Nicopolis

Delphi

Thebes

Athens

Rhegium

Corinth

Sicily

Olympia

ACHAEA

Syracuse

Sparta

Malta

Phoenix
Fair Hav

0   150 km
0   100 miles

Cyrene

CYRENAICA

Map of the first-century Mediterranean world